# MEDICINAL HERBS OF CALIFORNIA

## A Field Guide to Common Healing Plants

**Lanny Kaufer**

Guilford, Connecticut

An imprint of Globe Pequot, the trade division of
The Rowman & Littlefield Publishing Group, Inc.
4501 Forbes Blvd., Ste. 200
Lanham, MD 20706
www.rowman.com

Falcon and FalconGuides are registered trademarks and Make Adventure Your Story is a trademark of The Rowman & Littlefield Publishing Group, Inc.

Distributed by NATIONAL BOOK NETWORK

Unless otherwise noted, photos by Lanny Kaufer
White Sage, pictured on the front cover, is vulnerable to overharvesting and illegal resale. Please read Sustainable Collecting section, source from ethical suppliers, or grow your own. Front cover photo: Jess Starwood

British Library Cataloguing in Publication Information available

**Library of Congress Cataloging-in-Publication Data available**
Names: Kaufer, Lanny, author.
Title: Medicinal herbs of California : a field guide to common healing
   plants / Lanny Kaufer.
Other titles: Field guide to common healing plants | Falcon guide.
Description: Lanham, MD : Falcon, [2021] | Series: Falcon | Includes
   bibliographical references and index. | Identifiers: LCCN 2021037895 (print) | LCCN 2021037896 (ebook) |
   ISBN 9781493058020 (paperback) | ISBN 9781493058037 (epub)
Subjects: LCSH: Medicinal plants--California. | Field guides.
Classification: LCC RS431.M37 K38 2021  (print) | LCC RS431.M37  (ebook) |
   DDC 615.3/2109794--dc23
LC record available at https://lccn.loc.gov/2021037895
LC ebook record available at https://lccn.loc.gov/2021037896

$\infty$™ The paper used in this publication meets the minimum requirements of American National Standard for Information Sciences—Permanence of Paper for Printed Library Materials, ANSI/NISO Z39.48-1992.

The author and The Rowman & Littlefield Publishing Group, Inc., assume no liability for accidents happening to, or injuries sustained by, readers who engage in the activities described in this book.

This book is a work of reference. Readers should always consult an expert before using any foraged item. The author, editors, and publisher of this work have checked with sources believed to be reliable in their efforts to confirm the accuracy and completeness of the information presented herein and that the information is in accordance with the standard practices accepted at the time of publication. However, neither the author, editors, and publisher nor any other party involved in the creation and publication of this work warrant that the information is in every respect accurate and complete, and they are not responsible for errors or omissions or for any consequences from the application of the information in this book. In light of ongoing research and changes in clinical experience and in governmental regulations, readers are encouraged to confirm the information contained herein with additional sources. This book does not purport to be a complete presentation of all plants, and the genera, species, and cultivars discussed or pictured herein are but a small fraction of the plants found in the wild, in an urban or suburban landscape, or in a home. Given the global movement of plants, we would expect continual introduction of species having toxic properties to the regions discussed in this book. We have made every attempt to be botanically accurate, but regional variations in plant names, growing conditions, and availability may affect the accuracy of the information provided. A positive identification of an individual plant is most likely when a freshly collected part of the plant containing leaves and flowers or fruits is presented to a knowledgeable botanist or horticulturist. Poison Control Centers generally have relationships with the botanical community should the need for plant identification arise. We have attempted to provide accurate descriptions of plants, but there is no substitute for direct interaction with a trained botanist or horticulturist for plant identification. **In cases of exposure or ingestion, contact a Poison Control Center (800-222-1222), a medical toxicologist, another appropriate health care provider, or an appropriate reference resource.**

# ADVANCE PRAISE

"Amazing work! What a joy to dip into such a concentrated yet accessible resource! Here we have a field guide that in its thorough, accurate and comprehensive coverage crosses the boundary from field guide to outright herbal." —Carol Wade, Founder/Director, Earth Island Herbs and Ojai School of Herbal Studies

"Lanny Kaufer's exquisite attention to botanical science is balanced with respect for Indigenous systems of healing wisdom. Whether you are a beginner or a Ph.D., I trust that this will be your favorite new field guide. I love this book!" —Amanda McQuade Crawford, MA, MFT; Author, *Herbal Remedies For Women*; Director, PhytoHumana: Integrative Medicine

"Lanny Kaufer brings together all the best elements to create a classic compendium of ethnobotany." —David Crow, Licensed Acupuncturist, Herbalist, Founder of Floracopeia, Inc.

"This book is one of the best herb manuals I've seen in over a decade." —Jake F. Felice, N.D., L.M.P.

"This is a well-documented field guide for layperson and herbalist alike, excellent for responsible gatherers to find and use helpful medicinal plants. So, get the book, put on a hat, and go out into our glorious California wild areas. Happy hunting!" —Mary Hardy, MD, Integrative Medicine Physician; Founder/Director, Wellness Works; Coauthor: *Best Remedies: Breakthrough Prescriptions that Blend Conventional and Natural Medicine*

"This is an outstanding book! As a professional field botanist, I really appreciate the author's focus on the conservation status of the plants that he discusses, his many years of experience with these plants, his inclusion of propagation hints so that readers can avoid over-harvesting plants in the wild, the references that are cited, and the extensive bibliography that empowers the serious readers to do further study and research on their own." —Steve Junak, Author, *A Flora of Santa Cruz Island;* Research Associate, Santa Barbara Botanic Garden

"This is an outstanding resource for any herbalist, botanist, or conservationist in California! … Both practical and humorous, the tales of our local herbal allies are beautifully illustrated and brought to life. I will be recommending this book to my students for years to come!" —Emily Sanders, Founder/Director, Artemisia Academy of Herbal Arts & Healing

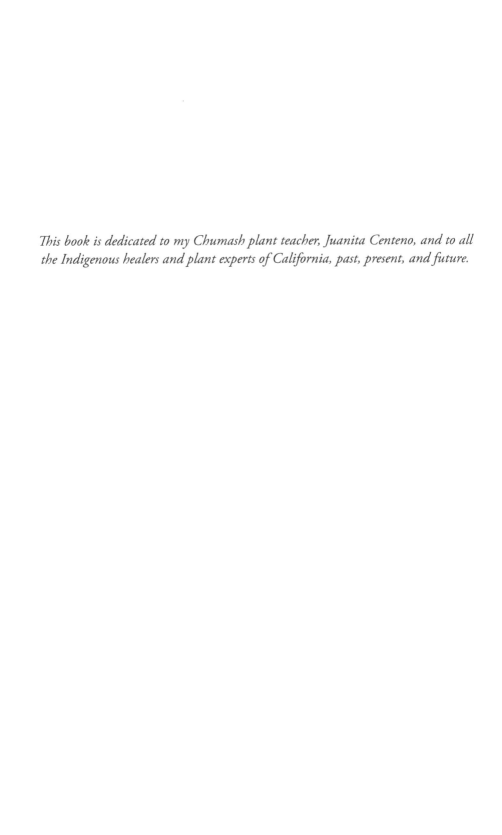

*This book is dedicated to my Chumash plant teacher, Juanita Centeno, and to all the Indigenous healers and plant experts of California, past, present, and future.*

# CONTENTS

Acknowledgments . . . . . . . . . . . . . . . . . . . . . . . . . . . . . . . . . .xii
Introduction . . . . . . . . . . . . . . . . . . . . . . . . . . . . . . . . . . . . 1
A Brief History of Medicinal Herbs in America. . . . . . . . . . . . . . . . . . 5
Sustainable Collecting . . . . . . . . . . . . . . . . . . . . . . . . . . . . . . 8
Native Plant Conservation . . . . . . . . . . . . . . . . . . . . . . . . . . . . 10
Collecting, Drying, and Storing Herbal Home Remedies. . . . . . . . . . . . . 14
Preparing Herbal Home Remedies . . . . . . . . . . . . . . . . . . . . . . . . 16
How to Use This Guide. . . . . . . . . . . . . . . . . . . . . . . . . . . . . . 18

LICHENS . . . . . . . . . . . . . . . . . . . . . . . . . . . . . . . . . . . . . .24
Shield Lichen family (Parmeliaceae) . . . . . . . . . . . . . . . . . . . . . . . 25
   *Usnea* genus . . . . . . . . . . . . . . . . . . . . . . . . . . . . . . . . . 25
      Usnea (*Usnea* spp.) . . . . . . . . . . . . . . . . . . . . . . . . . . . 25

GYMNOSPERMS . . . . . . . . . . . . . . . . . . . . . . . . . . . . . . . . .28
Cypress family (Cupressaceae) . . . . . . . . . . . . . . . . . . . . . . . . . . 29
   Cedar group . . . . . . . . . . . . . . . . . . . . . . . . . . . . . . . . . 29
      Incense-Cedar (*Calocedrus decurrens*) . . . . . . . . . . . . . . . . . 29
      Western Red-Cedar (*Thuja plicata*) . . . . . . . . . . . . . . . . . . 30
   *Juniperus* genus. . . . . . . . . . . . . . . . . . . . . . . . . . . . . . . 35
      California Juniper (*Juniperus californica*) . . . . . . . . . . . . . . . 36
      Common Juniper (*Juniperus communis*) . . . . . . . . . . . . . . . . 37
      Sierra Juniper (*Juniperus grandis*) . . . . . . . . . . . . . . . . . . . 38
      Western Juniper (*Juniperus occidentalis*) . . . . . . . . . . . . . . . . 39
      Utah Juniper (*Juniperus osteosperma*) . . . . . . . . . . . . . . . . . 40

Ephedra family (Ephedraceae) . . . . . . . . . . . . . . . . . . . . . . . . . . 44
   *Ephedra* genus . . . . . . . . . . . . . . . . . . . . . . . . . . . . . . . 44
      California Ephedra (*Ephedra californica*) . . . . . . . . . . . . . . . 44
      Nevada Ephedra (*Ephedra nevadensis*) . . . . . . . . . . . . . . . . . 44
      Green Ephedra (*Ephedra viridis*). . . . . . . . . . . . . . . . . . . . 45

Pine family (Pinaceae) . . . . . . . . . . . . . . . . . . . . . . . . . . . . . . 49
   *Pinus* genus . . . . . . . . . . . . . . . . . . . . . . . . . . . . . . . . . 49
Pines (*Pinus* spp.). . . . . . . . . . . . . . . . . . . . . . . . . . . . . . . . 49

**MAGNOLIIDS** . . . . . . . . . . . . . . . . . . . . . . . . . . . . . **57**
Laurel family (Lauraceae) . . . . . . . . . . . . . . . . . . . 58
  *Umbellularia* genus. . . . . . . . . . . . . . . . . . . . . 58
    California Bay (*Umbellularia californica*) . . . . . . . . . . . . . . . 58

Lizard-tail family (Saururaceae) . . . . . . . . . . . . . . . . 62
  *Anemopsis* genus . . . . . . . . . . . . . . . . . . . . . 62
    Yerba Mansa (*Anemopsis californica*) . . . . . . . . . . . . . . 62

**MONOCOTS** . . . . . . . . . . . . . . . . . . . . . . . . . . . . . **66**
Grass family (Poaceae) . . . . . . . . . . . . . . . . . . . . 67
  *Avena* genus . . . . . . . . . . . . . . . . . . . . . . . 67
    Wild Oats (*Avena fatua*) . . . . . . . . . . . . . . . . . . 67

**EUDICOTS** . . . . . . . . . . . . . . . . . . . . . . . . . . . . . **71**
Muskroot family (Adoxaceae) . . . . . . . . . . . . . . . . 72
  *Sambucus* genus . . . . . . . . . . . . . . . . . . . . . 72
    Blue Elderberry (*Sambucus nigra* subsp. *caerulea*) . . . . . . . . 72
    Black Elderberry (*Sambucus racemosa* var. *melanocarpa*) . . . . . . . . 73
    Red Elderberry (*Sambucus racemosa* var. *racemosa*) . . . . . . . . . . 73

Carrot family (Apiaceae) . . . . . . . . . . . . . . . . . . 78
  *Foeniculum* genus . . . . . . . . . . . . . . . . . . . . 78
    Fennel (*Foeniculum vulgare*) . . . . . . . . . . . . . . . . . 78

Sunflower family (Asteraceae) . . . . . . . . . . . . . . . . . 82
  *Achillea* genus . . . . . . . . . . . . . . . . . . . . . . 82
    Yarrow (*Achillea millefolium*) . . . . . . . . . . . . . . . . 82
  *Artemisia* genus . . . . . . . . . . . . . . . . . . . . . 86
    Coastal Sagebrush (*Artemisia californica*) . . . . . . . . . . . . 86
    Estafiate (*Artemisia ludoviciana*) . . . . . . . . . . . . . . . 87
    Great Basin Sagebrush (*Artemisia tridentata*) . . . . . . . . . . . 88
    Mugwort (*Artemisia douglasiana*) . . . . . . . . . . . . . . 92
  *Grindelia* genus . . . . . . . . . . . . . . . . . . . . . 95
    Grindelia (*Grindelia camporum*) . . . . . . . . . . . . . . . . 96
  *Matricaria* genus . . . . . . . . . . . . . . . . . . . . . 99
    Pineapple Weed (*Matricaria discoidea*) . . . . . . . . . . . . . .100
  *Pseudognaphalium* genus . . . . . . . . . . . . . . . . . .104
    California Everlasting (*Pseudognaphalium californicum*) . . . . . . . .104
  *Solidago* genus . . . . . . . . . . . . . . . . . . . . . .109
    Goldenrod (*Solidago velutina* subsp. *californica*) . . . . . . . . . . .109

Borage family (Boraginaceae) . . . . . . . . . . . . . . . . . . . . . 113
  *Eriodictyon* genus. . . . . . . . . . . . . . . . . . . . . . . . . . . 113
    California Yerba Santa (*Eriodictyon californicum*) . . . . . . . . . . 113
    Thick-Leaved Yerba Santa (*Eriodictyon crassifolium*) . . . . . . . . . . . 114
    Woolly Yerba Santa (*Eriodictyon tomentosum*) . . . . . . . . . . 114
    Sticky Yerba Santa (*Eriodictyon trichocalyx*) . . . . . . . . . 115

Cactus family (Cactaceae) . . . . . . . . . . . . . . . . . . . . . . 121
  *Opuntia* genus . . . . . . . . . . . . . . . . . . . . . . . . . . . . 121
    Prickly-Pear Cactus (*Opuntia* spp.) . . . . . . . . . . . . . . . 121

Heath family (Ericaceae) . . . . . . . . . . . . . . . . . . . . . . . 126
  *Arctostaphylos* genus . . . . . . . . . . . . . . . . . . . . . . . . 126
    Manzanita (*Arctostaphylos manzanita*) . . . . . . . . . . . . . . . 126
    Bearberry (*Arctostaphylos uva-ursi*). . . . . . . . . . . . . . . . 127

Pea family (Fabaceae) . . . . . . . . . . . . . . . . . . . . . . . . . 132
  *Glycyrrhiza* genus . . . . . . . . . . . . . . . . . . . . . . . . . 132
    American Licorice (*Glycyrrhiza lepidota*). . . . . . . . . . . . . . 132

Beech family (Fagaceae). . . . . . . . . . . . . . . . . . . . . . . . 136
  *Quercus* genus . . . . . . . . . . . . . . . . . . . . . . . . . . . 136
    Oak (*Quercus* spp.) . . . . . . . . . . . . . . . . . . . . . . . 136

St. John's Wort family (Hypericaceae). . . . . . . . . . . . . . . . . 142
  *Hypericum* genus. . . . . . . . . . . . . . . . . . . . . . . . . . . 142
    Tinker's Penny (*Hypericum anagalloides*). . . . . . . . . . . . . 142
    Gold-Wire (*Hypericum concinnum*) . . . . . . . . . . . . . . . . . 142
    Klamathweed (*Hypericum perforatum* subsp. *perforatum*) . . . . . . . . 143
    Scouler's St. John's Wort (*Hypericum scouleri*) . . . . . . . . . . . 143

Walnut family (Juglandaceae). . . . . . . . . . . . . . . . . . . . . . 147
  *Juglans* genus. . . . . . . . . . . . . . . . . . . . . . . . . . . . 147
    Southern California Black Walnut (*Juglans californica*) . . . . . . . . 147

Mint family (Lamiaceae) . . . . . . . . . . . . . . . . . . . . . . . . 151
  *Clinopodium* genus. . . . . . . . . . . . . . . . . . . . . . . . . . 151
    California Yerba Buena (*Clinopodium douglasii*) . . . . . . . . . . 151
  *Marrubium* genus . . . . . . . . . . . . . . . . . . . . . . . . . . 154
    Horehound (*Marrubium vulgare*) . . . . . . . . . . . . . . . . . . 154

*Mentha* genus . . . . . . . . . . . . . . . . . . . . . . . . .158
   Wild Mint (*Mentha arvensis* and *Mentha canadensis*) . . . . . . . . .158
*Prunella* genus . . . . . . . . . . . . . . . . . . . . . . . .161
   Self-Heal (*Prunella vulgaris*) . . . . . . . . . . . . . . .161
*Salvia* genus . . . . . . . . . . . . . . . . . . . . . . . . .163
   White Sage (*Salvia apiana*) . . . . . . . . . . . . . . . .165
   Blue Sage (*Salvia dorrii*) . . . . . . . . . . . . . . . . .169
   Purple Sage (*Salvia leucophylla*) . . . . . . . . . . . . .170
   Black Sage (*Salvia mellifera*) . . . . . . . . . . . . . . .171
   Hummingbird Sage (*Salvia spathacea*) . . . . . . . . . . . .176
*Scutellaria* genus . . . . . . . . . . . . . . . . . . . . . .179
   Skullcap (*Scutellaria californica*) . . . . . . . . . . . .179
*Trichostema* genus . . . . . . . . . . . . . . . . . . . . . .182
   Woolly Blue Curls (*Trichostema lanatum*) . . . . . . . . . .182

Myrtle family (Myrtaceae) . . . . . . . . . . . . . . . . . . . .186
*Eucalyptus* genus . . . . . . . . . . . . . . . . . . . . . . .186
   Eucalyptus (*Eucalyptus globulus*) . . . . . . . . . . . . .186

Poppy family (Papaveraceae) . . . . . . . . . . . . . . . . . . .190
*Eschscholzia* genus . . . . . . . . . . . . . . . . . . . . . .190
   California Poppy (*Eschscholzia californica*) . . . . . . . .190

Rose family (Rosaceae) . . . . . . . . . . . . . . . . . . . . .194
*Heteromeles* genus . . . . . . . . . . . . . . . . . . . . . .194
   Toyon (*Heteromeles arbutifolia*) . . . . . . . . . . . . .194
*Prunus* genus . . . . . . . . . . . . . . . . . . . . . . . . .199
   Bitter Cherry (*Prunus emarginata*) . . . . . . . . . . . .199
   Hollyleaf Cherry (*Prunus ilicifolia* subsp. *ilicifolia*) . . . . . . . . .199
   Catalina Cherry (*Prunus ilicifolia* subsp. *lyonii*) . . . . . . . . .200
   Western Chokecherry (*Prunus virginiana* var. *demissa*) . . . . . . . .200
*Rosa* genus . . . . . . . . . . . . . . . . . . . . . . . . . .205
   California Wild Rose (*Rosa californica*) . . . . . . . . . .205
   Bald-Hip Rose (*Rosa gymnocarpa*) . . . . . . . . . . . . .205
   Woods' Rose (*Rosa woodsii*) . . . . . . . . . . . . . . . .206
*Rubus* genus . . . . . . . . . . . . . . . . . . . . . . . . .208
   Whitebark Raspberry (*Rubus leucodermis*) . . . . . . . . . .209
   Thimbleberry (*Rubus parviflorus*) . . . . . . . . . . . . .209
   Salmonberry (*Rubus spectabilis*) . . . . . . . . . . . . .210
   California Blackberry (*Rubus ursinus*) . . . . . . . . . . .210

Nightshade family (Solanaceae). . . . . . . . . . . . . . . . . . . . . . . . . 214
    *Datura* genus. . . . . . . . . . . . . . . . . . . . . . . . . . . . . . . . 214
        Sacred Datura (*Datura wrightii*). . . . . . . . . . . . . . . . . . 214

Nettle family (Urticaceae). . . . . . . . . . . . . . . . . . . . . . . . . . . 218
    *Urtica* genus . . . . . . . . . . . . . . . . . . . . . . . . . . . . . . . 218
        Giant Stinging Nettle (*Urtica dioica* subsp.). . . . . . . . . . . . 218
        Dwarf Stinging Nettle (*Urtica urens*) . . . . . . . . . . . . . . . 218

Caltrop family (Zygophyllaceae) . . . . . . . . . . . . . . . . . . . . . . . 223
    *Larrea* genus . . . . . . . . . . . . . . . . . . . . . . . . . . . . . . . 223
        Creosote Bush (*Larrea tridentata*) . . . . . . . . . . . . . . . . . 223
    *Tribulus* genus . . . . . . . . . . . . . . . . . . . . . . . . . . . . . . 227
        Goathead (*Tribulus terrestris*) . . . . . . . . . . . . . . . . . . . 227

*Recipes* . . . . . . . . . . . . . . . . . . . . . . . . . . . . . . . . . . . . 231
*Endnotes* . . . . . . . . . . . . . . . . . . . . . . . . . . . . . . . . . . . 250
*Bibliography* . . . . . . . . . . . . . . . . . . . . . . . . . . . . . . . . . 264
*Plant Index* . . . . . . . . . . . . . . . . . . . . . . . . . . . . . . . . . 276
*Recipe Index* . . . . . . . . . . . . . . . . . . . . . . . . . . . . . . . . . 279
*Contributors* . . . . . . . . . . . . . . . . . . . . . . . . . . . . . . . . . 281
*About the Author* . . . . . . . . . . . . . . . . . . . . . . . . . . . . . . 283

# ACKNOWLEDGMENTS

The writing of this book was made possible by many people. Starting close to home, I thank my wife, Rondia, for her love and support throughout a project that took much more of my time than either of us realized going into it. Likewise, I thank my son and daughter, Aran and Mara; brother, Michael; sister, Gilda; step-daughter, LaVeane; daughter-in-law, Melissa; and all of their families for their continual love and support.

I say "thank you" to my mentors and teachers who walked beside me on my medicinal plant path over the years. They include Juanita Centeno, William LeSassier, Henry Hilgard, Michael Tierra, Ken Littlefish, Julie Tumamait-Stenslie, Carol Wade, Fred Siciliano, and Amanda McQuade Crawford. Michael Moore's monumental three volumes on medicinal plants of the West have been guiding lights throughout my career.

Christopher Nyerges's experience as an author and his willingness to share it were essential in the completion of this book. Steve Junak deserves special recognition for his generosity in sharing botanical information, photographs, and essential contacts. James D. "Jim" Adams went above and beyond the call in every aspect of putting this book together, including sharing botanical and pharmacological information, photos, and recipes. Jess Starwood always found the time to contribute photos, recipes, and moral support. Thanks also to Carol Wermuth and Tonantzin Guerra-Rennick for their contributions from the Menache Inter-Tribal Council.

Many fine photographers and curators of photographs added imagery to this guide. Photographically, this book would not be the same without the help of Randy Wright of Santa Barbara Botanic Gardens. A few others who deserve special recognition for their time and generosity in sharing photos are Jim Adams, Ben Grangereau, Keir Morse, and Steven Norris.

Additional photo and recipe contributors are credited at the end of the book. Thank you all for sharing!

For their help in reviewing and critiquing this book as well as their professional and moral support, I am indebted to Roy Upton, David Magney, JiLing Lin, Enrique Villaseñor, and Sarah Karinja, in addition to others already mentioned above. Anyone else who contributed a piece of the editing puzzle here and there, you know who you are. Know also that I appreciate you!

Thanks to Don Edwards, Mike Swimmer, John Hickey, Burton Lang, Christine Lemming, and Marco Rojas for their friendship and their support of the project and to Kevin Curran for setting me on this writing path. Last but not least, my gratitude goes out to Katie O'Dell, my exceptional editor at Globe Pequot, for her seemingly infinite patience with this first-time author.

# INTRODUCTION

In 1967, while traveling in New Mexico, I gave a man a ride up into the mountains to his home in the Jemez Pueblo. In gratitude, he invited me and my companion to stay for several days as his guests. During that time, I came down with a cold. His older relative brought me a bag of dried leaves he called "cedar tea." He instructed me on how to prepare it and told me to inhale the steam and drink the tea. My cold quickly subsided, and a lifelong curiosity about medicinal herbs began.

Upon returning to Santa Barbara, I began to explore the local mountains with whatever plant identification guides I could find. I searched for books on herbal medicine, realizing quickly that almost all the books available were about herbs of the eastern United States or Europe. I needed a teacher, but I didn't know how to contact any local Chumash who might have traditional plant knowledge. My first herb mentor appeared in 1971 when William LeSassier[1] moved in next door to me for a while before settling on the East Coast, where he had a distinguished career as an herbalist and teacher.

Not long after William left, I was fortunate to attend a series of classes taught by Chumash plant expert Juanita Centeno[2] through University Extension at UC Santa Barbara. By 1976 I had completed a biology degree at UC Santa Cruz and was living in Ojai, leading herb walks (a term William coined). I invited Juanita to co-teach some classes with me. Our friendship grew, and with it my knowledge of local plant use and a deep appreciation for the Indigenous perspective on the relationship between humans and the Earth. "Destroy Nature and you destroy yourself," Juanita warned us.

Over the years, thanks to immersing myself in nature as much as possible and having many excellent teachers, mentors, and colleagues, my enthusiasm for medicinal plants has grown. This book is the product of that enthusiasm. It is intended to be a tribute to the Indigenous knowledge of California's original inhabitants, complemented by the latest scientific studies on medicinal plants. It is an introduction to some common California plants that can be sustainably collected and safely used as what I call "ancient over-the-counter remedies." These plants are not meant to replace the services and prescriptions of licensed medical practitioners. Rather, they are presented as alternatives to the nonprescription medicines that anyone can purchase in a drug store.

As much as I believe that scientifically validated herbs deserve to be classified as medicines alongside other drugs, their current designation by the Food and Drug Administration as "dietary supplements" is also fitting. Over thousands of years of evolution, our bodies have learned to digest and assimilate plants, including medicinal herbs, as part of our diets. As explained in the section on how to use this book, we use some compounds created by plants, their primary metabolites, for nourishment. Plants also produce non-nutrient, secondary metabolites that can trigger natural healing processes in our bodies. Those secondary metabolites enable plants to become medicinal herbs.

Many of the plants in this book can be purchased as dried herbs processed to varying degrees, but there is a deep satisfaction in getting to know them in the field well enough to positively identify them and be able to collect small quantities to stock your own medicinal pantry. If you do that, you will find their freshness, quality, and potency surpass what is usually commercially available. And you may find a connection to nature that no book, not even this one, can provide.

## The Scope of This Guide

This book is not an exhaustive list of every possible medicinal plant that grows in California. It is a selection of some of the most common and useful medicinal herbs in the state. My writing process began by compiling a list of about 200 native and non-native plants found growing wild in California that are known, or believed, to have medicinal properties. The list was pared down to what you hold in your hand based on five criteria:

- Is the plant common enough in California to justify small-scale, sustainable collecting?
- Is a good part of the plant's range within California, or is California on the fringes? In other words, is it a better fit in a neighboring state's book on medicinal herbs?
- Is it a non-native "weed" so common throughout the United States that it is sufficiently covered in many other books?
- Is there sufficient evidence of Native American medicinal use of the plant?
- Is there sufficient modern scientific validation of its Native American uses?

In addition, an attempt was made within these few pages to present plants that reflect the incredible diversity of California's plant communities, habitats, and climate zones. One could make the argument that, biologically and geographically, California is made up of several quite different states or bioregions crammed together inside its political state borders. Think of this field guide as a starting point to explore the enormous potential of California's medicinal herbs.

Fortunately, Californians are lucky to have some excellent botanical resources, in print and online, to supplement this book. The University of California at Berkeley's Jepson Herbarium maintains the Jepson eFlora at ucjeps .berkeley.edu/eflora/. Based on *The Jepson Manual: Vascular Plants of California*, second edition, the website is an indispensable reference for the taxonomy and identification of native and non-native wild plants in California. Also out of UC Berkeley, the Berkeley Natural History Museums provide the CalPhotos website at calphotos.berkeley.edu/, with 400,000 plant photos at latest count. For a focus on cultivating native plants, see the California Native Plant Society's CalScape website at calscape.org.

The FalconGuides series includes two other books to complement this one in your library. Like this book, both arrange the plants botanically. Christopher Nyerges's *Foraging California* will help you find, identify, and prepare wild edible foods. *Plants of Northern California: A Field Guide to Plants West of the Sierra Nevada* by Eva Begley is a beautifully photo-illustrated guide to identifying more than 500 species of native and non-native California plants.

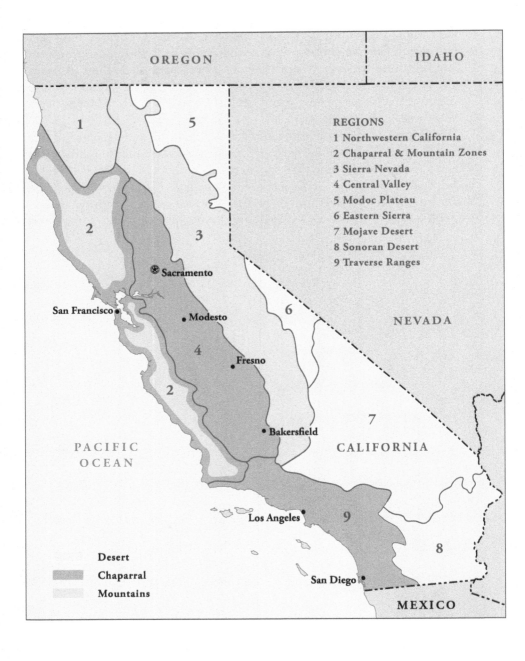

OREGON

IDAHO

REGIONS
1 Northwestern California
2 Chaparral & Mountain Zones
3 Sierra Nevada
4 Central Valley
5 Modoc Plateau
6 Eastern Sierra
7 Mojave Desert
8 Sonoran Desert
9 Traverse Ranges

1

5

2

3

⊛ Sacramento

San Francisco •

• Modesto

4

Fresno •

6

NEVADA

2

Bakersfield •

7

CALIFORNIA

PACIFIC
OCEAN

Los Angeles •

9

8

San Diego •

Desert
Chaparral
Mountains

MEXICO

# A BRIEF HISTORY OF
# MEDICINAL HERBS IN AMERICA

In 2012 researchers studying dental calculus on the teeth of 50,000-year-old Neanderthal skulls in a Spanish cave made a surprising discovery. They were looking for—and finding—evidence of the plant foods that made up the diet of early humans, but they also found remains of two not-very-tasty plants, chamomile and yarrow, known today as medicinal herbs. The researchers suggested that self-medication is the best explanation for this finding.[1] It is highly likely that as long as humans have inhabited the Earth, we've used herbs for self-healing, probably from observing animals such as bears do the same. Today, the World Health Organization estimates that 60 percent of the world's population—80 percent in developing countries—rely on herbal medicines for their primary health care.

As humans evolved, Indigenous tribes created their own localized herbal medicine traditions, based on trial and error and passed down orally. At the same time, two major herbal medical systems developed in India and China that are still in use today. The Ayurvedic system of herbal medicine in India was first described in writing about 3,500 years ago and may have been developing for thousands of years before that. It continues today uninterrupted, with practitioners around the world. The earliest recorded Chinese pharmacopoeia (catalog of medicines), the *Pen Tsao Ching*, dates back to the second century AD but is thought to be based on thousands of years of oral teachings. The Chinese plant medicine system continues to this day in the form of traditional Chinese medicine (TCM), practiced by acupuncturists and Doctors of Oriental Medicine (OMDs) worldwide.

A different story unfolded in Europe, where for thousands of years, in the absence of a unifying system, folk healers (mostly women) treated people with local herbs. Those herbalists whose remedies worked gained followers and apprentices. Herbal knowledge spread by word of mouth. Meanwhile, a more formal herbal medical tradition evolved in Greece around the writings of two physicians: Hippocrates (c. 460–c. 370 BC), known as the "Father of Medicine," and Dioscorides (c. AD 40–90), who wrote the first Western pharmacopoeia. In the early days of the Roman Empire, another Greek physician and author, Galen (AD 129–c. 210), used his newfound knowledge of anatomy and physiology to become the emperor's physician. His teachings, which dominated Western medicine for more than 1,000 years, included complex and expensive herbal formulas, as opposed to the single-herb remedies of the folk herbalists known as "simples."

After the fall of Rome, the European tradition of plant medicine was squelched by the Catholic Church and replaced with religious beliefs about the source and treatment of illness. Throughout the Dark Ages, local herbalists continued their work in secret, often paying for their "witchcraft" with their lives. Meanwhile, monks in monasteries transcribed the Greek medical writings. Their manuscripts fueled a renewed interest in herbs when the Renaissance blossomed in Europe in the 1500s with a flurry of lavishly illustrated books called "herbals." The result today is an ongoing European interest in time-honored plant medicines.

North America was an entirely new frontier for Western herbal medicine. The English and other European settlers in the eastern part of the continent and Spanish missionaries and pioneers in the West brought an assortment of herbs and recipes with them from their homelands. They soon discovered that Indigenous tribes already had well-developed medical traditions based on herbs they gathered, cultivated, or acquired through trade. Native American herbal remedies and healing practices had been tested in the crucible of time for thousands for years. Unfortunately for the future of American medicine, most of the Indigenous knowledge was lost as tribal lands were overrun in what can only be described as a genocide. Furthermore, a racist bias prevented most Europeans from accepting medical advice from people they deemed to be inferior or, even worse, subhuman.

A few early American physicians did, however, value Indigenous medicine. Aided by the observations of pioneering anthropologists and ethnographers who recorded American Indian healing practices, these physicians began to establish a uniquely American brand of medicine by combining European and Native American herbalism. They wrote books and started medical schools, practicing what was known as Eclectic Medicine, physio-medical therapeutics, and naturopathy, among other names. These schools and the doctors they produced rode a wave of popularity that was peaking in the late 1800s and into the early 1900s.

This promising evolution came to a halt in 1910 with the release of "Medical Education in the United States and Canada" by Abraham Flexner, now known as the Flexner Report.[2] Commissioned by Andrew Carnegie and funded by John D. Rockefeller, the report was promoted as a scientific attempt to assess the unregulated state of medical education in the United States, which was, indeed, in need of improvement. While at the time it seemed a worthy philanthropic cause for the public good, today's historical perspective reveals another possible motive. Carnegie, Rockefeller, J. P. Morgan, and other millionaire industrialists and bankers of their day were invested in oil and mineral extraction that produced the ingredients used in place of plants by the fledgling pharmaceutical industry to create synthetic chemical drugs. The Rockefeller fortune soon became heavily invested in the pharmaceutical industry—and remains so to this day.

The Flexner Report resulted in the elimination of more than half the existing medical schools, including those who taught herbal or naturopathic medicine as well as those who trained Black and women doctors. Schools that survived and became accredited were the beneficiaries of generous funding by the Rockefeller Foundation.

Similar changes already under way in the *US Pharmacopoeia* (USP) picked up steam after the Flexner Report. Following the isolation of morphine from the opium poppy in 1805, whole-plant drugs were gradually replaced with laboratory versions based on a plant's "active constituent." This so-called "biomedical" approach focused on one isolated component while overlooking the synergy of the many compounds found in a whole herb.

In the first USP, published in 1820, 70 percent of the drugs listed were derived from plants. By the eleventh edition of 1936, the number had dropped to 45 percent.[3] Between 1870 and 1970, the total number of plant-derived drugs in the USP fell from 636 to 68, while hundreds of synthetic compounds were added.[4] This trend resulted in part from the inability of pharmaceutical companies to patent a whole plant.

Ironically, the very word "drug" is derived from the Old Dutch *drōgi*, referring to dry herbs. Yet today, the Food and Drug Administration (FDA) defines a drug as "a substance recognized by an official pharmacopoeia or formulary" and, secondly, as "a substance intended for use in the diagnosis, cure, mitigation, treatment, or prevention of disease." The result is that even though many herbs have a history of use and a few still exist in some form in the USP, they cannot be considered medical drugs unless they are approved by the FDA. Herbs are now placed in the regulatory category of "dietary supplements." Since they cannot prescribe them, physicians do not learn about herbs in medical school and pharmacists no longer learn about them in pharmacy school. In California, only licensed acupuncturists and naturopaths can prescribe whole herbs. The botanical medicines they prescribe will be found in their own herbal pharmacies or in retail health food stores, but not in medical pharmacies or drug stores.

The legal status of medicinal herbs, or lack of it, did not stop American consumers from spending $8.8 billion on herbal supplements in 2018. Meanwhile, Native American communities continue to tap into their legacy of plant medicine. Hopefully, by bringing together the long-standing contributions of California Indians and the latest studies in plant pharmacology, this book will be able to play some part in restoring the status of medicinal herbs. At the same time, it may empower you, its readers, to learn how to identify and sustainably collect some common California herbs to create your own herbal pharmacy of home remedies.

# SUSTAINABLE COLLECTING

Once you're confident about identifying a wild plant and know the right time of year to collect various parts, the best way to acquire it for personal use is to grow it yourself or harvest it from a farm or from a friend who has it growing on their land. If you choose to collect small quantities in the wild, please do so in a mindful and respectful way.

Here are some guidelines:

- Learn about the conservation status of your chosen plant within the pages of this book or on the California Native Plant Society's Inventory of Rare and Endangered Plants.[1] Is it native or non-native? Harvest native plants only where they are abundant or, at the very least, not rare or endangered. See the "Native Plant Conservation" section for more information on conservation status.

- Pick where local laws allow it and only where sufficient quantities of your intended plant are growing. California Penal Code Section 384a outlaws cutting or removing plants on state public lands, with an exemption for plants declared to be a public nuisance.[2] Plant gathering is not permitted on public and private preserves or in national parks, national monuments, and USDA Forest Service (USFS) designated wilderness areas and campgrounds. Most national forests do not have an official written policy but do allow for gathering small quantities of aboveground parts for personal use—i.e., what will fit in a grocery bag. Check with your local jurisdiction.

- Collect only the aboveground parts unless you are on private land with owner permission or you are in possession of a USFS collecting permit for educational purposes. Federal commercial harvesting permits are also available, for a price.

- In any case, never take more than 10 percent of the mass of any single plant. Prune carefully while picking to try to encourage new growth and leave the plant looking better than you found it.

- Take your cue from Indigenous peoples of the Americas, who have a tradition of giving thanks and asking permission of the plants before picking. This may be done in the form of a prayer, a song, or a small offering of a sacred herb or something biodegradable that symbolizes the plant's value to you. Juanita Centeno, my Chumash teacher, instructed her students to take a moment to do this upon encountering the first specimen of a plant we intended to harvest. She told us to then continue looking for an abundant population of that plant before collecting any of it. That is basic environmental responsibility in action.

- Jacque Tahuka Nunez of the Acjachemen tribe of the Orange County region offers this simple three-step advice:

    1. "Don't take more than you need."

    2. "Give back."

    3. "Be resourceful."[3]

- For your own protection, do not pick where there are signs of pollution, spraying of herbicides, or alongside paved roads and highways (where most spraying takes place). Dust can be washed off before preparing fresh herbs or drying them for storage.

# NATIVE PLANT CONSERVATION

All the plants included in this field guide were vetted to ensure that no rare, endangered, or threatened plants were included. A number of highly regarded medicinal plants did not make the cut because their populations, while plentiful in other states, are too small in California to support collecting. Hopefully, they will appear in FalconGuides for those other states.

Two essential and iconic California herbs found in this book, yerba mansa (*Anemopsis californica*) and white sage (*Salvia apiana*), are on United Plant Savers' "Species At-Risk" list. While neither plant is currently recognized as threatened or endangered by the US Environmental Protection Agency or any of the other organizations listed below, please refrain from collecting them in the wild, and discourage others from doing so. Grow your own, or find a reputable source. The California Native Plant Society's CalScape website (calscape.org) has a complete list of all native plant nurseries in California.

Here are the sources used to determine conservation status, with a brief explanation of each:

1. **The International Union for Conservation of Nature's Red List of Threatened Species**
   IUCN's Red List of Threatened Species is widely recognized as the world's most comprehensive information source on the global conservation status of animal, plant, and fungi species. Because IUCN has a global perspective, they may deem certain California native plants as threatened worldwide simply because they are found only in California and nowhere else (iucnredlist.org).

2. **California Native Plant Society's Inventory of Rare and Endangered Plants**
   CNPS's Inventory of Rare and Endangered Plants is another widely recognized resource for rare plant protection and conservation planning in California. Today, the eighth edition is available online (cnps.org/rare-plants/cnps-inventory-of-rare-plants).

3. **NatureServe Explorer**
   The NatureServe conservation status system tracks 100,000 species and ecosystems worldwide. Developed and maintained by The Nature Conservancy, it is a premier resource for information on rare and endangered species and ecosystems in the Americas. NatureServe Explorer is its search tool (explorer.natureserve.org).

4. **United Plant Savers "Species At-Risk" list**
   UpS is a nonprofit organization whose goal is to "assure the increasing abundance of the medicinal plants which are currently in decline due to expanding popularity and shrinking habitat and range." UpS provides a "Species At-Risk" list of wild medicinal plants that it feels are currently most sensitive to the impact of human activities. The group also initiates programs to preserve those plants (unitedplantsavers.org).

Invasive plants, such as fennel and horehound, are rated for severity by the California Invasive Plant Council (Cal-IPC) as "high," "moderate," "limited," or "watch."

Here are the ranking systems that you will see under "Conservation status rankings" in the brief specs section for each plant. For further details on these organizations, visit them online.

## The IUCN Red List Categories and Abbreviations
**Note:** When a plant included in this field guide does not appear on the IUCN list, it is described as "Not listed."

1. **Extinct (EX)**

2. **Extinct in the Wild (EW)**

3. **Critically Endangered (CR)**

4. **Endangered (EN)**

5. **Vulnerable (VU)**

6. **Near Threatened (NT)**

7. **Least Concern (LC)**

A taxon is of "Least Concern" when it has been evaluated against the criteria and does not qualify for Critically Endangered, Endangered, Vulnerable, or Near Threatened status. Widespread and abundant taxa are often included in this category.[1]

## CNPS Rare Plant Ranks
- **California Rare Plant Rank 1A:** Plants presumed extirpated in California and either rare or extinct elsewhere
- **California Rare Plant Rank 1B:** Plants rare, threatened, or endangered in California and elsewhere

- **California Rare Plant Rank 2A:** Plants presumed extirpated in California but common elsewhere
- **California Rare Plant Rank 2B:** Plants rare, threatened, or endangered in California but more common elsewhere
- **California Rare Plant Rank 3:** Review List: Plants about which more information is needed
- **California Rare Plant Rank 4:** Watch List: Plants of limited distribution

## CNPS Threat Ranks

The CNPS ranks at each level also include a threat rank after a decimal point (e.g., CRPB 4.3) and are determined as follows:

- **0.1:** Seriously threatened in California (over 80 percent of occurrences threatened / high degree and immediacy of threat)
- **0.2:** Moderately threatened in California (20–80 percent occurrences threatened / moderate degree and immediacy of threat)
- **0.3:** Not very threatened in California (less than 20 percent of occurrences threatened / low degree and immediacy of threat or no current threats known)[2]

## NatureServe State Rankings

This field guide lists only the state, not the global, rankings for California's medicinal herbs. The state rank (S-rank) refers to the imperilment status only within California's state boundaries.

**S1: Critically Imperiled**—Critically imperiled in the state because of extreme rarity (often five or fewer populations) or because of factor(s) such as very steep declines making it especially vulnerable to extirpation from the state.

**S2: Imperiled**—Imperiled in the state because of rarity due to very restricted range, very few populations (often twenty or fewer), steep declines, or other factors making it very vulnerable to extirpation from the state.

**S3: Vulnerable**—Vulnerable in the state due to a restricted range, relatively few populations (often eighty or fewer), recent and widespread declines, or other factors making it vulnerable to extirpation from the state.

**S4: Apparently Secure**—Uncommon but not rare in the state; some cause for long-term concern due to declines or other factors.

**S5: Secure**—Common, widespread, and abundant in the state.

**SNR: Unranked.**

**SNA: Not Applicable** (used mainly for non-native species).[3]

## United Plant Savers (UpS)

UpS uses a Species At-Risk Assessment Tool to assign scores from 0 to 100 to plants on its "Species At-Risk" list. Only two plants from their list are included in this field guide. Yerba mansa (*Anemopsis californica*) has a score of 41. White sage (*Salvia apiana*) has a score of 49. Several other herbs found in California that are on the UpS list were purposely omitted from this book for conservation reasons, despite their considerable medicinal value.[4]

# COLLECTING, DRYING, AND STORING HERBAL HOME REMEDIES

Before attempting to collect parts from any plant, be sure to read the "Sustainable Collecting" section. Then get to know the growth pattern of the plant so that you can prune or harvest it for increased growth as you would any other plant growing in your garden.

### Collecting, Drying, and Storing Aboveground Parts (leaves, flowers, and berries)

Select healthy plants that are thriving where plenty of that species is growing. As a general rule, do not take more than 10 percent of the foliage of an individual plant or 10 percent of the total plants in a colony or patch. Using clean hand pruning shears, clip outer leafy stems no closer to the center of the plant than necessary. When possible, clip just above a growth bud to stimulate new growth at that point. Arrange the clipped stems facing in the same direction, and bundle them by wrapping with rubber bands or jute garden twine near the cut ends. Tie twine tightly or it will loosen as the herbs dry and shrink. The drier the leaves, the larger the bundles can be. Moist herbs will mold if too many are bundled too close together. Bunches of berries can simply be placed in a paper bag for transporting rather than bundling. Carry all collected herbs in paper or cloth bags, never plastic, to prevent molding.

Hang bundles of leafy or flowering stems in a dark, dry, well-ventilated place to air-dry. Individual leaves and clusters of flowers and berries can be spread out in shallow cardboard flats, which can then be stacked crossways on one another to allow air circulation. You can also use recycled framed window screens covered with cheesecloth as makeshift drying shelves. Stack them with bricks or blocks of wood at the corners to provide air space between them. You can also tack cheesecloth or netting onto empty window frames or across the tops of cardboard boxes. Be resourceful with the space you have to work with. In very moist climates, a fan may be necessary to prevent spoilage.

Once thoroughly dry, herbs should be stored in airtight containers in a cool place away from light. I use clean mason jars, recycled glass jars with clean lids, and recycled holiday cookie tins. Store herbs in as whole a form as possible, and crumble or grind just before using. Aboveground parts will be good for at least one year, often longer if properly stored. Aromatic herbs will lose their potency faster through oxidation. The smell test will let you know if they are still good. Modern high-tech folks can use a vacuum sealing device to preserve herbs much longer, but I prefer glass over plastic bags for long-term storage.

## Collecting, Drying, and Storing Tree Bark

The inner bark closest to the wood is the part you want. If you're able to find freshly cut or fallen limbs or a woodcutter provides some for you, great! They must be fresh, though, as all bark will harden quickly, and some barks start to ferment within a couple of days. Otherwise, for the health of the tree, harvest small branches rather than taking bark from the trunk. Choose small to medium branches that you can cut with clean hand pruning shears. Ideally, they will have at least ⅛ inch of bark. Using a sharp knife or heavy-duty vegetable peeler, scrape off as much as you can of the thin outer layer of the bark, but don't stress if you can't remove it all. Starting at the cut end of the branch and working a section at a time, score ½-inch-wide strips lengthwise with your knife. Score another shallow cut around the circumference of the branch several inches down, and use your knife to pry up and peel back strips of bark to that line. If the bark won't peel easily, carefully slice it off with your knife or peeler, trying not to dig into the wood. Repeat this process up the branch. Bark should be transported in a paper or cloth bag and dried as soon as possible to prevent fermentation.

Spread out pieces of bark in cardboard trays or screen/netting shelves as described above to dry. Turn each day to prevent spoilage. You can pierce larger strips and hang with twine. If the right drying conditions are not available, use a dehydrator to dry bark. Cut or break bark into smaller pieces when dry to store.

As with all herbs, be sure bark is completely dry before storing. Barks will usually store for two to three years unless cut or ground down to powder or very small pieces. Wait until just before use for final processing into smaller units.

## Collecting, Drying, and Storing Roots

To collect roots from shrubs or trees, dig up a few root sections as far from the trunk as you can find them. If you must dig up whole smaller plants for their roots, do so in the fall or winter after seeding, and choose the largest plants of the patch, leaving the smaller ones to grow. Fill in your holes, and make sure those plants you leave behind are still firmly rooted in the soil. Do not remove more than one-fourth of the plants in a group. Transport roots in paper or cloth bags.

Thoroughly wash all dirt off the roots, and towel dry. Cut roots into medium-size pieces, and start drying immediately in well-ventilated shade. Larger roots should be split lengthwise before cutting into pieces. When completely dry, store roots in that form, as described above for other herbs, and then cut into small pieces or run through a grinder just before using. Larger pieces will keep for several years. Some roots must be cut smaller before drying; otherwise, they will become too hard to cut or grind when fully dry.

# PREPARING HERBAL HOME REMEDIES

## Infusion

An infusion is the standard way to prepare a tea of most leaves, flowers, and berries. To make a hot infusion, pour just-boiled water over herbs in a cup, mug, saucepan, or teapot. Cover right away and let it sit (steep) for 10–15 minutes for a beverage tea or 20–30 minutes for a medicinal tea. Use approximately 1 teaspoon dried herbs per cup (8 ounces) water for a beverage tea or 1 tablespoon per cup for a medicinal tea. Double the amount of herbs if using fresh material, since hydrated leaves do not allow water to penetrate their cells as easily. A more accurate way to measure herbs is by weight—1 ounce herbs to 1 quart water.

You can also make a hot infusion by putting the herbs in cold water in a covered saucepan and bringing it to a boil. Immediately turn off the heat and let steep. Strain and drink.

A cold infusion is made by steeping 1 ounce herbs in 1 quart cold water overnight. Strain, compost the herbs, and drink the tea. If you make a larger amount, refrigerate the rest and use it within the same day.

## Decoction

A decoction is the preferred method for preparing most roots, barks, and seeds for tea. To make a decoction, put 1 ounce herbs and 1 quart water in a covered saucepan and bring to a boil. Boil gently for 10 minutes; cool to drinking temperature, strain, and drink. It's worth noting here that the traditional Chumash are known for weaving coiled baskets so tight they can be used to boil water by adding heated rocks.

## Tincture

Alcohol tinctures are used mainly for extracting compounds that are not water-soluble. In my opinion, most of the herbs in this book to be taken internally should be prepared as infusions or decoctions for home use. Tinctures, being much more concentrated, pose a greater risk of overdosing. They are better suited for the professional herbalist. If you have reason to prepare a tincture, the general rule is to combine one part by weight of dried herb with five parts by volume of 70 percent (140 proof) alcohol in a glass jar with a tight-fitting lid. Let it sit for at least two weeks. Up to six weeks is better. Strain, squeeze, or press out the liquid and discard the rest. Label and store the tincture in brown glass eyedropper bottles or in the dark if in clear glass. Alcohol tinctures will keep indefinitely. For recommended proportions and alcohol strengths for specific herbs, see Michael Moore's "Herbal Tinctures in Clinical Practice" online.[1]

## Syrup

A syrup is made by cooking down a prepared herb tea with sugar or honey to a syrupy consistency. Some herbs, like wild cherry (*Prunus* spp.), require an infused tea as a base. Others can be decocted. See Elderberry Immune Syrup, Horehound Cough Syrup, and Wild Cherry Cough Syrup in the "Recipe" section for three syrup recipes.

## Poultice

A poultice is an external application usually made with mashed, warmed fresh herbs. Dried herbs can be steeped in hot water for a poultice if fresh material is not available. The warm moist herbs are wrapped in a dampened muslin or cotton cloth and laid over the affected part. If you have tea from steeping dry herbs, dip the cloth in it and wring out before wrapping the herbs. Cover this with a towel to trap the heat, and leave on until it is no longer warm.

## Salve, Ointment, or Balm

"Ointment" and "balm" are alternate words for a salve. A salve is made by infusing herbs in oil and then adding beeswax to harden it to the desired consistency. For two salve recipes, see Medicinal Ointments and Pinyon Pine Salve in the "Recipes" section of this book.

# HOW TO USE THIS GUIDE

Each plant chapter in this field guide includes the following sections, including a "brief specs" section:

## FAMILY (–ACEAE)

Plants are presented in alphabetical order by plant families, then in alphabetical order by genus and species within the families. Common (English) and scientific (Latin) names of plant families and short descriptions precede the plant chapters. Plants in the same family usually share similar physical characteristics and sometimes have similar phytochemistry, resulting in similar uses. **Note:** All currently accepted plant family scientific names end in "–aceae." Family names are not written in italics; genus and species names are.

## COMMON NAME

The late Tom Bostrom, an Ojai landscape architect legend, once correctly observed that "there is no such thing as a wrong common name for a plant." Phrased in the opposite way, you could say there is no such thing as an exact common name that everyone can agree on. Common names are usually traced back to the original English or Spanish speaker who first encountered the plant and tried to name it. It may have been a translation of a Native American name or simply a descriptive term that made it easier for that person to remember the plant. Many more explorers and settlers followed in their footsteps, sometimes making up new names they felt better described the plant.

The advantage of common names is that they are easy to say and remember and often draw on a main feature of the plant. The disadvantage is that there are many of them for each plant, reflecting local preferences and the history described above. Common names may also contain misleading words, such as "sage" in sagebrush or "pineapple" in pineapple weed—which, by the way, is also not a "weed" unless it's growing where you don't want it in your garden. Both examples were named for their aromas, not for any relation to the other plants named.

This book will use the common name I am most familiar with for each plant. Some other common names will be listed in the brief specs section. Common names will be used throughout the text, except where it's necessary to use the scientific name for clarity. Some chapters include multiple species, with corresponding common and scientific names for each.

**Note:** Given the number of California's Indigenous tribes and languages, it is not possible in a book of this size to list every plant's California Indian names.

## SCIENTIFIC NAME

The scientific (Latin) name is the most current genus-and-species name agreed upon by botanists and taxonomists. This book uses the Jepson eFlora,[1] managed by the Jepson Herbarium at UC Berkeley, as the primary source of scientific names. The eFlora is regularly updated to reflect the latest revisions of *The Jepson Manual: Vascular Plants of California.* It is essential to know or have access to these names and be able to spell them correctly if you hope to make a positive identification supported by multiple sources.

Being able to correctly pronounce the scientific names can help the flow of reading this book. If you don't already have another resource to help with that, you may find the free online article "Pronunciation of Biological Latin" by Peter Ommundsen useful.[2]

## THE BRIEF SPECS SECTION OF THE PLANT CHAPTER

**Synonyms:** Synonyms are alternate, usually less-current, scientific names that may still be in use or found in older reference books. It's helpful to know these synonyms when expanding your plant research beyond this book.

**Other common names:** Just a few of the more commonly used alternate common names are listed here.

**Origin:** Plants known to be growing in California at the time of first European contact are considered native plants. All others are non-native.

**Range:** This is the geographic range within California, including elevations, where the plant is likely to be found. Bear in mind that this range category may include locations at the extremes of where you're likely to see the plant. You have a much better chance of finding any quantity of a plant as you move into the middle of the range. You may also find an occasional specimen outside that range, but usually not enough of a population to justify sustainable collecting.

**Habitat:** Habitat is another name for the plant community in which the plant lives. In a state as large and diverse as California, there are at least thirty such habitats or communities, each of which may have, for example, southern, northern, coastal, or interior versions. For each plant in this book, a few of the most common habitats are listed. The plants may also be found in other habitats not listed. It is beyond the scope of this guide to list every possible habitat on record for a plant. Here are a few of the larger, more-common native plant communities you may find referenced in this book:

- Chaparral
- Coast Redwood Forest
- Coastal Sage Scrub
- Coastal Salt Marsh
- Coniferous Forest

- Creosote Bush Scrub
- Great Basin Sagebrush
- Mixed-evergreen Forest
- Mountain Meadow
- Northern Coastal Scrub
- Oak Woodland
- Pinyon-Juniper Woodland
- Riparian Rivers and Creeks
- Sagebrush Scrub

**Related species in California:** This category is for listing resident California species that are closely related to the plant but did not warrant a chapter of their own. They are often mentioned in the text of the plant chapter and may have similar properties.

**Related species globally:** Same as above for related plants of interest found in other parts of the world.

**Conservation status rankings:** See the "Native Plant Conservation" chapter on page 10 for a complete rundown of these important rankings.

**Uses:** A brief description of some of the most common functions and uses of the herb.

**Parts used:** A brief listing of the plant parts most commonly used.

**Edibility:** Edible or not edible.

## CHAPTER TEXT

### Description
A description of the plant will be found here, including range, habitat, size, color, leaf and flower shapes, and other identifying characteristics. In some cases the range and habitat are already described in the brief specs section and not repeated here.

### Conservation Status
This section expands on the rankings in the brief specs section, including native or non-native status, prevalence (common or rare), and other concerns around the sustainability of the plant's population in California. See also "Native Plant Conservation" and "Sustainable Collecting" for more details as well as general considerations about collecting plants.

## Traditional Uses

Historical uses by California tribes are the focus here, based on an exhaustive study of all existing data recorded or shared directly by Indigenous people or journaled by anthropologists, ethnographers, and other observers. Much of the information in this section includes citations indicating the print and online sources. Where not otherwise noted, much of the record of traditional Native American uses is taken from Daniel Moerman's book *Native American Medicinal Plants: An Ethnobotanical Dictionary*.[3] The book is also accessible online, courtesy of the author, under the title "Native American Ethnobotany Database."[4]

This section may also include global uses for those plants with a long history of use in other parts of the world.

Continuing use of a plant over time is a good indicator that it has proven to be of some benefit. If not, it likely would have fallen out of use. The record of successful historical uses is what scientists call empirical evidence, based on experience rather than on theories proven through laboratory and clinical studies that define modern medicine.

## Modern Uses

This section covers current uses by contemporary tribal members and descendants, modern American and European herbalists, acupuncturists, Ayurvedic doctors, naturopaths, and others. The information in this section relies heavily on the writings of the late herbalist, author, and educator Michael Moore, who is widely considered the unparalleled expert on medicinal plants of the western United States. I had the pleasure of spending time in the field with Michael when herbalist Amanda McQuade Crawford and I hosted him for a multiday workshop in Ojai in the mid-1990s.[5]

Another oft-cited book in this section is *Healing with Medicinal Plants of the West*, third edition, by Chumash herbalist Cecilia Garcia and pharmacologist James D. Adams Jr.[6]

This section also references the German Commission E, a scientific advisory board of Germany's medical regulatory agency, *Bundesinstitut für Arzneimittel und Medizinprodukte* (Federal Institute for Drugs and Medical Devices). Between 1984 and 1994, Commission E published 380 monographs on medicinal plants, some of which are found growing in California as native or non-native species. These monographs were published in English by the American Botanical Council and sourced for this book at their website (herbalgram.org/resources/commission-e-monographs/).

## Phytochemicals/Mechanisms of Action

Plant chemicals are referred to here as phytochemicals. Plants, like all organisms, produce chemicals called metabolites as products of their normal metabolic processes. There are two forms of metabolites. Primary metabolites, such as carbohydrates, lipids, and proteins, are essential for the growth and development of the plant. They are what food foragers are seeking from plants. Secondary metabolites are by-products of primary metabolites. They are not necessary for growth but serve other important functions, such as protecting plants from disease, defending against herbivores, and interacting with other species. Plants produce powerful, concentrated, secondary metabolites such as terpenes, phenols, alkaloids, sterols, and tannins to prevent disease and deter insects and other animals from eating them. Over time, humans discovered that these chemicals are able to create responses in the human body when ingested or applied topically. They are what herbalists are seeking.

In this section we "follow the science" and explore the inner workings of medicinal herbs to see which phytochemicals they contain and how they work to account for the traditional and modern uses described above. This is, by necessity, the most technical section of each plant chapter. As my UC Santa Cruz neuroanatomy professor once warned me and the rest of his students, "Biologists have the biggest words to describe the smallest things." The aim of this book is to present the plant pharmacology in a digestible form, but it's impossible not to sometimes choke on a mouthful of complex chemical names for which there are no simple substitutes.

## Cultivation

While complete gardening information is outside the scope of this book, this section is meant to encourage the reader to explore cultivating California natives. Along with conservation and sustainable collecting practices, growing these plants is the best way to ensure they will be here for future generations. A great free online resource for information on cultivating California natives is the California Native Plant Society's CalScape website.[7] The site features a statewide list of native plant nurseries, including map locations.

## Cautions

There are potential hazards to visiting or using some of the plants described in this book, including mistaking them for look-alike plants, lack of awareness of contraindications, or otherwise misusing them. Hopefully, common sense and a cautious approach will protect you from those concerns not included in this section of the plant chapters.

## Notes

This is a catchall section for miscellaneous harvesting and preparation tips, origin of name, non-medicinal uses, interesting plant lore, etc.

# HERBS

# Lichens

A lichen is a composite organism made up of a fungus and an alga growing in symbiosis. The fungus provides the structure. The alga (singular form of "algae") contains chlorophyll and provides nutrition for the organism through photosynthesis. Lichens are classified as part of the fungus kingdom. Each species is given its scientific name from its fungal component. Lichens are not parasites; they do not draw nutrients from their hosts.

# SHIELD LICHEN FAMILY (PARMELIACEAE)

Parmeliaceae is the largest family of lichens, with 87 genera and more than 2,000 species worldwide in a variety of climates and habitats.

## Usnea genus

*Usnea*, commonly known as beard lichen, is one of the largest genera in the Shield Lichen family, including over 600 species worldwide. It is a grayish-green, fruticose lichen that hangs like a beard from the branches of hardwood and evergreen trees throughout the temperate forests of the world. Usnea is one of those plants, like eucalyptus, whose scientific name is also its most-used common name.

## USNEA
### *Usnea californica*

**Other common names:** California beard lichen, old man's beard

**Origin:** Native

**Habitat:** Oak and coniferous forests

**Related species in California:** Several, including warty beard lichen (*Usnea ceratina*) and Methuselah's beard (*Dolichousnea longissima*; formerly *U. longissima*), now considered rare

**Related species globally:** Old man's beard (*U. barbata*); found worldwide

**Conservation status rankings:**

    **IUCN Red List:** Not listed

    **CNPS Rare Plant Rank:** Only *U. longissima* is listed (as 4.2).

    **NatureServe State Rank:** SNR

**Uses:** Antimicrobial, antifungal

**Parts used:** Whole lichen

**Edibility:** Edible in small amounts, preferably first soaked in water

*Beard lichen, probably* Usnea californica
KYRA EPSTEIN

## Description

Usnea is a grayish-green, fruticose lichen that hangs like a beard from the branches of hardwood and evergreen trees throughout the temperate forests of the world. Usnea can be found in Northern California in cool, damp forests on old-growth oaks, Douglas-firs, pines, and other conifers. Although it generally avoids direct sun, usnea is often found on dying trees, presumably because the loss of canopy allows more sun to reach it and stimulate its growth. There are several very similar species of *Usnea* in California, with *Usnea californica* among the most common. Even some lichen experts have trouble telling the various usneas apart.

On top of that, usnea resembles other tree-dwelling lichens, such as oak-moss (*Evernia prunastri*) and lace lichen (*Ramalina menziesii*), the California state lichen. What distinguishes usnea from other lichens is the white, elastic "cord" running through it. This filament stretches when gently pulled, whereas other lichens will break apart. Any *Usnea* species can be used for the purposes described below.

## Conservation Status
Usneas and lichens in general are susceptible to excess nitrogen, sulfur dioxide, and other toxic chemicals in air pollution. Once common and widespread, the population of the related lichen species Methuselah's beard (*Dolichousnea longissima*) has declined severely due to air pollution. The USDA Forest Service has a National Lichens & Air Quality Database and Clearinghouse to help them assess the ecological impacts of air pollutants.

Even in the best conditions and where plentiful, this lichen grows very slowly, so please be extra careful not to harvest more than you need. An ecological way to harvest usnea is to pick it up off the forest floor after a storm and dry it thoroughly before storing.

## Traditional Uses
The Nitinaht of Vancouver Island, British Columbia, use usnea as a wound dressing and for bandages.[1] California tribes use it as diaper material. Over time, they probably observed its antifungal effect on diaper rash. Usneas have a long history of use in Europe and Asia as antibacterial and antifungal remedies.

## Modern Uses
The American Botanical Council (ABC) reports that local species of *Usnea* are used by American herbalists as an infusion or a diluted alcoholic tincture to treat lung infections, tuberculosis, urinary tract infections, *Candida albicans*, and strep throat. Based on its longtime use by European herbalists for mucus membrane infections, the German Commission E studied *U. barbata* and reported antimicrobial activity. They approved it for mild inflammation of the oral and pharyngeal mucosa. It is usually taken in lozenge form.[2] Usnea ointments are commonly sold in Europe for treating topical fungal infections such as athlete's foot and ringworm.

In 1986 California herbalist Christopher Hobbs wrote a book that is still the ultimate resource on all aspects of usnea, including its uses and phytochemistry. The book is now out of print, but he has made it available online.[3] The

Kaiser Permanente website includes usnea in a list of "herbs that directly attack microbes." The list includes several other herbs covered in this field guide: creosote bush, eucalyptus, sage, and St. John's wort.[4]

## Phytochemicals/Mechanisms of Action

All *Usnea* species contain lichenic acids, including usnic acid, a secondary metabolite (a by-product of plant metabolism produced for some purpose other than growth). Usnic acid may possibly protect the lichen from unwanted effects of sunlight exposure and deter grazing with its bitter taste. Usnea's antimicrobial and antifungal chemicals probably inhibit the growth of harmful microorganisms on the lichen. According to a study mentioned on the ABC website, *U. barbata*, the common species of commerce, has demonstrated a broad antibiotic spectrum.[5] Studies have shown that usnic acid is effective against Gram-positive bacteria such as *Streptococcus* and *Staphylococcus*.

A species of *Usnea* was cultured in a laboratory in India with a goal of generating enough material for pharmaceutical research. Researchers were looking for evidence of its antioxidant potential but also found it to be antibiotic, antimycobacterial, antiviral, anti-inflammatory, analgesic, antipyretic, antiproliferative, and cytotoxic.[6]

## Cultivation

While lichenologists have been able to transplant other Shield family lichens, such as oakmoss, I am not aware of any attempts to transplant usnea. If it's even possible, it would be very difficult to simulate the unique conditions in which usnea chooses to grow in the wild.

## Cautions

Lichens accumulate airborne toxins, such as mercury in ocean fog, so it's important to keep up with research on local air quality if you plan to collect usnea. Although a few cases of liver toxicity were reported from ingesting a weight-loss product containing usnic acid, usnea is considered safe to take internally in the traditional manner as a tea. Despite its bitterness and mild acidity, some people eat small amounts, usually first soaking it in water. More than a small amount could cause digestive upset.

## Notes

Usnea can be mistaken for other fruticose lichens hanging on trees. The pull test on the tough and elastic central cord will distinguish it.

A tincture of usnea is a common way to preserve it as a liquid for external use. See "Recipes" for Usnea Antibacterial Double Extraction.

# Gymnosperms

"Gymnosperm" means "naked seed." These are primitive plants in the evolutionary time line whose exposed seeds are often held in cones and are fertilized by pollen that lands directly on them. Conifers and ephedra are members of this group. (Angiosperms, the other plant subgroup, evolved much later and enclose their seeds in ovaries.)

The plants in this section are arranged alphabetically, first by the family's scientific (Latin) name and then by the species' scientific name.

# CYPRESS FAMILY (CUPRESSACEAE)

The Cypress family consists of 27 genera with about 130 woody, aromatic species worldwide. Most are trees and shrubs with rot-resistant wood. In addition to those listed in this section, the cypress family also includes redwoods.

## Cedar Group

While the two Cypress family trees described below are commonly known as cedars and share similar medicinal properties and aromatics with true cedars of the genus *Cedrus* of the Pine family, neither is a true cedar. Those are found only in the Mediterranean region and western Himalayas. The naming confusion arose in England hundreds of years ago when imported boxes made from the wood of the aromatic northern white-cedar (*Thuja occidentalis*) were all that were known of that American tree and its cousins. The boxes smelled like those made from true cedar (*Cedrus* spp.), and the cedar name was borrowed. The name stuck when northern white-cedar trees were imported into England and its other relatives were discovered in North America. The hyphen before "cedar" in the common names of our two native California "cedars" indicates that they are not true cedars.

## INCENSE-CEDAR
### *Calocedrus decurrens*

**Synonym:** *Libocedrus decurrens*
**Other common names:** California post cedar, California white cedar
**Origin:** Native
**Range:** Throughout the state except Central Valley and Mojave Desert, 1,100 to 8,200 feet elevation
**Habitat:** Mixed conifer and yellow pine forests

*Incense-cedar sapling.* LANNY KAUFER

*Western red-cedar (*Thuja plicata*).* JEAN L. PAWEK

## WESTERN RED-CEDAR
*Thuja plicata*

**Synonym:** *Thuja gigantea*
**Other common names:** Western arborvitae, giant arborvitae
**Origin:** Native
**Range:** Near the coast of northwestern California to 6,000 feet elevation
**Habitat:** Coastal conifer forest
**Related species in California:** Alaska yellow-cedar (*Callitropsis nootkatensis*), Port Orford white-cedar (*Chamaecyparis lawsoniana*), Monterey cypress (*Cupressus macrocarpa*), junipers (*Juniperus* spp.)
**Related species globally:** Northern white-cedar (*Thuja occidentalis*), Mediterranean cypress (*Cupressus sempervirens*)
**Conservation status rankings:**
    **IUCN Red List:** LC
    **CNPS Rare Plant Rank:** Not listed
    **NatureServe State Status:** SNR
**Uses:** Antifungal, antibacterial, analgesic; for colds, coughs, fungal infections, sore joints
**Parts used:** Leaves
**Edibility:** Not edible

## Description

Incense-cedar (*Calocedrus decurrens*) is a large evergreen tree, 70 to 200 feet tall, with a range extending from all of California into Oregon and Nevada. It has a classic pyramidal shape. The aromatic bark is reddish brown and smooth when young, eventually forming longitudinal fissures that peel off in fibrous strips as it thickens with age. The spreading branches end in flattened, vertical sprays of decurrent, scalelike, bright green, aromatic leaves ⅛ to ½ inch long. Light brown pollen cones on the tips of the branches release their contents around December. Dark reddish-brown seed cones that resemble duckbills with a tongue sticking out are ⅔ to 1⅓ inches long and appear on the same

*Incense-cedar (*Calocedrus decurrens*)*
ENRIQUE VILLASEÑOR

tree as the pollen cones. They ripen in the fall and remain on the tree until spring.

Western red-cedar (*Thuja plicata*) is another large aromatic conifer of similar appearance, reaching heights of 100 to 230 feet. Its extended range includes the Pacific Northwest and Alaska. The only habitat it shares with incense-cedar in California is in the far northwestern corner of the state. Western red-cedar also develops thick, fibrous, reddish-brown bark with shallow fissures that peel easily. Its branches also form flat, fanlike sprays, but they are not vertical like those of incense-cedar. The upper surface of the young shoots is glossy dark green; the underside is streaked with white. The scalelike, decurrent leaves are ¹⁄₁₆ to ¼ inch long. Most of the pollen cones are found on the foliage on the sunny side of the tree. The light brown seed cones are found midway down the branches on the same tree as the pollen cones. They are football shaped and only ⅜ to ¾ inch long until they open and spread out like wooden flowers.

*Western red-cedar leaves and cones*
J. R. "BOB" HALLER, COURTESY OF SANTA BARBARA BOTANIC GARDEN

## Conservation Status

Both trees are common and unthreatened within their ranges at this time. Thousands of acres of giant old-growth incense-cedar trees were logged in the past to produce . . . get ready for it . . . pencils. Apparently, the wood has all the right characteristics of straightness and density for a perfectly sharpened pencil. While incense-cedar is still the preferred pencil wood, improved forestry practices have created a sustainable supply of second- and third-growth trees for the pencil industry.

## Traditional Uses

The Yuki drink a decoction of incense-cedar leaves to relieve stomach problems.[1] The Oregon Paiute inhale the steam from the leaf infusion for colds, and the Oregon Klamath inhale the purifying steam in the sweat lodge.[2] Train reports some Nevada Paiute people drinking a decoction as a protection against infectious

Fragrant, peeling bark of incense-cedar, the source of its common name
BEN GRANGEREAU

diseases.[3] Historically, the Miwok prepared a bath for smallpox patients with a decoction of incense-cedar leaves. This was said to cure the pustules and prevent more-serious skin eruptions. The bath was also used for ague (alternating chills and fever).[4] For another external use, see "Recipes" for Carol Wermuth's antifungal cedar balm from the Tübatulabal people.

Moerman cites several tribes of the Pacific Northwest drinking an infusion or decoction of the leaves of western red-cedar for coughs and colds. A decoction or poultice of the leaves is applied to sore joints or sore backs and to the upper back for bronchitis.[5] The related Cypress family trees mentioned above, as well as juniper, have been used worldwide for centuries for similar medicinal purposes as incense-cedar and western red-cedar.

## Modern Uses

While incense-cedar is not used much in modern Western herbalism, western red-cedar is still in use, often in tincture form to better extract the essential oil compounds. To clear bronchial mucus, steam is inhaled from the infused leaf tea or from simmering water to which a teaspoon of tincture has been added. The cold infusion can be drunk for chronic bladder and urethra irritation. Women can take it for achy, long menstrual cycles or vaginal irritation. The same tea is used by men for an enlarged prostate. Small daily doses can build immunity against chronic respiratory and intestinal infections. Externally, the tincture (or the cedar balm in the "Recipes" section) can be applied two or three times a day to fungal infections such as ringworm, tinea versicolor, and athlete's foot.[6]

## Phytochemicals/Mechanisms of Action

The medicinal properties of these two resinous trees derive mainly from their essential oils, found throughout the entire plants and concentrated in the wood. They provide these conifers with their characteristic aromas and protect them against herbivores and fungi.[7] The oils are composed mainly of terpenes known to be antifungal, antimicrobial, and pain-relieving. Incense-cedar oil contains about fifty such compounds. The highest concentrations are the monoterpenes limonene, carene, pinene, and terpinolene.[8]

The essential oil of western red-cedar leaf contains over eighty compounds. The main constituent by far is the monoterpene thujone, named for the *Thuja* genus. There also are significant amounts of the monoterpene fenchone and the diterpene beyerene. Also present in smaller amounts are other monoterpenes, such as sabinene, camphor, and terpinen-4-ol.[9]

Research has shown that certain plant families, including the Cypress family, show exceptional antibacterial activity. The similarity in phytochemical makeup of the various Cupressaceae species mentioned here is a good predictor of new antibacterial drugs.[10] Plant pharmacologists, are you listening?

*Incense-cedar branch.* BETTY (POTTS) RANDALL, COURTESY OF SANTA BARBARA BOTANIC GARDEN

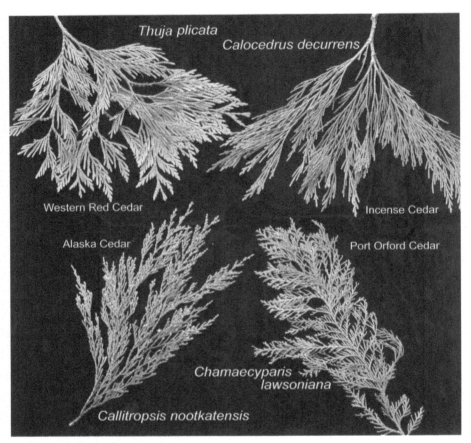

*Four California "cedars" compared.* PATRICK BREEN

## Cultivation

If you have rich, loamy soil and the right space for a tall evergreen, you can find incense-cedar at many nurseries. It will get by on 10 inches of rain a year, but likes more, and will tolerate up to 150 inches with good drainage in its natural habitat. Western red-cedar enjoys 40 to 120 inches of rain a year and a cool climate in its home forests. Few nurseries in California carry it. Both can be started from seed. See the California Native Plant Society's CalScape website (calscape .org) for more information on growing both trees.

## Cautions

Due to its thujone content, western red-cedar should not be ingested in strong concentrations or for extended periods of time, especially by those with known kidney conditions. Pregnant women should not ingest it at all. While thujone has not been found in incense-cedar, it's probably safest to observe similar precautions with it.

## Notes

In the traditional leaching of acorns by Indigenous Californians, the stone-ground meal is laid on incense-cedar branches on a bed of sand before water is poured through it. This removes the tannin and imparts a mild cedar flavor to the finished product.

The leaves of both of these "cedars" are used to smudge participants in ceremonies of the Native American Church, where the trees are considered purifying plants, physically and spiritually. They are referred to as "flat cedar," as opposed to "round cedar" (*Juniperus* spp.). The branches are dried and meticulously "cleaned" by eliminating all stems and breaking the leaves into tiny pieces for sprinkling on the coals of the ceremonial fire. The bark, the most fragrant part when burned at home as an incense, is what gave the tree its common name. The bark can be ethically collected from the ground around the tree rather than breaking it off the trunk.

*Calocedrus* means "beautiful cedar," from the Greek *kalos* ("beautiful") and *kedros* ("cedar"). The genus *Thuja* is derived from the Greek *thuia*, also the common name of a resinous, aromatic African tree. The species name, *plicata*, means "folded in plaits" in Greek, referring to the overlapping, scaled pattern of its leaves. Its other common name, arborvitae, translates as "tree of life" in Latin.

## *Juniperus* genus

The *Juniperus* genus includes sixty-seven species and twenty-eight varieties worldwide, almost all in the Northern Hemisphere. There are eight species and varieties in California. The five species described below are the most common ones in California. They represent the two types of junipers: low-growing shrubs with flat, pointy leaves in whorls of three as in common juniper (*J. communis* varieties) or large shrubs and trees with small scalelike leaves that overlap one another to form round, twiglike structures, as in all the rest listed below.

*Singleleaf pinyon pine (*Pinus monophylla*), left, and California juniper (*Juniperus californica*), right, the namesakes of the pinyon-juniper woodland plant community* STEVE JUNAK

# CALIFORNIA JUNIPER
## *Juniperus californica*

**Other common names:** None
**Origin:** Native
**Range:** Western, southern, and southeastern California from 160 to 5,000 feet elevation
**Habitat:** Pinyon-juniper woodland, dry slopes

*Pale blue California juniper berries (*Juniperus californica*) with brown male pollen cones showing among the overlapping scalelike leaves*
JAMES DAVID ADAMS JR.

*Depressed juniper (*Juniperus communis var. depressa*).* KEIR MORSE

*Depressed juniper.* KEIR MORSE

## COMMON JUNIPER
### *Juniperus communis* varieties

**Other common names:** Varieties include depressed juniper (*Juniperus communis* var. *depressa*), Jack's juniper (*Juniperus communis* var. *jackii*), and mountain juniper (*Juniperus communis* var. *saxitilis*).

**Origin:** Native
**Range:** Northern and northeastern California from 2,000 to 11,000 feet elevation
**Habitat:** Rocky places

*Sierra juniper* (Juniperus grandis). LANNY KAUFER

# SIERRA JUNIPER
## *Juniperus grandis* (formerly *J. occidentalis* var. *australis*)

**Other common names:** Grand juniper, Sierra western juniper
**Origin:** Native
**Range:** East side of the Sierra Nevada from 300 to 10,000 feet elevation
**Habitat:** Dry, rocky slopes; forests; pinyon-juniper woodland

*Western juniper* (Juniperus occidentalis) STEVE JUNAK

# WESTERN JUNIPER
## *Juniperus occidentalis*

**Other common names:** Yellow juniper, Canada juniper
**Origin:** Native
**Description:** Tree, 15 to 50 feet high with brown bark
**Range:** Northeastern California from 2,300 to 7,500 feet
**Habitat:** Dry slopes, sagebrush, juniper woodland

*Western juniper berries* (Juniperus occidentalis)
J. R. "BOB" HALLER, COURTESY OF SANTA BARBARA BOTANIC GARDEN

Gymnosperms    39

*Utah juniper berries (*Juniperus osteosperma*)* LANNY KAUFER

# UTAH JUNIPER
## *Juniperus osteosperma*

**Synonym:** *J. utahensis*
**Other common names:** Utah cedar, shaggy-bark juniper
**Origin:** Native
**Range:** Eastern California from 4,300 to 8,500 feet elevation
**Habitat:** Pinyon-juniper woodland
**Related species in California:** All listed above
**Related species globally:** Many in the United States and worldwide, including *J. communis* in Europe and elsewhere
**Conservation status rankings:**
    **IUCN Red List:** LC
    **CNPS Rare Plant Rank:** Not listed
    **NatureServe State Status:** SNR
**Uses:** Antiseptic, aquaretic, carminative; for urinary tract conditions, colds, coughs, poor digestion
**Parts used:** "Berries" (cones), leaves
**Edibility:** Sun-ripened berries of California juniper are sweet and edible.

## Description

All junipers are evergreen and produce similar-looking, hard "berries" (actually fleshy female seed cones) ranging in color from light blue to purple. The berries are usually covered with a white bloom of wild yeast. Some age to a reddish-brown color, others to a dark purplish black. California juniper (*Juniperus californica*) is a shrub or small tree to 13 feet high with layers of thin gray bark. Common juniper (*J. communis*) varieties are spreading, mat-like ground covers. Sierra juniper (*J. grandis*) is a large tree, 25 to 65 feet high, with reddish-brown bark. Western juniper (*J. occidentalis*) is also a tree, 15 to 50 feet high, with brown bark. Utah juniper (*J. osteosperma*) is a small tree, up to 25 feet high, with layers of thin, grayish-brown bark. The berries and leaves of all juniper species can be used for medicinal purposes.

## Conservation Status

All five species are common enough in California to be considered secure. Common juniper (*J. communis*) and its subspecies and varieties have the largest global range of all woody plants on Earth. They are found throughout the cooler regions of the entire Northern Hemisphere.

## Traditional Uses

In California the Atsugewi, Achomawi, Cahuilla, and Maidu chew local juniper berries or make a berry tea to treat colds and fevers. They use the bark to prepare teas for treating colds and fevers. The Modoc drink an infusion of the leaves for coughs and colds and an infused tea of leaves or berries to relieve urinary problems. The Chumash make a decoction of the berries for rheumatism as well as problems in the genitourinary system. The Ohlone prepare a decoction of the leaves to relieve pain and cause sweating.[11] [12] [13] [14] [15]

Farther east, the Shoshone and Paiute consider Utah juniper the herb of choice for cold and cough remedies. They usually boil the branch tips to make a tea, sometimes adding the berries or cooking just the berries alone. This tea is also used for fevers and stomachaches and, boiled with pine resin, for kidney ailments. The berries are preferred for kidney problems and to induce urination. Nine berries are boiled in 1 quart of water and the tea taken in half-cupfuls three to four times a day.[16] In Arizona and Nevada, the White Mountain Apache and the Gosiute make an infusion of California juniper leaves for colds and coughs. Apache women also drink it to relax uterine muscles prior to childbirth.[17]

## Modern Uses

In Europe, herbalists have long used juniper berries as a carminative and digestive stimulant to treat indigestion and flatulence and to increase the appetite. Citing its history of use, German Commission E approved juniper berry for dyspepsia (indigestion). They also reported an increase in urine excretion and a direct effect on smooth muscle contraction in animal experiments, but stopped short of approving juniper berry for those purposes. For the most part, modern herbalists use juniper for increasing urination and disinfecting the urinary tract. Michael Moore recommends a teaspoon of crushed berries or a rounded teaspoon of leaves, steeped in a cup of water for 15 minutes, to be taken one to three times a day. He suggests mixing it with bearberry or manzanita leaves. To stimulate stomach secretions for improved digestion, he suggests eating a few berries about 1 hour before meals.[18] Herbalist Stephen Buhner prefers to treat urinary tract infections with five to twenty drops of a berry tincture up to three times a day or an infusion of the leaves three to six times a day.[19]

As with pines and cedars, a steam inhalation of the leaves is helpful for upper respiratory conditions. Externally, the essential oil is applied to sore joints and muscles to treat arthritis and rheumatism. The same can be done with a homemade balm (ointment). See "Recipes" section for steam inhalation and ointment instructions. According to Buhner, any dried, powdered part of the plant can be used externally to prevent or cure wound infections.[20]

### Phytochemicals/Mechanisms of Action

Thanks to its long history of use, common juniper is one of the most studied of all plants. Its antiseptic activity is derived mainly from its essential oil when it is excreted through the urinary tract. Almost 60 percent of the oil consists of antimicrobial monoterpenes, including pinene, sabinene, myrcene, camphene, camphor, cineole, cymene, cadinene, limonene, terpinene, thujene, and borneol.

The main active ingredient is terpinen-4-ol, a monoterpene alcohol. It works as an irritant, stimulating the glomerular filtration rate in the kidneys to increase urination. It is considered aquaretic because, unlike some other diuretics, it does not cause loss of electrolytes in the urine. Juniper also contains sesquiterpenes such as cedrene, cedrol, caryophyllene, cadinene, and elemene, which may provide added antioxidant and anti-inflammatory activity. A flavonoid, amentoflavone, has shown antiviral properties in tests.[21]

It is likely that most, if not all, these compounds from common juniper are found in the other junipers listed above. The essential oil of western juniper, for example, showed strong wound healing and anti-inflammatory activity when applied externally in an animal study.[22]

### Cultivation

Junipers are drought tolerant and will grow in most soils, but they are not easy to start from seed. California juniper and common juniper plants are sometimes available in native plant nurseries. The others may be hard to find in California.

## Cautions

The essential oil of juniper creates antiseptic aquaresis by irritating the kidneys. Therefore, juniper preparations of any kind should not be ingested by those with kidney disease or by pregnant women. While simple home preparations are otherwise safe for short periods, internal use of this or any essential oil should be done under the supervision of a medical herbalist, integrative physician, or other certified practitioner.

## Notes

Common juniper berries are gathered in their second year; the other species, at the end of the first year. Leaves can be harvested at any time. Fully ripe juniper berries are eaten as is or sun-dried and processed into a flour by several California tribes. Some enjoy it; others consider it a survival food. I have found the berries to be sweet and delicious when they are so ripe that they are falling off the trees.

Dried juniper leaves are placed on hot coals in the same manner as incense-cedar (*Calocedrus decurrens*) leaves for a calming and purifying smudge in Native American Church services and other tribal ceremonies. They are sometimes referred to as "round cedar" while incense-cedar leaves are called "flat cedar." The smoke is also used as a fumigant in the home after illness.

Gin gets its name from the juniper berries used to flavor it. The genus name *Juniperus* comes from the Latin *junio* ("young") and *parere* ("to produce"), meaning "youth-producing," a fitting tribute to this healing herb.

# EPHEDRA FAMILY (EPHEDRACEAE)

*Ephedra* is the only genus in the Ephedra family. Along with the coniferous trees described in this book, it is a gymnosperm—an ancient subgroup of seed plants named for their exposed, or naked, seeds formed on the scales of their cones. Angiosperms, the other plant subgroup, evolved much later and enclose their seeds in ovaries.

## *Ephedra* genus

*Ephedra* species prefer arid, desertlike habitats. They are basically leafless, densely branched shrubs that are able to photosynthesize through thin, green, jointed stems that form in whorls on the woody lower branches and then reach straight for the sky. Nodes at the stem joints produce pollen cones on male plants and seed cones on female plants.

## CALIFORNIA EPHEDRA
### *Ephedra californica*

**Other common names:** California desert tea, California Mormon tea, California joint-fir, Indian tea
**Range:** Merced County (central California) and Inyo County (eastern California) to the Mexican border from 230 to 4,300 feet elevation
**Habitat:** Dry grassland, chaparral, creosote bush scrub

## NEVADA EPHEDRA
### *Ephedra nevadensis*

**Other common names:** Gray ephedra, Nevada Mormon tea, Nevada joint-fir
**Range:** Kern County (southern California) and Mono County (eastern California) to the Mexican border below 3,600 feet elevation
**Habitat:** Rocky and sandy soils in creosote bush scrub, desert grassland, and Joshua tree woodland

*Nevada ephedra (*Ephedra nevadensis*)* STEVE JUNAK

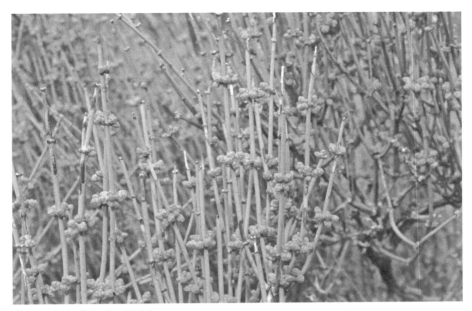

*Green ephedra (*Ephedra viridis*).* JAMES DAVID ADAMS JR.

# GREEN EPHEDRA
## *Ephedra viridis*

**Other common names:** Mountain ephedra, mountain tea, green Mormon tea, green joint-fir, *cañutillo* (Spanish)

**Origin:** Native

**Range:** San Luis Obispo County (western California) and Lassen County (eastern California) to the Mexican border from 3,000 to 7,500 feet elevation

**Habitat:** Sandy soils in sagebrush scrub, creosote bush scrub, Joshua tree woodland, pinyon-juniper woodland

**Related species in California:** Boundary ephedra (*E. aspera*), Death Valley ephedra (*E. funerea*), longleaf ephedra (*E. trifurca*)

**Related species globally:** Chinese ephedra or ma huang (*E. sinica*) and about 50 other species in arid regions worldwide

**Conservation status rankings:**

    **IUCN Red List:** LC

    **CNPS Rare Plant Rank:** All are unlisted except Torrey's Mormon tea (*E. torreyana*), which is 2B.1.

    **NatureServe State Status:** SNR

**Uses:** Astringent urinary tract cleanser, possible decongestant

**Parts used:** Stems

**Edibility:** Beverage tea

*Green ephedra (*Ephedra viridis*).* EDWIN R. CHANDLER, COURTESY OF THE SANTA BARBARA BOTANIC GARDEN

## Description

California ephedra (*E. californica*) grows up to 5 feet high, with very thin grooves running all along the length of the stems. The stems are bright green when young, turning yellow-brown with age. They are the thickest stems of these three species. Eventually, the bark turns grayish brown on the lower branches that produce the green stems. California ephedra sprouts three tiny (barely visible), scalelike leaves at the stem joints, setting it apart from the other two species, which make pairs of tiny leaves. Male plant stems produce one to three orange-yellow, ovoid pollen cones per joint node, each about ⅓ inch long. Slightly larger seed cones on female plants also form in nodes, usually one per node but sometimes more. Each cone usually holds one smooth brown seed, sometimes two. Coning season occurs between March and May.

Nevada ephedra (*E. nevadensis*) is a shorter plant, reaching 4 feet in height. Its pale, olive-green stems age to yellow and finally to gray. Males produce one to three ovoid pollen cones ⅛ to ⅓ inch long. Female seed cones are round, ¼ to ½ inch in diameter, and usually produce two seeds.

Green ephedra (*E. viridis*) grows 2 to 5 feet high and 2 to 3 feet in spread, with dense clusters of thin, deep green stems that sometimes age to yellow-green. The stems are also finely ridged like California ephedra. The bark on the lower branches is reddish brown at first, eventually turning gray. Ovoid male cones are about ¼ inch long. Female seed cones are obovoid, ¼ to ⅜ inch long, and produce two smooth, three-angled seeds each.

## Conservation Status

These three species are common and widespread within their ranges; no conservation concerns.

## Traditional Uses

Many native people throughout the Southwest value ephedra as both a beverage and a medicine. The Kawaiisu, Tübatulabal, Cahuilla, Luiseño, and Diegueño use their local species of ephedra in a tea as a blood purifier, a term used to describe an herb that helps the liver or, in this case, the kidneys to remove toxins and waste material from the blood. It is also drunk for backaches associated with kidney problems. The Diegueño drink California ephedra tea for stomachaches caused by overeating or bad food. The Salinan use the tea to treat bladder problems. The Chumash also drink ephedra tea for urinary tract infections, often combining it with corn silk, which was historically acquired through trade with tribes to the east. Some Indigenous groups also use it for stomachaches and many have used it in earlier times to treat venereal diseases. Dried and powdered ephedra stems are used by several tribes as a wound or burn dressing.[23][24][25][26][27]

The Kawaiisu, Tübatulabal, Paiute, and Shoshone drink the tea for colds and the congestion that comes with them. According to Garcia and Adams's *Healing with Medicinal Plants of the West*, the Chumash chew a piece of stem the length of the longest finger to clear up nasal congestion for about an hour and a half.[28][29][30]

## Modern Uses

It's important to clarify that our North American ephedras have not been shown to contain any of the alkaloids found in Chinese ephedra, the source of the drug ephedrine. There is no scientific evidence supporting the use of North American ephedras for asthma, nasal or lung congestion, or other conditions treated with that drug. That being said, the fact that they lack ephedrine compounds (and the dangerous side effects that come with them) combined with their long history of use by Native Americans make North American ephedras safe choices as home remedies. At the least, any of them can be taken as an astringent and diuretic tea for increasing urination and cleansing the urinary tract or for treating diarrhea.

Legendary Southwest herbalist Michael Moore and a graduate of his school, herbalist Michael Cottingham, both attest to the likely presence of trace amounts of ephedrine-like compounds in our native ephedras. Cottingham believes that some species growing in the right soil and conditions have a taste similar enough to Chinese ephedra to make them usable as decongestants and mild stimulants. Moore also recommends trying the tea to reduce congestion related to allergies, especially if taken before the allergic symptoms kick in.[31][32] Once again, as stated throughout this book, further studies are needed. In the meantime, the two Michaels' points of view are a good reminder that plants can speak to us about their phytochemistry with their own language of smell and taste. It takes time and experience in the plants' habitats to learn that language. We await further scientific studies on California's *Ephedra* species.

## Phytochemicals/Mechanisms of Action

Aside from the question of possible ephedrine alkaloids, California's ephedras still have some noteworthy phytochemistry. Studies on the *Ephedra* genus as a whole revealed phenolic compounds, tannin, flavonoids, lignans, proantho-cyanidins, and seven amino acid derivatives.[33] Many of these compounds are likely present in our local species and could account for most of their uses by traditional and modern healers. The only phytochemical analysis that focused on a California species (*E. viridis*) showed four forms of lariciresinol, a phenylpropanoid lignan with antioxidant activity that could prove to be useful for treating several cancers.[34] Another compound, kynurenic acid, a by-product of the amino acid tryptophan, shows promise in the treatment of brain disorders such as schizophrenia.[35] Ephedra tea is a good source of dietary calcium due to a protective coating of calcium oxalate on the plant's exposed stems.

## Cultivation

Ephedras can be propagated by seeds planted in the spring or by division and replanting of the root clump. They must be grown in the type of well-drained, sandy soil of their native habitats. Ephedras prefer full sun but will grow in half shade. They are extremely drought-tolerant once established.

## Cautions

Ephedra tea from these California species is generally considered safe. Because of historical accounts of its Indigenous use to induce abortions, pregnant women should avoid it out of an abundance of caution.

## Notes

Ephedra tea brews to a nice red color, reminding me of a light Pinot Noir. Coincidentally, its mild astringency and pleasant taste make green ephedra tea a nice substitute for red wine or Chinese tea (*Camellia sinensis*) when sipped with a meal. The astringent quality of Chinese green or black tea, red wine—and ephedra—makes them all good palate cleansers when drunk between mouthfuls to enhance the flavor of food.

The name *Ephedra*, like the plant, is ancient. Its meaning in Greek is lost in time. The species name *viridis* is Latin for "green." Some consider alkaloid-containing ephedras to be the world's oldest medicinal plants, with garlic coming in second. The remains of local ephedra stems have been found in Chumash burial sites, placed in baskets with the flowers of California everlasting (*Pseudognaphalium californicum*).

# PINE FAMILY (PINACEAE)

The Pine family includes 10 genera and 193 species worldwide. Not counting subspecies, California is home to seven species of fir (*Abies*), three spruces (*Picea*), seventeen pines (*Pinus*), two Douglas-firs (*Pseudotsuga*), and two hemlocks (*Tsuga*). All are natives, and most are found in cold, wet mountains. The needles and resins of all these Pinaceae species can be used interchangeably as described below for *Pinus*, the family's type genus.

## *Pinus* genus

*Pinus* is the type genus for which the Pine family is named. There are ninety-four species of *Pinus* worldwide, all found in the Northern Hemisphere. California is home to twenty-eight species, subspecies, and varieties of *Pinus*.

### PINES
### *Pinus* spp.

*Jeffrey pine (*Pinus jeffreyi*).* LANNY KAUFER

**Origin:** Native

**Range:** Throughout the state, mostly in the mountains or by the northern coast

**Habitat:** Mainly in colder climates among other conifers

**Related species in California:** Firs (*Abies* spp.), Douglas-firs (*Pseudotsuga* spp.), and other conifers in the Pine family

**Related species globally:** Many pines and Pine family members

**Conservation status rankings:**

**IUCN Global Red List:** All LC except *P. albicaulis* (EN), *P. balfouriana* (NT), *P. coulteri* (NT), *P. monticola* (NT), *P. muricata* (VU), *P. radiata* (EN), *P. torreyana* (CR)

**CNPS Rare Plant Rank:** All unlisted except *P. radiata* (1B.1), *P. contorta* subsp. *bolanderi* (1B.2), *P. edulis* (3.3), *P. longaeva* (4.3), *P. torreyana* (1B.2)

**NatureServe State Rank:** SNR except *P. contorta* subsp. *bolanderi* (S2), *P. edulis* (S3), *P. longaeva* (S3), *P. radiata* (S1), *P. torreyana* (S1)

**Uses:** Respiratory conditions, sore throats, rheumatism, sore muscles

**Parts used:** Needles and resin

**Edibility:** Pine nuts are edible and nutritious; inner bark is cooked for survival food.

*Singleleaf pinyon pine (*Pinus monophylla*), right, alongside California juniper (*Juniperus californica*), center left, in the pinyon-juniper woodland plant community*
STEVE JUNAK

## Description

The focus here is on trees of the *Pinus* genus. Space does not allow for descriptions of all the Pine family genera and species found in California. As stated above, all can be used for the medicinal purposes described below. Pine nuts are the only seeds of Pine family species commonly eaten by humans.

Pines are evergreen, resinous conifers with cone-shaped crowns when young. The number of needles in a bunch, length of needles, and size and shape of cones are the primary indicators of the species. Pine needles occur in bunches of two or more, except for singleleaf pinyon pine (*P. monophylla*), the preferred species for large pine nuts. Other common pines in California include whitebark pine (*P. albicaulis*), lodgepole pine (*P. contorta*), Jeffrey pine (*P. jeffreyi*), sugar pine (*P. lambertiana*), ponderosa pine (*P. ponderosa*), and gray pine (*P. sabiniana*).

## Conservation Status

Other than the species and subspecies listed in "Conservation status rankings" above, pines are not threatened in California. Although some tribes traditionally used bark preparations, please do not take bark from living trees, as it requires pruning or debarking the tree, potentially inviting insects or disease. When gathering pitch in the wild, do not cut into the bark or remove any pitch that is serving as a protective layer on a wound. Use the extra resin dripping below the cut or exuding naturally from other places on the trunk.

## Traditional Uses

Native Americans, including most of California's tribes, use the needles or resin (pitch, sap) of pines and other members of the Pine family such as firs and Douglas-firs to make medicinal decoctions, including teas and steam inhalations, for coughs, fevers, sore throats, and rheumatism. The pitch is sometimes chewed and the saliva swallowed for sore throats. Maidu eat one ponderosa pine needle for heartburn.

Several tribes apply warmed or chewed pitch to the skin to remove splinters, bring boils to a head, or as a poultice on cuts, sores, swellings, and insect bites. Some tribes apply a salve of boiled pine pitch and grease to sore muscles and joints. (See pine pitch salve recipes.)

## Modern Uses

Pine sprouts are German Commission E approved for internal use as teas, syrups, and tinctures for catarrhal (inflamed) conditions of the upper and lower respiratory tract and externally as alcoholic solutions in oils or ointments for mild muscular pain and neuralgia. See "Recipes" for two pine salve recipes.

*Mixed conifer forest at sunset on Pine Mountain in Ventura County with white firs (*Abies concolor*) on left and right, alongside Jeffrey pines (*Pinus jeffreyi*), center.* BRYANT BAKER

*Needles of Jeffrey pine (*Pinus jeffreyi*).* LANNY KAUFER

The essential oil obtained from fresh needles, or fresh boughs with needles and tips, is Commission E approved in hot water as a steam inhalation for catarrhal (inflammatory) diseases of the upper and lower respiratory tract or rubbed on the skin as an ointment for rheumatism and neuralgia.

According to Jan Timbrook's *Chumash Ethnobotany*, some contemporary Chumash people add pine needles to hot bathwater as a treatment for rheumatism.

Pine pollen contains over twenty amino acids, including the nine essential ones, many vitamins and minerals, flavonoids, and plant sterols. It has been esteemed as a restorative "Jing" tonic in Chinese medicine for thousands of years, used for adrenal and sexual exhaustion, hormonal imbalance, and fatigue.

*Jeffrey pine bark showing sap (resin) dripping in lower right quadrant.* LANNY KAUFER

## Phytochemicals/Mechanisms of Action

The monoterpenes alpha- and beta-pinene, named for *Pinus*, are among the most common terpenes in nature. They have shown antitumor, antimicrobial, antimalarial, antioxidant, anti-inflammatory, antianxiety, and analgesic effects.[36] The diterpene abietic acid has shown antimicrobial, antiulcer, and cardiovascular activities.

One of the identifying traits of Jeffrey pine is the vanilla-like scent you can smell in the crevices of the bark when the sun shines on it. This is no accident. Coniferin, a glycoside found in the cambium resin of pines, is used to make synthetic vanillin, the primary flavor of vanilla beans.

*Cones of sugar pine (*Pinus lambertiana*), the longest cones of the pine family.* LANNY KAUFER

Two separate laboratory analyses revealed that shoots of eastern white pine (*P. strobus*) and black pine (*P. nigra*) contain significantly more vitamin C (ascorbic acid) than oranges, which have roughly 50 mg/100 g. *P. strobus* had 187 mg/100 g; *P. nigra* had 231 mg/100 g.[37]

*Singleleaf pinyon needles and cones, showing imprint of two nuts on each scale*
J. R. "BOB" HALLER, COURTESY OF SANTA BARBARA BOTANIC GARDEN

*The green cones of white fir (*Abies concolor*) will flake apart when mature and dry.* STEVE JUNAK

## Cultivation

Pines can be grown from seed (unshelled nuts) or seedlings purchased from nurseries. Their potential size and water needs require careful consideration as to which species, if any, are right for your property.

## Cautions

Frequent use of pine teas may cause kidney irritation. Also, in *A Field Guide to Western Medicinal Plants and Herbs*, Foster and Hobbs warn that when cows ingest some pines, a "pine needle abortive factor" can cause decreased uterine blood flow, abortion, and retained placenta in late pregnancy.

## Notes

*P. lambertiana* is named sugar pine because its pitch is sweeter than that

*Needles of red fir (*Abies magnifica*), extending horizontally on younger stem and upright on older stem.* JEAN L. PAWEK

*Rondia Kaufer, the author's wife, with a Jeffrey pine behind her on left of photo, points out a stunted white fir that seems to be growing out of solid rock.* LANNY KAUFER

of other pines. Several tribes chew it like gum. The Karok add it to yerba santa tea as a sweetener.

The inner bark of pines, preferably sugar pine, can be stripped, shredded, boiled, and eaten as a survival food of last resort. Did the Donner party's Miwok guides suggest this? If they did, the idea fell on deaf ears, and Luis and Salvador became the only members of the group purportedly murdered for their flesh.

Traditionally, the Southern Maidu burned dwarf mistletoe (*Arceuthobium* spp.), which grows on several Pine family species, as a healing smudge for patients with coughs, colds, and rheumatism. It's in the Sandalwood family and can be burned simply as an aromatic incense. By harvesting it, you are ridding the pines of a destructive parasite.

*Cones of bigcone Douglas-fir (*Pseudotsuga macrocarpa*), soon to go down in flakes*
J. R. "BOB" HALLER, COURTESY OF SANTA BARBARA BOTANIC GARDEN

# Magnoliids

Magnoliids are an early-evolving group, or clade, of flowering plants (angiosperms) that share magnolia trees as a common ancestor. They are often aromatic and are represented here by California bay and yerba mansa.

The plants in this section are arranged alphabetically by the family's scientific (Latin) name.

# LAUREL FAMILY (LAURACEAE)

This aromatic family boasts 3,500 species worldwide, including sassafras, cinnamon, spicebush, camphor, avocado, and the family's namesake, the European bay laurel (*Laurus nobilis*). Most of the Laurel family are found in tropical and subtropical regions. California bay is the only Lauraceae native to California.

## *Umbellularia* genus

The *Umbellularia* genus has only one species, *Umbellularia californica*. It is the only Laurel family plant native to California.

## CALIFORNIA BAY
### *Umbellularia californica*

**Other common names:** California bay-laurel, pepperwood, Oregon myrtle

**Origin:** Native

**Range:** Widespread throughout California in all but the deserts and Central Valley from sea level to 5,000 feet; also grows in southern Oregon

**Habitat:** Riparian canyons and valleys

**Related non-native species in California:** Avocado (*Persea* spp.)

**Related species globally:** European bay laurel (*Laurus nobilis*)

**Conservation status rankings:**
  **IUCN Red List:** LC
  **CNPS Rare Plant Rank:** Not listed
  **NatureServe State Rank:** SNR

**Uses:** Antiseptic, anodyne, insecticide; for headaches and pain relief

**Parts used:** Leaves

**Edibility:** The mature roasted nuts are edible and high in protein, fats, B vitamins, and minerals.

*California bay (*Umbellularia californica*)* STEVE JUNAK

## Description

California bay is a common and widespread evergreen tree in riparian and related habitats from San Diego to southwest Oregon. It can be found from sea-level coastal streams to 5,000 feet in the mountains. In arid southern California it almost always grows close to the water in canyons with year-round streams.

Farther north, it spreads out from the creeks into riparian valleys, onto damp slopes, and into coniferous forests. It can grow up to 100 feet in height, with a spread of up to 50 feet.

The strongly aromatic leaves are lanceolate, usually 3 to 5 inches long, and resemble willow, but wider and glossier. The top side of the leaf is shinier than the underside. The leaves release their spicy aroma with the slightest rubbing. California bay blooms from December to June in clusters of five to ten flowers in pale yellow, ⅝-inch umbels; hence the Latin name for the genus, *Umbellularia*. The shiny fruits look like smaller, ovoid versions of its Laurel family relative, the avocado. The fruits go through the same color changes as some avocado varieties—from green to dark purple when ripe, at which point they resemble a large olive 1 inch or more in length.

### Conservation Status
This tree's preference for steep, wet canyons and dense forests puts it mostly outside of the terrain favored by developers. Because of that and its natural insect resistance, it is common and unthreatened.

### Traditional Uses
California bay is used by the Tongva and many other California tribes to treat headaches. A tea of the leaves is drunk or the fresh leaves applied to the head as

a poultice by the Ohlone, and the smoke from burning leaves is used to get rid of fleas.[1] A decoction of bay leaves is used by several tribes as an insecticidal wash. Traditionally, branches were buried in the coals with other herbs in a pit fire to fumigate homes when colds or other sickness was present.[2]

The fruit looks like its Laurel family cousin, the avocado, except in this case you shuck the fruit and roast and eat the pit. DIETER WILKEN, COURTESY OF SANTA BARBARA BOTANIC GARDEN

My teacher, Chumash plant expert Juanita Centeno, showed me how to cut a small branch and chew on the cut end to fashion an antiseptic, cooling, and slightly anesthetic toothbrush, especially useful for toothaches.[3]

For migraines and other headaches, Chumash herbalist Cecilia Garcia recommends tearing and deveining sixteen leaves, placing them in a cloth, and inhaling the vapors. Sucking on the end of a torn leaf may also stop some migraines. For general pain relief and aromatherapy, a handful of leaves can be steeped in a

*California bay (*Umbellularia californica*) with ripening bay nuts.* LANNY KAUFER

hot bath for 15 minutes. To strengthen immunity at the change of the seasons, she suggests an infusion of the leaf tea drunk four nights in a row.[4] [5]

Traditional Karok, Miwok, and Pomo, among others, parch the "pepper-nuts" in the ashes of a fire, stir them around, crack them open, and eat them.

### Modern Uses
California bay is a powerful pain-relieving herb. Herbalist Michael Moore echoes the native use of bay leaf infusion for headaches, especially for painful cervical-occipital or neuralgic headaches.[6]

### Phytochemicals/Mechanisms of Action
California bay contains the phenolic compounds safrole and methyl eugenol, the monoterpenes umbellulone and sabinene, and other monoterpenoids such as eucalyptol (cineole) and thymol. These compounds collectively have shown insecticidal, antibacterial, anesthetic, and pain-relieving activity. Safrole is used as an ingredient in insecticides, acting to inhibit insects' defense mechanisms.

It is also the main component in sassafras oil. In 1960, following studies that showed safrole at high doses caused liver cancer in rats, the FDA banned safrole and sassafras oil from foods. Prior to that, safrole was the primary flavoring agent in root beer and was used in toothpaste and other products.

A 2013 study comparing leaves of European bay (*Laurus nobilis*) and California bay for their insecticidal and larvicidal potential found that essential oil of California bay showed biting deterrent activity against *Aedes aegypti*, the notorious yellow fever mosquito. It also killed the mosquito larvae. One of the compounds responsible, umbellulone, is not found in European bay, which may explain why it does not show the same insecticidal activity as its California cousin.[7]

### Cultivation
California bay can be started by planting the unhulled nuts in moist, well-drained, loamy soil. It likes shade in hot climates. It has no serious pests or diseases other than aphids, particularly in damper situations. Sooty mold fungus grows on the aphid honeydew, leaving black powder on the leaves.

### Cautions
Be forewarned: Crushing and smelling fresh bay leaves close to your nose will almost always result in a painful, cold sensation in the sinuses. Applying fresh leaves or essential oil directly on the skin is likely to cause irritation. Because California bay contains safrole, not found in European bay, it is advisable to dry California bay leaves before use in cooking or drinking a tea.

While it may be tempting—and probably effective—to burn the leaves as a fumigant to rid your house of fleas, if not done properly and with adequate protection, it could expose you to toxic smoke.

### Notes
Years ago, I first learned about the vermicidal properties of bay leaves from my Italian stepfather, Frank Landucci. He places the dried leaves in containers of pasta, flour, or grains to ward off weevils. On that note, a 2002 California study found evidence that dusky-footed wood rats place bay leaves around their nests, apparently to kill flea larvae.[8] [9]

Bay wood is used for making bowls and other items. Known in the trade as Oregon myrtle wood, it is a highly prized, fine-grained tonewood, considered an exceptional material for guitar backs and sides.

California bay nuts are an important food in the traditional diet of California and Oregon Indigenous peoples. Modern foragers enjoy them too. When roasted and removed from their outer covering, they have a nutty, dark chocolate flavor with a spicy bay taste. See Christopher Nyerges's *Foraging California* for more on that.

# LIZARD-TAIL FAMILY (SAURURACEAE)

The Lizard-tail family has only five genera and seven species worldwide.

## *Anemopsis* genus

The genus *Anemopsis* consists of just one species, *Anemopsis californica*. It is native to California, the southwestern United States, and northern Mexico.

## YERBA MANSA
### *Anemopsis californica*

**Synonyms:** *A. berlanderi, Houttuynia californica*
**Other common names:** Swamp root, apache beads, lizard tail, *yerba del manso* (Spanish)
**Origin:** Native
**Range:** Central and southern California, from the Bay Area south, below 6,500 feet elevation
**Habitat:** Wet saline or alkaline soils, fresh- and saltwater marshes
**Related species in California:** None
**Related species globally:** None
**Conservation status rankings:**
    **IUCN Red List:** Not listed
    **CNPS Rare Plant Rank:** Not listed
    **NatureServe State Rank:** SNR
**Uses:** Antibacterial, antifungal, antispasmodic, anti-inflammatory; for wounds, sores, ulcers, chronic inflamed mucus membranes, arthritis
**Parts used:** Whole plant, especially the root
**Edibility:** Not edible

*Yerba mansa (*Anemopsis californica*)*
CAROL WADE

## Description

Yerba mansa is an aromatic, perennial herb that grows in colonies spread by rhizomes in wet, alkaline places. It has many hollow, hairy stems growing from white, peppery-tasting roots. Basal leaves are elliptic to oblong and 1½ to 8 inches long on long petioles (leaf stems) that may reach 2 feet high. Smaller ovate leaves up to 5 inches long clasp the lower to middle part of the flower stems. Many tiny white flowers appear on green, cone-shaped spikes ⅜ to 1½ inches long. Each spike is surrounded by what appears to be a whorl of six white petals. These are actually petallike bracts, up to 1¼ inches long. They turn red with age and often show red spots through the flowering season. Yerba mansa flowers

*Yerba mansa flower and leaves showing their red spots.* JAMES DAVID ADAMS JR.

from March to September, depending on location, and usually goes dormant after seeding until the winter rains.

## Conservation Status

Yerba mansa does not appear on any rare or endangered lists. Over time, Native Americans intentionally spread this medicinally important plant. Large patches became established in new locations such as California's Channel Islands. Nonetheless, United Plant Savers added it to their "To-Watch" list due to the current impact of collecting it for medicinal use. Also, much of its historical, California coastal habitat has been lost to development.

## Traditional Uses

Yerba mansa has a long history of use by Indigenous and Mexican people of California and the Southwest. In the late 1800s to early 1900s, several writers, including ethnographer J. P. Harrington, noted that the Chumash used a root tea internally for coughs and as a "blood purifier." Externally, they washed cuts and ulcerated sores with it and applied it as a hot bath or poultice for rheumatism.[10] The Cahuilla drink an infusion of the whole plant for colds, chest congestion, and stomach ulcers. The Kawaiisu and Tübatulabal use a decoction of the roots for colds, coughs, and flus. They and the Shoshone also drink this decoction for indigestion, while the Ohlone take it for menstrual cramps and as a general pain remedy. The root is chewed or a strong tea is used by the Kawaiisu as a mouthwash for canker sores or sores of the mucus membrane.

Topically, the Paiute make a bath with a decoction of the leaves for muscular pains and sore feet. The Ohlone wash sores with an infusion of the plant and apply the dried, powdered plant on wounds as a disinfectant. The Kawaiisu make a leaf salve for cuts and wounds and use a poultice or hot soak of the whole plant for arthritis or as a first-aid treatment for venomous spider or rattlesnake bites.

The Shoshone apply a poultice of boiled, mashed roots to swellings and use a decoction of the roots as an antiseptic wash.[11] [12] [13] [14] [15] [16]

## Modern Uses

Some contemporary Chumash continue to wash sores with a tea of the root and drink it for colds, asthma, and kidney problems.[17] In their article "Chumash Treatments for Broken Bones and Sprains," Adams and Garcia describe lightly wrapping the injured area with yerba mansa leaves, binding them in place with a cloth. This may relieve the pain and speed the healing.[18] Margarita Artschwager Kay, author of *Healing with Plants in the American and Mexican West*, describes widespread continuing use of yerba mansa by native tribes for all the purposes mentioned above and more, including as a douche for excessive bleeding after childbirth. In fact, she reports that she has more entries for yerba mansa in her data collection than for any other species in the book.[19]

Michael Moore praises yerba mansa root tea for healing chronic, congested, inflamed, and/or infected conditions of the mouth, lungs, upper and lower gastrointestinal tracts, and urinary tract. He recommends it for mouth, gum, and throat sores as well as stomach and duodenal ulcers. See "Recipes" for a throat gargle. Like the Indigenous healers before him, he advocates drinking the tea for arthritis and similar problems and cites two actions: excretion of nitrogenous wastes (like uric acid) through the urine and anti-inflammatory effects within the joints. He also seconds the Indigenous uses of the root tea as an antibacterial first-aid treatment for scrapes and bruises, and the application of the dried root powder as an antifungal dust for diaper rash and athlete's foot.[20]

## Phytochemicals/Mechanisms of Action

Yerba mansa contains thirty-eight phytochemical compounds found throughout the plant but mainly concentrated in the root. The essential oil contains phenolic compounds created by the plant as antibacterial and antifungal protectants, which may be useful for surviving the swampy habitats it prefers. The primary compound, methyl eugenol, sometimes known as allylveratrole, makes up 57 percent of the essential oil and is believed responsible for much of yerba mansa's antibacterial and antifungal effects. Methyl eugenol is found in over 450 other aromatic species, including California bay, and also has shown antispasmodic, anti-inflammatory, and pain-relieving activity.[21]

Also present in the oil are antibacterial and pain-relieving monoterpenoids such as thymol (13.8 percent) and piperitone (8 percent). Additional monoterpenoids in the oil with similar properties include pinene, sabinene, phellandrene, and eucalyptol (cineole), among others. In laboratory studies, the oil showed antimicrobial activity against the bacteria *Staphylococcus aureus* and *Streptococcus pneumoniae* and the fungus *Geotrichim candidum*.[22] [23]

*A typical colony, or patch, of yerba mansa (*Anemopsis californica*)* STEVE JUNAK

## Cultivation

Yerba mansa is well-suited for pond edges, water features, streams, and wet areas. It can be propagated by transplanting runners into damp soil or sowing seed in pots for later transfer to the landscape.

## Cautions

The methyl eugenol in yerba mansa may interact with sedative-hypnotic prescription drugs. The plant should not be taken internally during pregnancy.

## Notes

The aboveground parts can be harvested at any time of year before they go dormant. The roots can be gathered at any time for using fresh, although Moore and most others consider the roots to be at their strongest when the plant dies back in the fall. Herbalist Carol Wermuth, a student of Kawaiisu healer Rose Barneche, says the whole fresh plant, including the root, can be simmered for a light tea after thorough washing to remove clay and silt. The plant, or the roots alone, must be brewed much stronger for poulticing or other external use. The roots are sliced into thin disks and dried thoroughly for later use.[24] Moore recommends wilting the roots for several weeks with good ventilation before cutting them into small pieces to finish drying.[25]

The scientific name *Anemopsis* was most likely derived from the plant's resemblance to the cone-shaped flowers of the genus *Anemone*. Its common name, yerba mansa, supposedly began as *yerba del manso*, which translates literally as "herb of the tame [domesticated] Indian." This doesn't make immediate sense. What seems more plausible is that *manso* is short for *remanso* ("backwater"), a description of the plant's preferred habitat.

# Monocots

Monocots are a group, or clade, of flowering plants (angiosperms) with one embryonic leaf (cotyledon) as compared with eudicotyledons (eudicots), which have two. Although there is no consensus, some botanists consider monocots to be earlier than eudicots on the evolutionary time line. There are 60,000 species of monocots. The Orchid and Grass families are the largest groups of monocots. Lilies, onions, and garlic are also monocots.

# GRASS FAMILY (POACEAE)

The Grass family is a large, worldwide family of monocotyledons, or monocots. Poaceae is the fifth-largest family of plants and includes the cereal grains, sugarcane, bamboo, and the many grasses of lawns, meadows, pastures, and prairies. Important edible grass seeds, known as grains or groats, include oats, wheat, corn, barley, rye, and millet. Many plants may have the word "grass" in their common names, but only those of the Poaceae family are true grasses.

## *Avena* genus

There are twenty-nine species of *Avena,* or oats, in the temperate regions of the world, including cultivated oats (*A. sativa*), the source of oatmeal. None are native to California. Wherever they are found growing wild, they are simply called wild oats.

## WILD OATS
### *Avena fatua*

**Other common names:** Common wild oats, spring wild oats
**Origin:** Non-native
**Range:** All of California except the deserts, on disturbed soil up to 8,000 feet elevation
**Habitat:** Roadsides, grassland, disturbed soil
**Related species in California:** Cultivated oats (*A. sativa*)
**Conservation status rankings:**
    **IUCN Red List:** LC
    **CNPS Rare Plant Rank:** Not listed; invasive, naturalized species
    **NatureServe State Rank:** SNA
**Uses:** Nervine, antispasmodic, tonic, mineral supplement
**Parts used:** Green stems and unripe seeds
**Edibility:** Oat groats are an important cereal grain; oatstraw tea is rich in minerals.

*Flowering stalks of wild oats (*Avena fatua*) with immature green seeds.* LANNY KAUFER

## Description

Wild oats (*Avena fatua*) and its cousin, cultivated oats (*A. sativa*), are non-native, winter annual grasses found in many habitats wherever there is disturbed soil or grazing land, especially on native grassland sites. They can often be seen on

*Wild oat stalks before cleaning*
LANNY KAUFER

*Wild oat stalks after stripping away blades*
LANNY KAUFER

roadsides, with upright leaves (blades) reaching 2 to 3 feet tall and flowering stems up to 6 feet in a good rain year. Across California's diverse geography, they can flower anytime in the spring, with the seeds ripening a month or two later. While oats share common, easily recognizable traits with other cereal grasses—green blades, a hollow stem, and clusters of seeds near the top—they are easily distinguished from most other grasses by the way the bristly seeds dangle separately on short stems branching off at more or less right angles from the main stalk. Over centuries, the seeds of cultivated oats were bred to be larger for eating. The blades of oats, like all grasses, are sandpapery rough when "rubbed the wrong way," an indication of the high silica content.

## Conservation Status

Wild oats were originally introduced to California as livestock forage and are considered an invasive weed wherever they interfere with farming of cultivated oats or crowd out native plants. They are a main culprit in the "type conversion" of plant habitats from natives to non-natives that happens after too-frequent wildfires. Cultivated oats are a naturalized escapee from farms. It's safe to say that native plant enthusiasts are happy to see both of these invasive species removed before the seeds mature.

## Traditional Uses

There is no Indigenous history of the use of oats prior to European contact in the 1500s. Once oats became naturalized, Native Americans recognized their value as a food, and many tribes made pinole (seed meal) with the groats (seeds).

A tincture of green, unripe oat seeds has a long history of medicinal use in Western herbalism for its sedative and nerve-restoring properties. Herbalist Michael Moore quotes the 1929 *Handbook of Pharmacy and Therapeutics* by Eli Lilly and Company: "Tonic, laxative, and nerve stimulant. Used in chorea, epilepsy, nervous exhaustion."[1]

## Modern Uses

Contemporary herbalists use either of these species for oatstraw tea. Alcohol tinctures, prepared with the immature, milky seeds, are employed to restore the nervous system and adrenal glands, assist convalescence, and strengthen a weakened constitution. The seeds are tinctured while still fresh and milky in two parts 190 proof alcohol (or as close as you can find to that strength). Oatstraw tea is a mild, nutritive remedy that does its work over a period of time.

The German Commission E approves oatstraw for topical use only, allowing oatstraw baths for inflammatory and seborrheic skin diseases, especially those with itching. A decoction made with 3½ ounces oatstraw in 3 quarts water is added to a full bath.

## Phytochemicals/Mechanisms of Action

Oatstraw and oat groats (seeds) contain protein (avenin), amino acids (ergothioneine), flavonoids, alkaloids (avenanthramides, hordenine, trigonelline), vitamins (B1, B2, D, E), and plant sterols. Studies confirm that all these compounds can nourish the nervous system.

Wild oat seeds, on right, compared with compact wild barley seed head (Hordeum *spp.*)
LANNY KAUFER

Oatstraw and oat groats are rich in silica, calcium, magnesium, iron, manganese, zinc, and other minerals important for good health and essential for bone, cartilage, and connective tissue. Several of these minerals are known to have sedative effects and are considered nerve tonics to soothe the nerves and smooth muscles, treating both exhaustion and restlessness.

Oat groats are high in beta-glucans, complex carbohydrates that play an important role in preventing chronic, noncommunicable diseases and also can lower cholesterol levels, according to a study published in the *American Journal of Clinical Nutrition*.[2]

## Cultivation
You can easily harvest your own mature wild oats for replanting. Seed for cultivated oats is readily available. Sow in full sun in well-drained soil in the fall to make use of winter rainfall.

## Cautions
Wild oats is a mild herb with no toxicity. Oatmeal is considered safe for gluten-free diets. It's still best for gluten-sensitive people to test oats or oatstraw in a small dose at first.

## Notes
The hollow green stalks and unripe seed clusters are the parts dried for oatstraw baths and tea. The fresh or dried unripe, milky seeds are used for tincturing. When processing oatstraw for tea, the blades must be stripped away from the stalks. They're a great nitrogen source for the compost pile. The remaining stalks and seed heads can be cut into small pieces with kitchen scissors and used fresh or dried for future use. In this "cut and dried" state they are best prepared as a decoction for baths and teas. If you grind these pieces to a finer, more powdery state, they can be steeped in an infusion rather than decocted. (See "Recipes.")

Some herbs, like ginseng, are household words and earn fortunes in the marketplace. The humble oatstraw tea had its one brush with fame when it was featured in the 1971 dark comedy *Harold and Maude*. I highly recommend the film, considered a cult classic, as well as the delicious tea.

Oatmeal is an excellent source of protein, carbohydrates, and healthy fats, making it a grounding food for building the constitution, especially after an illness or for those who are deficient or underweight. Cultivated oat groats are so small that it takes 12,000 to 17,000 seeds to make up 1 pound. Since the seeds of wild oats are even smaller, it's not practical to harvest them for food unless you have all the time in the world. Good thing oatmeal is in every grocery store.

# Eudicots

The modern term "eudicot," short for "eudicotyledon," is derived from the older "dicot" or "dicotyledon." It refers to plants whose embryos have two initial leaves instead of one (monocot). From an evolutionary perspective, eudicots are the most advanced group of flowering plants (angiosperms). They are the largest group of plants on Earth, estimated at around 280,000 species.

All plants in this section are arranged alphabetically, first by the family's scientific (Latin) name and then by the species' scientific name.

# MUSKROOT FAMILY (ADOXACEAE)

In 1994, DNA research led to Adoxaceae splitting off from Caprifoliaceae, the Honeysuckle family. The Muskroot family has only 5 genera and 220 species worldwide.

## *Sambucus* genus

The *Sambucus* genus includes twenty species found in the temperate and subtropical regions of the world. There are two native species of *Sambucus* in California. One of those is divided into two varieties. All three plants are commonly known as elderberry.

*The overall look from a distance of a flowering blue elderberry (*Sambucus nigra *subsp.* caerulea*)*
LANNY KAUFER

## BLUE ELDERBERRY
*Sambucus nigra* subsp. *caerulea*

**Synonym:** *S. mexicana*
**Other common names:** Mexican elderberry
**Origin:** Native
**Range:** Widespread throughout the western United States from sea level to 10,000 feet elevation
**Habitat:** Riparian habitats, oak woodland

# BLACK ELDERBERRY
## *Sambucus racemosa* var. *melanocarpa*

**Other common names:** Rocky Mountain elderberry
**Origin:** Native
**Range:** Widespread throughout western United States from 6,000 to 12,000 feet elevation
**Habitat:** Riparian habitats, meadows, coniferous forest

# RED ELDERBERRY
## *Sambucus racemosa* var. *racemosa*

**Other common names:** Mountain red elderberry
**Origin:** Native
**Range:** Widespread throughout the United States from sea level to 11,000 feet elevation
**Habitat:** Moist places
**Related species globally:** European black elderberry (*S. nigra*), European red elderberry (*S. racemosa*)
**Conservation status rankings:**
> **IUCN Red List:** LC
> **CNPS Rare Plant Rank:** Not listed
> **NatureServe State Rank:** SNR

**Uses:** Diaphoretic, antiviral; for colds and flus
**Parts used:** Flowers, berries
**Edibility:** The flowers and berries are edible, preferably cooked.

## Description

All three species of elderberry in California are native, deciduous, multistemmed shrubs that can become small trees. They have small, round fruits, ⅛ to ¼ inch in diameter, and pinnate, compound leaves with varying numbers of serrated, lanceolate or ovate leaflets. Blue elderberry (*S. nigra* subsp. *caerulea*) is the most common species in California. It has three to nine leaflets per leaf and dark purplish-blue fruits, can grow to 25 feet, and is found throughout the state up to 10,000 feet, although mostly at lower elevations. *S. racemosa* comes in two varieties named for the color of their fruits: red elderberry

*Blue elderberry (*Sambucus nigra *subsp.* caerulea*) flower cluster.* STEVEN MARK NORRIS

*Blue elderberry bush with berries.* LANNY KAUFER

(*S. racemosa* var. *racemosa*) and black elderberry (*S. racemosa* var. *melanocarpa*). Both are found in Northern California, have five to seven leaflets, and can occasionally reach heights of 20 feet but usually are smaller. Red elderberry grows in moist places up to 11,000 feet. Black elderberry prefers mountain streams and conifer forests from 6,000 to 12,000 feet.

Elderflowers appear in dense clusters of creamy-white to yellow flowers. Blue elderberry flowerheads are 2 to 10 inches across, often flat-topped, and bloom from March to July. Black and red elderberry flowerheads are smaller, ranging from 1½ to 5 inches in diameter, have a cone shape with the central stem dominating, and bloom in July and August.

Ripe elderberries are covered with a whitish bloom of natural yeast, also seen on ripe blueberries and grapes. Clusters may be so heavy that they hang upside down, bending the branches.

## Conservation Status

There are twenty-five species of *Sambucus* worldwide. All are considered secure at this time.

## Traditional Uses

The flowers, berries, and virtually all parts of blue elderberry (*S. nigra* spp.) have been used since ancient times in Europe, North Africa, west and central Asia, and here in North America. That is the species we are discussing here. There is no evidence of Indigenous medicinal use of red elderberry (*S. racemosa* var. *racemosa*) flowers or fruit and little evidence of use of black elderberry (*S. racemosa* var. *melanocarpa*). There are no pharmacological studies at this time on either plant.

The author displays the whitish yeast bloom on a bunch of ripe blue elderberries. HOLLY SHERWIN

The Miwok, Yuki, Kashaya, Cahuilla, Chumash, and most other California tribes use a hot elderflower tea for flus and colds; some, specifically to break a fever. The Kawaiisu and Chumash use it for fever in measles cases too. The Dieg-ueño consider it a safe tea for babies with fevers, adding wild rose petals. The Cahuilla boil the roots for constipation; the Kashaya Pomo, for a healing lotion on open sores and cuts. The Paiute apply a poultice of heated stems for rheumatic pains. Several tribes use a decoction of the leaves as an antiseptic wash.

Hippocrates, the "Father of Medi-cine," is said to have called elder his "medicine tree." Herbalists around the world have echoed his praise, giving the elderberry tree legendary status. In *A Modern Herbal* (1931), Mrs. Grieve devotes many pages to elderberry's his-tory and uses. Longtime English medici-nal recipes passed down to her include elderflower water, tea, lotion, salad, vinegar, and ointment. With the berries she prepares medicinal juice, wine, syrup, jam, ketchup, and chutney. She includes a recipe for making a thick syrup called a rob, the oldest English preparation of the berries for colds. Her book and recipes are now available free online.[1]

## Modern Uses

Elderflower tea and elderberry syrup are used by herbalists to treat the early stages of colds and respiratory flus. A long-standing European remedy still used today calls for drinking a hot infusion of equal parts of elder flowers and peppermint

*Ripe blue elderberries, center, with green unripe berries, upper left.* BEN GRANGEREAU

leaves, 1 tablespoon of the mixture steeped in 1 cup of boiled water, followed by going to bed under thick blankets. The idea is to raise the body's temperature beyond the virus's limits and then break the fever through sweating.

Citing diaphoretic activity and increased bronchial secretions, the German Commission E approved the use of elderflowers as an infusion, extract, or tincture for colds.

## Phytochemicals/Mechanisms of Action

Elderberry fruits and flowers are rich in healthful sugars, fiber, protein (including six essential amino acids), vitamin C, and minerals (potassium, calcium, iron, and many others). A protein in *Sambucus* can bind directly to the virus and neutralize a viral protein called influenza hemagglutinin that helps the virus attach to lung cells. The fruits and flowers also contain polyphenol compounds with antioxidant and immune system stimulating activity. These include anthocyanins (pigments), flavonoids, and terpenes. The anthocyanins and flavonoids can block the virus from attaching to dendritic cells in the lungs, allowing those protective cells to do their job of activating the immune system.[2][3][4][5]

Elderberry preparations are best used at the first sign of sickness. Several studies have shown that elderberry flowers, fruits, and products like Sambucol, a cold and flu product from Israel, can affect the onset, duration, and severity of colds and flus.[6][7] One prominent 2016 study found that a *Sambucus* extract reduced cold duration and symptoms in air travelers.[8]

*Processed blue elderberries cleaned of stems.* LANNY KAUFER

## Cultivation

Elderberry trees or shrubs can be started from seeds with the pulp removed. They can tolerate a variety of soil types and will grow in full sun or partial shade.

## Cautions

Avoid ingesting too many of the raw fruits. All fresh parts of elderberry plants contain cyanogenic glycosides, which convert to cyanide when cut, chewed, digested, or otherwise exposed to oxygen. These compounds are lowest in the berries and flowers but at potentially toxic, nausea-inducing levels in all other parts, including the seeds. Cooking, baking, or dehydrating the berries will evaporate the toxin from the seeds if they're left in. To be extra safe and to improve the flavor, I separate the berries from the stems and strain the juice from the seeds and skins before cooking it with sugar to make a syrup.

More cases of nausea are reported from ingesting the red berries, so it might be best to avoid them or test small amounts first for ill effects. One 2017 study found that the cyanogenic glycosides increase at higher altitudes.[9]

## Notes

Elderberry is also known as "the music tree." The genus name *Sambucus* comes from a Greek word for an ancient stringed instrument made from its wood. Many California tribes make clapper sticks, flutes, and whistles by hollowing out the pith in the center of the stem.

*The author separates blue elderberries from the stems.* RONDIA KAUFER

# CARROT FAMILY (APIACEAE)

The carrot family is one of the world's largest, consisting of about 446 genera and 3,820 species. Most are aromatic, and all flower in umbrellalike clusters called umbels. The family includes important foods and spices such as carrot, celery, parsley, parsnip, dill, anise, caraway, cumin, and coriander (cilantro). There are forty native and non-native carrot family species in California, including the non-native fennel presented here. At least two toxic species are found in California: non-native poison hemlock (*Conium maculatum*) and native water hemlock (*Cicuta* spp.).

## *Foeniculum* genus

The *Foeniculum* genus is composed of one species, sometimes divided into two varieties: the cultivated sweet fennel (*F. vulgare* var. *dulce*), of cooking and baking fame, and wild fennel (*F. vulgare* var. *vulgare*), the one found growing wild in California.

## FENNEL
### *Foeniculum vulgare*

**Synonyms:** *Foeniculum vulgare* var. *vulgare*

**Other common names:** Common fennel, wild fennel, bitter fennel (to distinguish it from sweet fennel)

**Origin:** Non-native

**Range:** Throughout California except the San Joaquin Valley to 5,000 feet elevation

**Habitat:** Roads, trails, disturbed places

**Related species in California:** None

**Related species globally:** Cultivated sweet fennel (*F. vulgare* var. *dulce*), anise (*Pimpinella anisum*)

**Conservation status rankings:**

> **IUCN Red List:** LC
> **CNPS Rare Plant Rank:** Not listed
> **NatureServe State Rank:** SNA
> **Cal-IPC Rating:** Moderate

*Wild fennel (*Foeniculum vulgare*)*
ANGELA ROCKETT KIRWIN

**Uses:** Digestive, carminative, antispasmodic, expectorant; aids digestion, relieves gas, promotes menstruation, expels phlegm from the lungs

**Parts used:** Seeds

**Edibility:** Seeds and peeled stems are edible; leaves used as a flavoring in small amounts.

## Description

Fennel (*Foeniculum vulgare*) is an introduced perennial from the Mediterranean region. It grows in disturbed soil along trails and roads throughout California, except in the San Joaquin Valley, to 5,000 feet elevation. Deep-rooted, it grows to 6 feet high. The entire plant has a strong odor of anise, a close relative. It may remind you of black licorice, which is flavored with anise oil. Alternate, compound leaves are ovate-triangular in shape and clasp the smooth main stem with a sheath. The leaves are made up of many finely dissected, threadlike, pinnate leaflets. Tiny yellow flowers appear from May to September in compound umbels made up of even smaller umbels. Oblong, brownish or greenish-gray seeds are ribbed, about ⅛ inch long, and ripen in the fall.

*Wild fennel (in my hand) with yellow flowers and poison hemlock (*Conium maculatum*), left, with white flowers.* RICHARD MARCELLIN

## Conservation Status

The California Invasive Plant Council (Cal-IPC) ranks fennel as moderately invasive, noting that "it can drastically alter the composition and structure of many plant communities."[10]

## Traditional Uses

As with other introduced plants, there is no evidence of traditional Native American use. Fennel has a long history of use in Europe, however, dating back to Hippocrates, who prescribed it for infant colic in the third century BC. Ancient Greeks used the seeds as an appetite suppressant for weight control or during fasting and to increase milk production in nursing mothers. Spreading around the world, fennel seed was adopted by European, Chinese, Ayurvedic, and Arabic herbalists, primarily for treating minor digestive complaints.

## Modern Uses

A tea of crushed or ground fennel seed is still in use worldwide, primarily as a digestive tract stimulant and to relieve stomach pains, bloating, and intestinal gas, as in colic. Herbalists often use it as a flavoring to offset bitter digestive herbs and add it to laxative herb formulas to prevent intestinal cramping. Fennel

*Wild fennel (*Foeniculum vulgare*)*. ANGELA ROCKETT KIRWIN

seed has mild expectorant and antibacterial properties that make it a pleasant-tasting addition to lung formulas and cough syrups. It is also used in formulas to increase breast milk.

Fennel seeds can be chewed as a naturally antibacterial breath aid to counteract halitosis. In the Ayurvedic tradition, East Indian restaurants often place a bowl of candied fennel seeds near the exit as a digestive aid and breath freshener.

Fennel seed is German Commission E approved for digestive problems such as mild spastic gastrointestinal afflictions, fullness, and flatulence. It is also approved for inflammation of the upper respiratory tract mucus membranes.

## Phytochemicals/Mechanisms of Action

Fennel's aroma and medicinal properties derive from its essential oil, composed mainly of the sweet-tasting organic compound anethole (50–80 percent) and, to a lesser degree, the bitter monoterpenoid fenchone (6–27 percent). Cultivated sweet fennel (*F. vulgare* var. *dulce*) and anise (*Pimpinella anisum*) contain higher amounts of the sweeter anethone. Fennel oil contains the organic compound estragole (3–20 percent), which also gives the unrelated herb tarragon its anise-like fragrance. The oil also includes the monoterpenes limonene, alpha-pinene, and alpha-phellandrene, as well as another sweet, anise-flavored organic compound, 4-anisaldehyde.

## Cultivation

Fennel can easily be grown from seed in the garden, but it should never be planted in the wild. Commercial cultivars of sweet fennel are popular for the edible bulbous stalks, commonly called "fennel root" or "finocchio."

## Cautions

At certain stages in its growth, fennel can be mistaken for the equally invasive and highly toxic poison hemlock (*Conium maculatum*). Poison hemlock tends to grow in damper soil and has white flowers. It also has purple splotches on the stems and lacks the sweet anise aroma of fennel. Be sure you have made a positive identification before harvesting fennel.

## Notes

Fennel is the host plant for the larvae of the anise swallowtail butterfly, *Papilio zelicaon*.

All aboveground parts of fennel are edible at some point in its yearly growth. See Christopher Nyerges's *Foraging California* for details.

# SUNFLOWER FAMILY (ASTERACEAE)

Asteraceae is also known as the Daisy or Aster family and was formerly named the Composite family (Compositae) for its characteristic flower heads composed of outer, petallike ray flowers and central, multiple disk flowers. (Picture a sunflower.) Asteraceae is the largest family of plants in California and the second-largest family worldwide, second only to the Orchid family (Orchidaceae). It includes over 32,000 species in more than 1,900 genera and is so big that botanists divide it into 13 subfamilies, which are further divided into numerous tribes.

## *Achillea* genus

The *Achillea* genus, known commonly as yarrow, is a member of the Anthemideae, or Chamomile, tribe of the subfamily Asteroideae of the Sunflower family. The Anthemideae tribe also includes two other genera covered in this field guide: *Artemisia* and *Matricaria*. There are about 115 species of *Achillea* found in North America, Europe, Asia, and North Africa.

### YARROW
### *Achillea millefolium*

**Synonyms:** *Achillea millefolium* var. *californica*
**Other common names:** Milfoil, soldier's woundwort
**Origin:** Native
**Range:** Up to 12,000 feet elevation throughout all California except the Mojave Desert
**Habitat:** A wide variety of habitats in Northern California; riparian woodlands and oak woodlands in southern California
**Related species in California:** None
**Related species globally:** Over 100 species in North America, Eurasia, and northern Africa
**Conservation status rankings:**
    **IUCN Red List:** LC
    **CNPS Rare Plant Rank:** Not listed
    **NatureServe State Rank:** SNR
**Uses:** Astringent, diaphoretic, styptic, antispasmodic, anti-inflammatory; for bleeding, wound healing, fevers, cramps, inflammation
**Parts used:** Flower heads, aerial parts
**Edibility:** Not edible

*Yarrow (*Achillea millefolium*) flowers.*
STEVE JUNAK

## Description

Yarrow (*Achillea millefolium*) is a low-growing, aromatic perennial that sends up flowering stalks 20 to 40 inches high. Its alternate leaves are dissected into many fine, often hairy, segments. The lower leaves are 4 to 6 inches long on long stems. The upper leaves on the stalks are small and have no stems. The flower heads are made up of many small flowers in a corymb-like structure. The individual composite flowers feature twenty-five to thirty disk flowers in the center surrounded by five or six white ray flowers. Yarrow blooms from March in warmer southern climates to September at cooler high altitudes.

## Conservation Status

Yarrow is common throughout the Northern Hemisphere and considered a native wherever it is found. There are no conservation concerns in California.

## Traditional Uses

Yarrow and chamomile residues were found in dental calculus on Neanderthal teeth dating back 50,000 years, presumably eaten for medicine, as they are not great foods.[11] James Adams includes those two plants, along with mugwort, elderberry, and stinging nettle, as staples in our migrating ancestors' medicine kits.[12] In the first century AD, two Greeks, naturalist Pliny the Elder and physician Dioscorides, wrote of the use of yarrow to stop internal and external bleeding, reduce inflammation, and treat diarrhea.

Mrs. R. F. Bingham reported to the Santa Barbara Society of Natural History in 1890 that the Santa Barbara Chumash use a poultice of yarrow to heal persistent open sores and the fresh plant to stop bleeding in recent wounds.[13] The Miwok, Pomo, Shoshone, Paiute, Washo, and others use the poultice for similar purposes. The traditional Karok considered it good medicine for an open arrow or gunshot wound, the soaked stalk and leaves applied directly. The Diegueño, Paiute, and Shoshone relieve toothache pain by inserting a small piece of yarrow root into the decayed tooth. The Mattole apply steamed leaves to soothe joint pain.

Many California natives and others around the country, including the Miwok, Maidu, Mattole, and Cherokee, drink a decoction of roots, leaves, and/or flowers for stomachaches, headaches, colds, and internal bleeding. The Cherokee drink the tea for its sweat-inducing property in order to reduce fevers in colds and flu.

## Modern Uses

According to the *American Herbal Pharmacopoeia*, an infusion of yarrow flower tea is one of the most widely used herbs to check bleeding.[14] David Hoffmann considers the hot tea one of the best diaphoretics and the standard remedy for helping the body to deal with fevers.[15] It is also used, like its Asteraceae cousin pineapple weed

(*Matricaria discoidea*), for gastrointestinal problems such as stomachache, inflammation, cramps, and diarrhea. More bitter than pineapple weed, yarrow tea also can stimulate appetite and bile secretion.

Yarrow's multiple astringent actions—stopping bleeding, stopping diarrhea, and healing external tissue—have earned it a reputation as a "heal-all herb" in Ayurvedic medicine.[16] The German Commission E approved yarrow flower tea for internal use for loss of appetite and digestive ailments, such as mild spastic discomforts of the gastrointestinal tract. They also approved its use in a sitz bath for painful, cramp-like conditions of psychosomatic origin in the lower part of the female pelvis.

## Phytochemicals/Mechanisms of Action

Yarrow contains many medicinal compounds that support its uses.[17] The challenge is knowing if they exist in the plant in front of you. Analyses of the essential oils of yarrow plants growing in different locations show a wide variation of phytochemicals, depending on different chromosome types, geographical locations, and times of year. Some of the compounds are not very water soluble, especially if using an infused tea of the plant. This may explain why many native tribes boil a decoction rather than steeping an infusion. Garcia and Adams suggest sucking on a fresh leaf rather than making an infusion.[18]

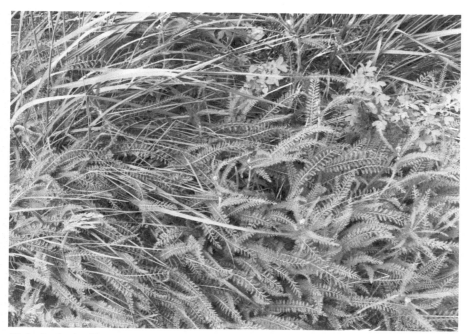

*Distinctive feather-like leaves of young yarrow plants.* LANNY KAUFER

Some of the active phytochemicals in yarrow include sesquiterpenoids (germacrane, rupicolin B, matricarin) known to relieve inflammation and swelling. Aromatic organic compounds (azulene and chamazulene) and flavonoids (cyanidin, apigenin) in the flowers are antispasmodics that help relax smooth muscle in the digestion tract and uterus. Monoterpenoids that are antimicrobial and also can relieve pain include isoartemisia ketone, sabinene, eucalyptol, pinene, camphor, and menthol. Yarrow contains a small amount of the sedative, pain-relieving monoterpene thujone. See *Artemisia* chapters for more on thujone. Salicylic acid is another phenolic compound in yarrow with anti-inflammatory and pain-relieving activity. It has been shown to bring down fevers and is the phytochemical basis for the development of aspirin.

Yarrow's long history of use for wounds is supported by the presence of alkaloids (achilletin and achilleine), known as hemostatics, that can help with blood coagulation. The high tannin content in yarrow leaves also contributes to wound cleansing and healing. The pain-relieving compounds mentioned above also treat external pain.

In 2011 Wendy Applequist and Daniel Moerman published a review, now available online, of all the ethnobotanical and biomedical research on yarrow to make a convincing case for more human clinical trials.[19]

## Cultivation

Yarrow can be easily grown from young transplants or from seed planted no more than ¼ inch deep. It likes some shade in warmer climates and, while drought tolerant, does best with regular watering. Native plant landscapers use it as a lawn substitute that can be mowed, walked on, and needs less water than standard turf grasses.

## Cautions

Some species of yarrow are known to cause allergic contact dermatitis in some people who are sensitive to the guaianolides (sesquiterpene lactones) that may be present in the fresh plant. This could be a concern for handling it or sucking on a leaf. Otherwise, yarrow is considered safe for use. One 2003 study on rats using a high dose raised an alarm about possible toxicity for pregnant women, but that single study has been questioned. Still, pregnant women should always apply an extra level of caution with medicinal substances. For everyone else, it's best to prepare the flowers as a standard infusion and take in moderation. With normal use, the small thujone content is not considered a problem.

## Notes

The genus name *Achillea* is derived from the legend of the mythological Greek warrior Achilles, who used the leaves to treat his soldiers' bleeding wounds.

Unfortunately, he wasn't able to poultice the deadly arrow wound to his own "Achilles' heel" tendon. The species name *millefolium* refers to the thousand dissections of the leaves.

Yarrow stalks are used for consulting the I Ching, an ancient Chinese oracle still in use today.

## *Artemisia* genus

About 400 species of *Artemisia* are found worldwide, mostly in the Northern Hemisphere. Perhaps the most famous, or infamous, is wormwood (*A. absinthium*), an ingredient in absinthe. There are twenty native species in California, not counting numerous subspecies. Mugwort and three species of sagebrush are included here for their medicinal properties. The *Artemisia* genus is named for Artemis, the Greek goddess of wild nature, the moon, and childbirth.

*California sagebrush leaves, showing the three thin lobes at the tips.* JAMES DAVID ADAMS JR.

## COASTAL SAGEBRUSH
### *Artemisia californica*

**Other common names:** California sagebrush, *romerillo* (Spanish)
**Origin:** Native
**Range:** Coastal California to 2,500 feet
**Habitat:** Well-drained soils in coastal sage scrub and chaparral

*Estafiate, also known as silver wormwood* (Artemisia ludoviciana *subsp.* ludoviciana*).* KEIR MORSE

## ESTAFIATE
### *Artemisia ludoviciana*

**Other common names:** Silver wormwood, mountain wormwood, white
sagebrush, *altamisa* (Spanish)
**Origin:** Native
**Range:** Dry inland and mountain
areas to 11,000 feet elevation
**Habitat:** Sandy or rocky soils in scrub
and conifer forest

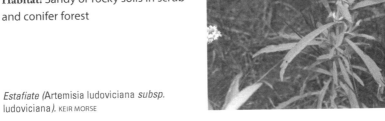

*Estafiate (*Artemisia ludoviciana *subsp.*
ludoviciana*).* KEIR MORSE

Great Basin sagebrush (Artemisia tridentata). ROBERT E. MERRITT

## GREAT BASIN SAGEBRUSH
### *Artemisia tridentata*

**Other common names:** Big sagebrush, old man sage
**Origin:** Native
**Range:** Higher elevation inland valleys and foothills to 7,000 feet elevation
**Habitat:** Sandy to loamy soils in inland valleys and mountain foothills
**Related species in California:** Many, including mugwort (*A. douglasiana*) and wild tarragon (*A. dracunculus*)
**Related species in Europe, Asia, North Africa:** Many, including wormwood (*A. absinthium*), common mugwort (*A. vulgaris*), and sweet annie (*A. annua*)
**Conservation status rankings:**
    **IUCN Red List:** Not listed
    **CNPS Rare Plant Rank:** Not listed
    **NatureServe State Rank:** SNR
**Uses:** Analgesic, anti-inflammatory, emmenagogue, anthelmintic, antifungal; for pain liniment, menstrual problems, intestinal parasites, diaper rash
**Parts used:** Leaves, stems
**Edibility:** Not edible

## Description

Despite the word "sage" in their common names, none of the sagebrushes are related to true sages in the genus *Salvia* of the Mint family. There are many species of *Artemisia* sagebrushes in California and throughout the Western states.

These three common ones will repre-sent the rest. They are perennials with a characteristic pungent aroma some-times referred to as "cowboy cologne." Coastal sagebrush (*Artemisia californica*) is found mainly in southern California in the coastal sage scrub plant commu-nity below 2,500 feet. It can grow 4 to 6 feet high and 3 to 4 feet wide. It has light grayish-green, threadlike leaves, 1 to 4 inches long, ending in three thin lobes. Estafiate (*Artemisia ludoviciana*) and Great Basin sagebrush (*Artemisia tridentata*) grow in the drier parts of the state from the mountains of east San Diego to the eastern deserts of North-ern California. Estafiate has weak stems and generally grows no more than 3 feet tall. Its fuzzy, whitish-gray leaves are 1 to 4 inches long and deeply lobed with pointed tips. Great Basin sagebrush grows 3 to 9 feet high, with a spread of 3 to 4 feet. Its ½- to 1½-inch grayish leaves have blunt ends with three tiny lobes that look like teeth, hence the Latin name, *A. tridentata*. Like other *Artemisia* species, these three species have tiny, inconspicuous flowers.

*Three-toothed leaf tips give* Artemisia tridentata *its scientific name.* JAMES DAVID ADAMS JR.

## Conservation Status

All three species are common and abundant within their ranges in California.

## Traditional Uses

Sagebrushes are among the most widely used medicinal plants for Indigenous Californians. They are universally considered cleansing and purifying plants. Chumash plant expert Juanita Centeno told me and her other students that coastal sagebrush is a purification plant for young women to drink from the onset of puberty until their first child.[20] The Tongva also consider it essential medicine for women of childbearing age, as do the Cahuilla, whose women use the tea for menstrual cramps. The Cahuilla chew the leaves for colds, and the Tongva, among others, brew a tea for asthma, coughs, rheumatic pains, and to help reduce fever.[21] [22] For bad colds, coughs, and bronchitis, the Diegueño boil fresh or dried leaves of Great Basin sagebrush for 5 minutes and drink hot three times a day.[23] Juanita also said that, traditionally, an infusion of coastal sagebrush tea was drunk for indigestion after overeating. Likewise, the Cahuilla drink Great Basin sagebrush for stomach problems.[24]

The Washo, Cahuilla, and others use a Great Basin sagebrush smudge as a fumigant after sickness in the home, while the Tongva use coastal sagebrush smoke in puberty and hunting rituals.[25] [26] Juanita Centeno also showed us how to strip the dead brown leaves from the lower stems

Wild tarragon (Artemisia dracunculus), a relative of sagebrush with a nice flavor but lacking the medicinal properties. LANNY KAUFER

of coastal sagebrush and rub or grind them into a moisture-absorbent, antifungal powder for diaper rash, athlete's foot, and other fungal infections. The leaves must be bone-dry for grinding.[27]

As the name implies, wormwood (*A. absinthium*) has long been used worldwide to get rid of intestinal parasites.

## Modern Uses

In their book *Healing with Medicinal Plants of the West*, Chumash healer Cecilia Garcia and pharmacologist James Adams describe the powerful pain-relieving properties of a sagebrush liniment. The monoterpenoids in sagebrush interact directly with the pain receptors in the skin to relieve pain quickly without the side effects of opioids or NSAIDs taken internally.[28] See "Recipes" for a sagebrush liniment recipe.

Garcia also says the pungent aroma of coastal sagebrush, smelled fresh or burned as a smudge, can bring back pleasant memories. The fresh leaves can be chewed for toothache.

Michael Moore recommends sagebrush tea drunk cold as stomach bitters for stimulating digestion or in a hot infusion to induce sweating to break a fever or to bring on delayed menstruation. The steam from the hot tea can be inhaled for lung congestion. He says estafiate is the most effective of the three for expelling pinworms.[29]

In Europe, a water infusion of the related wormwood, *A. absinthium*, is German Commission E approved as a digestive bitter.

## Phytochemicals/Mechanisms of Action

Coastal sagebrush's aroma comes from fifteen monoterpenoids, including six with proven pain-relieving properties: eucalyptol (cineole), camphor, camphene, β-pinene, borneol, and thujone. As mentioned above, these compounds are able to cross the skin barrier to affect neurotransmitters and break the pain cycle.[30]

Sesquiterpene lactones, known for their anti-inflammatory and analgesic activity, are also found in *Artemisia* species. A 2019 study found promise in the anti-inflammatory compounds extracted from *A. californica*.[31] One now-famous sesquiterpene lactone, artemisinin, became an important antimalarial drug after a Chinese researcher received a Nobel Prize in 2015 for discovering and effectively extracting it from sweet annie (*A. annua*).[32] It is now the principal treatment for malaria. There is no evidence that artemisinin is found in our native sagebrushes; if it were, it is not soluble in water, so a tea would not contain it.

## Cultivation

These three species can be propagated from seed, prefer full sun, and are drought tolerant.

## Cautions

Those allergic to the Asteraceae family should avoid using these plants. Sagebrush contains small amounts of thujone, a toxic phytochemical that may cause convulsions in large quantities. Internal use of sagebrush is contraindicated in pregnancy. Tincture or essential oil of sagebrush should be used only by a professional. Michael Moore reminds us that these sagebrushes make bitter teas, recommending estafiate as the least bitter and warning that Great Basin sagebrush is bitter to the point of causing vomiting in some people. A little goes a long way.

## Notes

Select healthy flowering branches to harvest in late summer or early fall, somewhat earlier for the delicate coastal sagebrush. Because sagebrushes produce their aromatic compounds to deter predation by insects and herbivores, a smudge bundle or the liniment in a spray bottle can be used as an insect repellent. Avoid spraying on clothing, as it may leave a green stain.

The green spirit absinthe is made with wormwood and is reputed to have psychoactive properties, possibly due to the thujone content. In reality, modern versions of absinthe contain a small fraction of the thujone present in Vincent van Gogh's day.

# MUGWORT
## *Artemisia douglasiana*

**Other common names:** Douglas' sagewort, dream sagebrush
**Origin:** Native
**Range:** Lower elevations throughout all of California, southwestern Oregon, and western Nevada
**Habitat:** Riparian habitat, wetlands
**Related species in California:** California sagebrush (*A. californica*), tarragon (*A. dracunculus*), Great Basin sagebrush (*A. tridentata*)
**Related species in Europe:** *A. vulgaris*
**Conservation status rankings:**
    **IUCN Red List:** Not listed
    **CNPS Rare Plant Rank:** Not listed
    **NatureServe State Rank:** SNR
**Uses:** Emmenagogue; for menstrual cramps, poison oak wash, moxibustion
**Parts used:** Leaves, stem
**Edibility:** Too bitter to be considered edible

*Patch of spring mugwort (*Artemisia douglasiana*).* LANNY KAUFER

## Description

Mugwort is a perennial colony plant, spreading by creeping rhizomes in the disturbed soil of the riparian habitat. It is often found growing alongside poison oak and blackberry up to 7,000 feet but is more common at lower elevations. The leaves are dark green above and furry white below, with pointy lobes on the larger, lower leaves and smooth margins on the smaller, upper ones. There can be a lot of variation in the lobes. The crushed leaves smell like sagebrush. Like its *Artemisia* relatives, mugwort has tiny, barely visible greenish flowers and equally small seeds. The flowering stems can reach 8 feet tall.

## Conservation Status

Mugwort is a very common native plant.

## Traditional Uses

California's Indigenous tribes drink mugwort tea for respiratory problems, stomachaches, fevers, dysentery; for easing menstruation; and for pain after giving birth. According to Cecilia Garcia and James D. Adams Jr. in *Healing with Medicinal Plants of the West*, California mugwort tea is still used by the Chumash for menopausal hot flashes. The patient takes either one leaf or cuts a finger-length piece of stem into small pieces and steeps it in a mug of hot water. One cup is drunk every day for about three weeks. To treat symptoms of premenstrual syndrome or dysmenorrhea (painful menstruation), this same tea is taken for four nights only. The authors also describe a toy made with dry mugwort leaves for children with attention deficit hyperactivity syndrome (ADHD). The leaves are stuffed into a star-shaped cloth toy sewn the size of the parent's hand. The child squeezes the star during the day and sleeps with it at night.[33]

Mugwort is often found growing next to poison oak (*Toxicodendron diversilobum*). The late Chumash plant expert Juanita Centeno showed me how to use the juice of fresh mugwort to stop the itching and dry up a case of poison oak rash in the early stages. She rolled several fresh leaves between her palms. Within seconds, she was dripping and patting dark green juice on the affected area. This method has been effective for many people, myself included, but is not recommended once pustules have formed and broken open. At that point, bacteria may be introduced.

European mugwort, *A. vulgaris*, has a long history of use as an aromatic bitter for stimulating digestion; for relieving difficult, suppressed, or painful menstruation; and for its dream-inducing properties.

## Modern Uses
The late herbalist William Le Sassier recommended drinking a mild infusion of mugwort and taking hot mugwort baths for menstrual cramps or any spasming in the low back or pelvic area.[34]

*The author formed this moxa cone by rolling dry leaves into a ball and then pinching and squeezing the ball into a pyramid shape.* ANGELINA SANCHEZ

European mugwort (*A. vulgaris*) is used by Western herbalists to stimulate gastric and liver secretions and to relieve suppressed menstrual flow. The latter use is echoed by Ayurvedic and traditional Chinese medicine (TCM) practitioners. TCM practitioners also prescribe the hot tea of *A. vulgaris* as a first treatment for the onset of colds on the theory that it has a warming effect by increasing blood flow.

Note the irregular pointed lobes at ends of mugwort leaves. LANNY KAUFER

## Phytochemicals/Mechanisms of Action

Mugwort contains water-soluble sesquiterpene lactones such as dehydroleucodine, vulgarin, and psilostachyin, which can bring down the body temperature in menopause and relieve the pain of dysmenorrhea.[35] Sesquiterpene lactones are a large group of natural compounds, found primarily in plants of the Asteraceae family. They show a wide range of biological activities, including antitumor, anti-inflammatory, analgesic, antiulcer, antibacterial, antifungal, antiviral, antiparasitic, and insect deterrent.[36] Mugwort also contains aromatic, pain-relieving monoterpenes, including camphor, eucalyptol, linalool, and thujone.

## Cultivation

Mugwort is easily grown from tiny seeds hidden in the clusters of dried flowers. Rub the dried clusters between your hands over a flat of potting soil, press down, and keep damp. After they sprout, transplant them to the garden, preferably in a shady or partially shady place, such as under the canopy of an oak. Once established, they are drought tolerant. A root barrier may be needed to prevent it from spreading beyond the desired area.

## Cautions

Due to the presence of thujone, which can cause seizures in large quantities, mugwort should only be consumed as an infusion, not as a decoction or as an alcoholic tincture or essential oil. Thujone is not water-soluble, so the mild infused tea is safe to drink. For those who are allergic to the Asteraceae family, caution must be used consuming any mugwort product, including mugwort mochi, a rice cake made from Japanese mugwort (*A. princeps*).

## Notes

Mugwort is best gathered for tea by topping younger plants or selecting healthy lower leaves from older plants before they go to seed. The fresh green branches have been called "dream sagebrush" for their reputed ability to stimulate dreaming when placed under one's pillow or hung over one's head. The dry brown leaves of mugwort that cling to the lower stems as the plant matures are used to make moxa for moxibustion by traditional Chinese and Japanese acupuncturists and healers. Moxa cones are placed directly on acupuncture points, or small pieces are attached to the top of acupuncture needles for their warming and sedative effect as they smolder. The smoke also is considered calming and therapeutic and can kill bacteria in the room. Moxa is an effective insect deterrent when burned in the backyard or at the campsite. Early European observers of the Chumash noticed that the elders often bore burn scars of frequent moxa treatments. The reason for its use is unknown, but it may have been to cauterize wounds. To make your own moxa cones, strip dry brown leaves from the lower stems, roll into a ball between your palms while removing stems, and pinch/twist the ball between the thumb and first two fingers to form a pyramid-shaped cone. Always observe fire safety precautions when burning moxa.

*Late-season mugwort showing white backs of leaves and dry brown leaves on lower stalks*
LANNY KAUFER

*A. douglasiana* is one of many California plants named for early nineteenth-century Scottish botanist David Douglas.

## *Grindelia* genus

About sixty species of *Grindelia* are found in western North America, Central America, and South America. Not including varieties, seven species are native to California. While the taxonomy can get confusing, the good news is that all grindelias produce gummy resin on the flowers and are interchangeable as medicinal herbs. We'll focus on the common gumplant (*G. camporum*), as it is the grindelia of commerce most often referenced in herbal literature under its old synonym, *G. robusta*. It's also the most common species in California.

*Oregon gumplant (*Grindelia stricta*).* STEVE JUNAK

## GRINDELIA
### *Grindelia camporum*

**Synonyms:** *Grindelia robusta, G. camporum* var. *bracteosa, G. camporum* var. *camporum*
**Other common names:** Common gumplant, bracted gumplant, Great Valley gumplant, gumweed
**Origin:** Native
**Range:** Throughout California below 4,500 feet elevation
**Habitat:** Wetlands, sandy or alkaline bottomlands
**Related native species in California:** Hairy gumplant (*G. hirsutula*), Idaho gumplant (*G. nana*), Oregon gumplant (*G. stricta*)
**Related non-native species in California:** Curly-cup gumplant (*G. squarrosa*)
**Conservation status rankings:**
    **IUCN Red List:** Not listed
    **CNPS Rare Plant Rank:** Not listed, except the 3 species listed below in the "Conservation Status" section
    **NatureServe State Rank:** SNR
**Uses:** Expectorant, antispasmodic, anti-inflammatory; for asthma, bronchitis, spasmodic coughing
**Parts used:** Flowers and upper (aerial) parts
**Edibility:** Not edible

## Description

Common gumplant is an erect, branching, perennial herb, sticky with resin. It grows from 1½ to 4 feet high with waxy, alternate, sharply toothed leaves up to 7 inches long near the base and smaller in the upper parts. The solitary flower heads are 1¼ to 2 inches across and covered with whitish, resinous exudate. They arise from an involucre—a spherical ring of curving, pointed bracts. The flowers are composed of many yellow disk flowers in the center surrounded by many bright yellow ray flowers. Common gumplant flowers from March to October.

## Conservation Status

Three grindelias have California Native Plant Society rare plant status. The rest are common. The three to avoid collecting are Ash Meadows gumplant (*G. fraxinipratensis*), San Diego gumplant (*G. hallii*), and San Francisco gumplant (*G. hirsutula* var. *maritima*).

## Traditional Uses

Several California tribes, including the Cahuilla, Chumash, Miwok, Paiute, Pomo, and Shoshone, drink a tea of grindelia's flowering tops to cure colds and treat lung problems. Some prepare a decoction; others prepare an infusion. Tribes use whichever species is found nearby.[37] Physio-medical physicians of nineteenth- and early twentieth-century America, having learned of it from Native Americans, adopted grindelia's upper leaves and flowers as an antispasmodic and expectorant for asthma, bronchitis, and dry bronchial coughs.[38] It was listed as an official drug in the *US Pharmacopoeia* from 1882 to 1926 and then in the US Formulary from 1926 to 1960.[39] Prior to 1960, grindelia was used in US and British hospitals and in several tuberculosis clinics in California.[40]

*Common gumplant (*Grindelia camporum*) flower showing recurving bracts below*
STEVEN MARK NORRIS

The Tübatulabal use a grindelia balm for hard-to-heal wounds. They believe it has superior tissue-healing properties, sometimes preventing or minimizing

*Common gumplant flower.* JAMES DAVID ADAMS JR.

scarring. They say it has great drawing power for boils and abscesses and regenerates new skin formation.[41] (See "Recipes.") The Chumash, Maidu, Miwok, and Shoshone prepare a warm poultice of the plant for treating wounds and sores. The decoction is also used as a cleansing wash.

The decoction or a poultice of grindelia has a great reputation as a cure for poison oak rash. It is used by the Cahuilla, Chumash, Maidu, and Miwok.

## Modern Uses

Many modern herbalists, such as Michael Tierra, Michael Moore, and David Hoffmann, recommend an infusion or tincture of the aerial parts for the plant's ability to relax smooth muscles in the lungs and heart while also reducing inflammation. They recommend it for treating asthmatic and bronchial conditions, especially when there is spasmodic coughing and rapid heartbeat.[42] [43] Moore suggests simply chewing on one of the fresh gummy flower heads.[44] It is often combined with yerba santa in cough syrup and tea formulas.

Like most of the herbs in this book with storied histories of use by Indigenous peoples, early physicians, and generations of herbalists, grindelia is no longer listed in the *US Pharmacopoeia* due to a lack of clinical evidence supporting its benefits. Across the pond, however, the German Commission E approved grindelia tea, extract, and tincture for catarrh (inflamed mucus membranes) of the respiratory tract.

The Indigenous use of grindelia for treating poison oak rash and other inflamed skin conditions lives on today. Researchers documented the successful treatment of the rash in the *Journal of Alternative and Complementary Medicine* in 2005.[45] Grindelia is the main ingredient in the over-the-counter line of Tecnu brand products for poison oak rash relief.

## Phytochemicals/Mechanisms of Action

The not-so-secret ingredient in all *Grindelia* species is the quite visible exudate (resin) on the flowers. *G. camporum* consists of about 10 percent resin, which is high for a plant that is not a tree. The resin contains anti-inflammatory diterpenes (camporic, grindelic, and oxygrindelic acids) with possible antimicrobial activity, as well as monoterpenes (borneol, alpha-pinene, limonene) known to be antimicrobial pain relievers. The whole plant contains anti-inflammatory flavonoids (kaempferol, quercetin), triterpenoid saponins (grindelia sapogenin) with expectorant and anti-inflammatory properties, polyacetylene compounds (matricarianol), and phenolic acids (chlorogenic acid) known to be anti-inflammatory. The plant also has tissue-cleansing and regenerating tannins.[46] [47]

## Cultivation

Grindelias can be propagated by seed. Starter plants, including a ground cover variety of Oregon gumplant, are available. Grindelia is a drought-tolerant pollinator attractant that provides flowers later in the year than many other natives.

## Cautions

There are no concerns with ingesting reasonable amounts of a standard infusion or tincture or with using externally as a decoction or poultice.

## Notes

As with other Asteraceae herbs with medicinal flowers, try to collect grindelia flowerheads and upper parts just as they bloom. They should be sticky and aromatic.

The genus *Grindelia* was named for the Latvian botanist David Grindel (1776–1836). It's one of those plants, like ephedra and eucalyptus, whose scientific name is also its best-known common name.

## *Matricaria* genus

Seven species of *Matricaria* are found in Europe, Asia, and North America. All are annuals, and most are aromatic. Two species are native to California, including pineapple weed (*M. discoidea*).

*Pineapple weed (*Matricaria discoidea*).* LANNY KAUFER

# PINEAPPLE WEED
*Matricaria discoidea*

**Synonyms:** *Matricaria matricarioides, M. suaveolens, Chamomilla suaveolens*
**Other common names:** Common pineapple weed, rayless chamomile, wild chamomile, manzanilla (Spanish)
**Range:** Throughout California and northwestern North America to 7,300 feet elevation
**Habitat:** Disturbed areas, often in compacted soil along roads and trails; vacant lots; riverbanks
**Related species in California:** Valley pineapple weed (*M. occidentalis*)
**Related species globally:** German chamomile (*M. chamomilla*; synonym *M. recutita*), Roman chamomile (*Chamaemelum nobile*)
**Look-alike species in California:** Common mayweed (*Anthemis cotula*)
**Conservation status rankings:**
    **IUCN Red List:** Not listed
    **CNPS Rare Plant Rank:** Not listed
    **NatureServe State Rank:** SNA
**Uses:** Anti-inflammatory, analgesic, anxiolytic, antispasmodic, carminative, and stomachic; for inflammation and spasms of the gastrointestinal tract, anxiety
**Parts used:** Flowers, whole plant
**Edibility:** The steeped flowers make a flavorful beverage tea.

## Description

Pineapple weed (*Matricaria discoidea*) is a short, erect, branching annual, 4 to 12 inches high, with a pleasant aroma reminiscent of pineapple. The ⅜- to 2-inch-long alternate leaves are finely, pinnately dissected. The ¼-inch-long cone-shaped flower heads appear at the ends of the branches from February to August, earlier at lower elevations. They are made up of only yellow disk flowers (no outer ray flowers) that fall apart at maturity. Pineapple weed makes its living growing in poor, hard-packed soils along roads and trails, in vacant lots, dirt driveways, and other places where few other plants can survive. It usually stays under 6 inches tall but can happily reach its maximum height, still only 1 foot high, with luxuriant growth in plowed fields and along riverbanks.

Pineapple weed's native cousin of the same genus, valley mayweed (*M. occidentalis*), is the same size and appearance but has slightly larger rayless flowers that stay intact when mature. It has little to no scent and is found only in alkaline soil around salt marshes and the like. A much more common look-alike, common mayweed (*Anthemis cotula*), grows to 2 to 3 feet high and is easily distinguished from pineapple weed by white ray flowers and a disagreeable stinky-cheese odor. Neither of these two plants is a substitute for pineapple weed in your herb pantry.

On the other hand, the non-native German chamomile (*M. chamomilla* or *M. recutita*) can be used in all the same ways described here for pineapple weed.

*A closer look at the flowers of pineapple weed (*Matricaria discoidea*) showing only disk flowers with no white ray flowers surrounding them.* KEITH FARRAR

It can be grown in your garden, occasionally found as a garden escapee in the wild, or easily purchased dried and ready for use. It has the same aroma and its growth habit is the same as pineapple weed, except that it has white ray flowers where pineapple weed has none.

## Conservation Status

Botanists disagree on whether pineapple weed is a California native. Given its recorded use by Native Americans, we'll consider it a native in these pages. Professor Emeritus James Adams of USC School of Pharmacy offers a theory that chamomile is one of five essential plants that humans have carried with them in their migrations for tens of thousands of years. The other four are elderberry, yarrow, mugwort, and stinging nettle. This could explain why all five are found worldwide and considered native wherever they grow.

## Traditional Uses

Along with yarrow (*Achillea millefolium*), chamomile residues were found in dental calculus on Neanderthal teeth dating back 50,000 years, presumably

*Common mayweed (*Anthemis cotula*), a look-alike plant with white ray flowers and a disagreeable odor.* BEN GRANGEREAU

eaten as medicinal foods.[48] Pineapple weed, known worldwide as wild chamomile, has been used medicinally for thousands of years. In California, the Maidu and Pomo use a decoction of the leaves and flowers to stop diarrhea. The Cahuilla make an infusion to do the same. The Ohlone use the tea for children and adults for gastrointestinal problems, to reduce fevers and treat pain, and externally as a disinfectant. The Diegueño brew a tea of the flowers for babies' fevers and a tea of the whole plant for adults. They also use it to treat stomachaches, colds, and menstrual cramps and give it to women following childbirth. The Maidu use an infusion of the flowers to relieve gastrointestinal cramps. To cure diarrhea, they make a decoction that also can be used to bring down fevers by producing profuse sweating.[49] In 1894, Oxnard physician C. L. Bard reported the Chumash using it to induce sweating as well as to treat pain.[50]

## Modern Uses

Pineapple weed continues to be used today as it has been for centuries. German chamomile flowers are Commission E approved for internal use for gastrointestinal spasms (cramps) and inflammatory diseases of the gastrointestinal tract. They are approved for external use for skin and mucous membrane inflammations, as well as bacterial skin diseases, including those of the oral cavity and gums; for inflammations and irritations of the respiratory tract (as inhalations); and for anogenital inflammation (as baths and irrigation).

Although the flower is considered the most concentrated medicinal part, herbalist Michael Moore recommends collecting and using the whole plant while the oldest flower is still yellow. The infusion method is used to make a tea. For external use, he describes steeping finely chopped, dried pineapple weed in olive oil for a week, one part herb in three parts (by volume) oil, then straining and squeezing out the oil to make a soothing emollient for inflamed skin.[51]

## Phytochemicals/Mechanisms of Action

The flowers contain several phenolic compounds, including the flavonoids apigenin, quercetin, patuletin, and luteolin. Apigenin is abundant in chamomile flowers, making up 68 percent of the flavonoid content. It is able to bind to central benzodiazepine receptors in the nervous system, giving it antianxiety and mild sedative activity. It acts as a natural COX-2 inhibitor, effectively making chamomile tea a type of nonsteroidal anti-inflammatory drug (NSAID), but without the potentially harmful side effects.[52]

The main components of the essential oil extracted from the flowers are the sesquiterpenes alpha-bisabolol, matricin, matricarin, and their derivatives, including azulene, chamazulene, and guaiazulene.[53] Bisabolol is known to have anti-irritant, anti-inflammatory, and antimicrobial properties. Chamazulene is reported to be anti-inflammatory, analgesic, antispasmodic, wound healing, and useful in treating eczema.

## Cultivation

Pineapple weed can be grown from seed. It's not picky about soil but is more likely to reseed itself in loose, tilled ground. Once established, as the name implies, it grows like a weed.

## Cautions

Those with known allergies to plants in the Asteraceae family should be wary of ingesting pineapple weed or applying it to the skin. The tea may stimulate uterine contractions so should not be used during pregnancy.

## Notes

The name "chamomile" is derived from the Greek *chamaimēlon* ("earth apple"), from *chamai* ("on the ground") plus *melon* ("apple").

## *Pseudognaphalium* genus

There are close to one hundred species worldwide of *Pseudognaphalium* (which I pronounce SUE-doe-nah-FAH-lee-um), eleven of which are native to California. The name translates as "false cudweed," referring to the *Gnaphalium* genus to which botanists once assigned it. Eleven species are native to California. Other than California everlasting, which has sticky green leaves, most in this genus are whitish, woolly plants. Some, including California everlasting, have a pleasant scent, described as maple syrup, butterscotch, oranges, curry, or some combination of those.

## CALIFORNIA EVERLASTING
### *Pseudognaphalium californicum*

*California everlasting.* STEVE JUNAK

**Synonyms:** *Gnaphalium californicum*

**Other common names:** Green everlasting, ladies' tobacco, California cudweed, *gordolobo* (Spanish)

**Origin:** Native

**Range:** Coastal California and Sierra foothills from Sonoma County south, below 2,500 feet

**Habitat:** Open areas in many plant communities

**Related species in California:** Pearly everlasting (*Anaphalis margaritacea*) and 10 other species of cudweed (*Pseudognaphalium* spp.)

**Related species globally:** Many cudweeds (*Pseudognaphalium* and *Gnaphalium* spp.)

**Conservation status rankings:**
    **IUCN Red List:** Not listed
    **CNPS Rare Plant Rank:** Not listed
    **NatureServe State Rank:** SNR

**Uses:** Astringent, antiseptic, analgesic; for respiratory and gastrointestinal inflammation

**Parts used:** Flowers for internal use; leaves for external

**Edibility:** Not edible

*Two young, pre-flowering California everlasting plants (*Pseudognaphalium californicum*).* LANNY KAUFER

## Description

California everlasting is a biennial, erect, branching herb that grows 16 to 32 inches tall and is found in open areas, mainly near the coast and in the Sierra foothills. The thin, oily leaves are green on both sides, 1½ to 4 inches long, and decurrent; i.e., the leaf bases clasp the stalk. The flowers emerge looking like clusters of white pearls, forming yellow centers as they mature. When they open throughout the spring and summer, they reveal thousands of tiny seeds, each crowned with a pappus (plural: pappi) of fine, bristly hairs that serve as a parachute. This makes the flower heads appear to be covered in wool. The flowers retain their scent for months as they turn into golden dried flowers, hence the name "everlasting."

The related medicinal species, pearly everlasting (*Anaphalis margaritacea*), is native to California but is also found nationwide. It arises from a horizontal system of rhizomes instead of the single taproot of the cudweeds. The leaves are green above with whitish-woolly undersides. The flowers look very similar and contain similar compounds, although they lack the strong scent of California everlasting. This could indicate different or lesser phytochemical activity. More studies are needed to verify this.

## Conservation Status

California everlasting is a common and widespread native plant throughout California, especially after wildfires. One related species, white rabbit-tobacco (*P. leucocephalum*), is on the CNPS Rare Plant Inventory.

*California everlasting flowers at gathering time.* BEN GRANGEREAU

## Traditional Uses

Over centuries, Native American and European herbalists have shown a consistent pattern of using *Pseudognaphalium* and the closely related *Gnaphalium* species for the same purposes. The Ohlone use an infusion of the leaves and flowers of California everlasting for colds and stomach pains. Miwok drink a decoction of the leaves for that reason. They also make a poultice of the plant for sores and swellings, sometimes heating it to make it stickier. Californian and northern Mexican tribes use their local species in similar ways. The Karok use an infusion of smallhead cudweed (*P. microcephalum*) as a wash for sore eyes. Many Eastern tribes use rabbit tobacco (*P. obtusifolium*) for the same uses noted above, as well as for nervousness, sleeplessness, sore throat, and fevers.

To decrease the duration of colds and flus, Chumash healer Cecilia Garcia prepares a hot tea by adding about 1 teaspoon of California everlasting flowers to a mug of water. This is brought to a boil, turned off, and steeped for 10 minutes. The tea is drunk four nights in a row at the first sign of sickness.[54] She also recommends an infused tea of the leaves drunk before meals as an appetite suppressant to help lose weight.[55]

The leaves and flowers of pearly everlasting (*Anaphalis margaritacea*) are used by tribes across the country for colds, throat infections, sore eyes, and as a poultice.

## Modern Uses

American herbalist Michael Moore considers *Anaphalis, Gnaphalium*, and *Pseudognaphalium* species equally effective for their anti-inflammatory and astringent activity in treating diarrhea, stomach flu, and the inflamed mucus membranes of respiratory conditions. He also recommends applying a poultice of leaves and flowers for soothing and healing sunburns.[56] For trailside first aid, the sticky leaves can be applied directly to minor scrapes for pain and to stop bleeding.

European herbalists use local species of *Gnaphalium* and *Pseudognaphalium* for respiratory and gastrointestinal inflammation. Marsh cudweed (*G. uliginosum*), a British native, is used as a tea and an astringent, antiseptic gargle for sore throats and upper respiratory conditions.[57]

## Phytochemicals/Mechanisms of Action

Although the phytochemistry of California everlasting has not yet been studied, many other *Pseudognaphalium* and *Gnaphalium* species contain anti-inflammatory flavonoids such as gnaphaliin, kaempferol, and quercetin. Several of these flavonoids are neuraminidase inhibitors, which can block an enzyme that viruses use to invade healthy cells. Everlasting flowers also contain anthocyanins, flavonoid pigments that can stimulate the immune system.

Scented species like California everlasting have aromatic oils in the leaves and flowers composed of mono- and diterpenes with antimicrobial and pain-relieving

*California everlasting flowers about to open.* JESS STARWOOD

Harvested California everlasting flowers showing "wool" of fine hairs (pappi). LANNY KAUFER

Harvested California everlasting flowers after winnowing out pappi. LANNY KAUFER

properties. Some species of *Gnaphalium* have inhibited *Streptococcus* and *Staphylococcus* bacteria in vitro. Biological studies have demonstrated antioxidant, antibacterial, antifungal, expectorant, anti-inflammatory, and other activities of *Gnaphalium* species.

## Cultivation
California everlasting can be propagated by spreading the tiny seeds in a flat and covering with a thin layer of soil. Plants are available in nurseries.

## Cautions
The pappi that carry the tiny seeds airborne can be irritating to breathe or to drink in a tea. For maximum medicinal potency, try to harvest the stalks when the flowers have just reached maturity—when the yellow centers have appeared but the flowers haven't fully opened. Dry them in a paper bag, shaking occasionally to release the seeds. Then put on a face covering, take the stalks outside in a breeze, and winnow them by waving them in the air. It's also possible to harvest the flowers shortly after they are completely open and naturally winnowed by the wind, as long as they still retain their scent.

## Notes
The common Spanish name for everlasting, *gordolobo*, is the source of some confusion, as it is also applied to several other woolly plants, especially mullein (*Verbascum thapsus*). I always recommend keeping up with the current scientific

names to be sure of an accurate ID. The online Jepson eFlora (ucjeps.berkeley.edu/eflora) is an excellent place to do that.

## *Solidago* genus

There are about one hundred species of *Solidago*, known commonly as goldenrod. They are found mainly in North America. Most are perennials. The genus *Solidago* is derived from the Latin *solidare* ("to make whole"), a tribute to goldenrod's wound-healing reputation.

## GOLDENROD
### *Solidago velutina* subsp. *californica*

*California goldenrod flower stalk.* STEVE JUNAK

**Synonyms:** *Solidago californica*
**Other common names:** California goldenrod, *oreja de liebre* (Spanish)
**Origin:** Native
**Range:** Throughout California; sparse in Central Valley
**Habitat:** Damp meadows, grasslands, riparian valleys and canyons
**Related native species in California:** Southern goldenrod (*S. confinis*), West Coast Canada goldenrod (*S. elongata*), coast goldenrod (*S. spathulata*), and others
**Related species globally:** Many, including Canada goldenrod (*S. canadensis*) and European goldenrod (*S. virgaurea*)
**Conservation status rankings:**
  **IUCN Red List:** Not listed
  **CNPS Rare Plant Rank:** Not listed, except 2 species mentioned below
  **NatureServe State Rank:** SNR
**Uses:** Aquaretic, anti-inflammatory, astringent; for urinary and respiratory tract inflammation, skin washes and compresses
**Parts used:** Flowering tops and upper leaves
**Edibility:** Young leaves are edible as a cooked vegetable.

## Description

The ten native species of goldenrod in California can vary in size, but they all share a similar appearance and can be used interchangeably as medicinal herbs. California goldenrod (*Solidago velutina* subsp. *californica*) is a stout, single-stemmed, densely downy, perennial herb that grows from 1 to 5 feet high in crowded colonies that spread by creeping rhizomes. Its alternate, grayish-green leaves are oblanceolate to obovate in shape, serrated, and 2 to 4½ inches long on the lower part of the plant. The upper leaves are much smaller. Goldenrod is easily recognized once its bright yellow flowers appear in long, compact, oval panicles at the tops of the stems. Depending on location and altitude, it can flower anytime from June to November.

### Conservation Status
All California species are secure except Guirado's goldenrod (*S. guiradonis*), CNPS 4.3, and Rocky Mountains Canada goldenrod (*S. lepida* var. *salebrosa*), CNPS 3.2.

### Traditional Uses
In California, the Chumash drink a decoction of California goldenrod for coughs, colds, and chest congestion. The Miwok use a root decoction as an eyewash and hold a plant decoction in the mouth for toothaches, but do not swallow it. The Maidu relieve sore throats by chewing on the flowers and drink the tea as a diuretic. Cahuilla women use the tea as a hair rinse and as a douche for feminine hygiene.

*Colony of California goldenrod (*Solidago velutina *subsp.* californica*)* STEVE JUNAK

Goldenrod is employed more often for external use by California tribes. The Cahuilla, Chumash, and Ohlone boil a decoction of the leaves for disinfecting and healing sores, wounds, and burns. The Kawaiisu use an infusion for the same purposes. Sometimes a leaf poultice or powdered dried leaves are also applied.

Across North America, many tribes use their local species of *Solidago* medicinally. For example, the Okanagan drink an infusion of the flower heads for diarrhea and a decoction for the flu. They give children the infusion for fevers. The Delaware drink an infusion or chew the green leaves for diarrhea and fevers. The Thompson drink a decoction of plant tops for diarrhea and use it as a bath for babies with diarrhea. The Potawatomi drink an infusion of the whole plant for fevers. The

*Close-up of California goldenrod flowers*
JAMES DAVID ADAMS JR.

Alabama take an infusion of the root for bad colds and place a root in dental cavities for toothache. The Chippewa and Blackfoot chew a root for sore throat. For external use, the Chippewa apply a compound poultice of flowers to burns.[58]

## Modern Uses

Modern herbalists use the aerial parts for lower urinary tract inflammation. Goldenrod is used as an aquaretic, a special type of diuretic that increases urine flow without loss of electrolytes. The German Commission E approved goldenrod for that use, as well as for helping to prevent and eliminate small kidney stones. Herbalists also believe it can reduce pain and inflammation in urinary tract infections, especially when coupled with antibiotic drugs or herbs that have stronger antimicrobial activity to actually fight the infection.

Goldenrod also is one of the first herbs of choice for European herbalists in treating inflammation of the mucus membranes of the upper respiratory tract in colds and flus, especially when combined with antimicrobial herbs. Externally, a tea of the upper parts of goldenrod is still used, as it long has been, for a mouthwash, throat gargle, and douche. It also has a reputation for soothing nettle rash and can be used as an astringent, tissue-shrinking wash, or compress for cuts and scrapes.

## Phytochemicals/Mechanisms of Action

Goldenrod's aquaretic effect is achieved by dilating glomerular arterioles in the kidneys, which, in turn, increases glomerular filtration rate and amount of water in the urine.[59] This function comes from goldenrod's combined content of flavonoids (quercetin and rutin) and saponins (triterpenoid glycosides, mainly bayogenin). Several studies have shown goldenrod to have anti-inflammatory and analgesic properties. Although California goldenrod has a higher content of flavonoids and saponins than the European goldenrod of commerce (*S. virgaurea*), it is lacking a key compound, leiocarposide, that gives European goldenrod its added antifungal activity.

Goldenrod contains the cleansing and healing tannins that you might expect from Asteraceae family plants. It also contains anti-inflammatory diterpenes and pain-relieving sesquiterpenes, including beta-caryophyllene, which works by binding to receptors in the endocannabinoid system of the central nervous system.

## Cultivation

California goldenrod can be started from seeds. Several California nurseries carry starter plants.[60] It is easy to grow if you can provide plenty of space and summer sun and water it in the spring. A root barrier will curb spreading.

## Cautions

Goldenrod tea is considered safe to use internally and externally, but it should not be ingested by those with chronic nephritis. It is generally prepared as an infusion for internal use.

## Notes

As with other Sunflower family plants used for their medicinal flowers, the flowering tops should be gathered just as they begin to open. The upper leaves are included in internal preparations. The large lower leaves can also be used for preparing external washes and poultices.

# BORAGE FAMILY (BORAGINACEAE)

The Borage family is made up of 120 genera and 2,300 species worldwide. Many can be found in temperate zones such as the Mediterranean region and western North America. Most members of this family have hairy or fuzzy leaves and flowers. The family includes the notable European herbs comfrey and borage.

## *Eriodictyon* genus

The *Eriodictyon* genus includes eleven species native to the southwestern United States and northern Mexico. All but one are commonly known as yerba santa. The genus name *Eriodictyon* comes from the Greek *erio* ("wool") and *dictyon* ("net"), referring to the woolly network of veins on the back side of the leaf.

*Thick-leaved yerba santa (*E. crassifolium *var.* nigrescens*).* LANNY KAUFER

## CALIFORNIA YERBA SANTA
### *Eriodictyon californicum*

**Other common names:** California mountain balm
**Origin:** Native
**Range:** Throughout California to 6,000 feet elevation
**Habitat:** Chaparral, woodlands, forests

# THICK-LEAVED YERBA SANTA
## *Eriodictyon crassifolium*

**Other common names:** Bicolored yerba santa
**Origin:** Native
**Range:** Southern California to 5,000 feet elevation
**Habitat:** Chaparral, pinyon-juniper woodland

*First-year thick-leaved yerba santa plant (*E. crassifolium *var.* nigrescens*) coming up after a fire.* LANNY KAUFER

*Woolly yerba santa (*Eriodictyon tomentosum*).* BRYANT BAKER

# WOOLLY YERBA SANTA
## *Eriodictyon tomentosum*

**Other common names:** Tomentose yerba santa
**Origin:** Native
**Range:** Western central California to 4,500 feet elevation
**Habitat:** Chaparral, foothill woodland

*Flowers of sticky yerba santa (*Eriodictyon trichocalyx*).* JAMES DAVID ADAMS JR.

## STICKY YERBA SANTA
### *Eriodictyon trichocalyx*

**Other common names:** Hairy yerba santa, shiny-leaf yerba santa
**Origin:** Native
**Range:** Southwestern California to 7,000 feet elevation
**Habitat:** Chaparral, yellow pine forest, pinyon-juniper woodland, Joshua tree woodland
**Toxic look-alike:** Poodle-dog bush (*E. parryi*)
**Conservation status rankings:**
    **IUCN Red List:** Not listed
    **CNPS Rare Plant Rank:** Not listed
    **NatureServe State Rank:** SNR
    **NatureServe Global Rank:** LC, except for *E. crassifolium* and *E. tomentosum*, which are G3
**Uses:** Expectorant, anti-inflammatory, antimicrobial
**Parts used:** Leaves
**Edibility:** Fresh leaves can be chewed like gum.

## Description
Yerba santa is an aromatic, perennial native shrub. It has purple flowers and alternate, lanceolate-ovate, coarsely-toothed leaves with a netlike pattern of veins on the underside of the leaf. Of the ten species of yerba santa in California, four are common enough for collecting:

1. California yerba santa (*Eriodictyon californicum*) has shiny, highly resinous leaves and is found throughout the state from near sea level to 6,000 feet elevation.

2. Thick-leaved yerba santa (*Eriodictyon crassifolium*) grows near the coast from San Diego north to the Santa Barbara backcountry. It's divided into two varieties. *E. crassifolium* var. *crassifolium* has downy, grayish-green leaves and is found from near sea level to 5,000 feet elevation. *E. crassifolium* var. *nigrescens* has somewhat-sticky, dark green leaves and grows from 300 to 8,000 feet elevation.

*Glossy, resinous leaves of California yerba santa* (Eriodictyon californicum). BEN GRANGEREAU

3. Woolly yerba santa (*Eriodictyon tomentosum*) has densely woolly, whitish-green leaves and grows from 200 to 5,000 feet elevation from San Luis Obispo County north to San Benito County.

4. Sticky yerba santa (*Eriodictyon trichocalyx*) can be found inland from the San Gabriel Mountains south to the Mexican border. It's also divided into two varieties. Both have white flowers. *E. trichocalyx* var. *lanatum* grows from 1,000 to 7,000 feet elevation. Its leaves have a densely woolly, white underside compared to *E. trichocalyx* var. *trichocalyx*, the stickier one, which grows from 400 to 8,500 feet elevation.

## Conservation Status

None of the species included here are threatened within their ranges. Because thick-leaved and sticky yerba santa have limited ranges and grow almost entirely within California, NatureServe ranks them globally as G3 (vulnerable).

## Traditional Uses

Yerba santa is one of the most important medicinal plants in California history, used by native tribes, European settlers, and modern herbalists alike. The Spanish named it *yerba santa* ("holy herb") in tribute to its effectiveness. The Cahuilla, Diegueño, Karok, Kashaya Pomo, Miwok, Kawaiisu, Luiseño, and others brew a tea of their local species for coughs, colds, stomachaches, and rheumatic pains. Katherine Siva Saubel of the Cahuilla offers this recipe: "Take 3 leaves of yerba santa, wash well, boil, put in ½ teaspoon of sugar, and administer 1 teaspoon every 4 hours for cough."[61] A similar Diegueño recipe for a cough calls for boiling the leaves for 10 minutes and drinking hot three times a day. An alternative is to cook the leaves briefly in honey and take by the teaspoonful.[62]

Some tribes chew fresh leaves for colds, coughs, and to quench thirst. It tastes bitter at first, but the saliva it creates brings a sweet, cooling aftertaste. The Atsugewi, Diegueño, Gabrielino, and Serrano use it in their sweat lodges for colds, rheumatism, and other illnesses. Before the advent of antibiotics, the Chumash used yerba santa for all breathing problems, including asthma, tuberculosis, and pneumonia.

A strong decoction or a poultice of the mashed leaves is used externally to heal sores, cuts, wounds, insect bites, sprains, and poison oak rash. Josefina López Meza of the Kumeyaay applies a sticky leaf directly to a cut when in the field or heats the leaf on a stove and presses it onto the wound to help with healing.[63]

Inspired by glowing reports from California settlers, physicians across the country adopted yerba santa for lung conditions. *E. californicum* was listed in the US Dispensatory for pharmacists at least as early as 1877 for "asthma, chronic bronchitis, and allied conditions."[64] In 1894 it was added to the *US Pharmacopoeia*, where it remained until 1945.[65] The *National Formulary* included it until 1970 as a flavoring agent in cough syrups and stomach tonics.

*Swallowtail butterfly on flowers of yerba santa (*E. crassifolium *var.* nigrescens*).* LANNY KAUFER

*Poodle-dog bush (*E. parry*), center, and yerba santa (*E. crassifolium *var.* nigrescens*), lower left*
ANNA SZYMKOWIAK-CHUNG

## Modern Uses

Modern Chumash descendants continue to use the tea to expel mucus in respiratory problems and as a general tonic.[66] Contemporary Chumash healer Cecilia Garcia recommends vaporizing over the steam of the boiled leaves for coughs and also drinking the tea for more serious conditions. She makes a poultice of the cooked leaves with crushed garlic cloves for applying to the chest. (See "Recipes" for steam inhalation instructions.)

In *Planetary Herbology*, herbalist Michael Tierra, LAc, describes an infusion of yerba santa tea as an excellent warming expectorant for the lungs and suggests combining it with grindelia in a cough syrup. He also recommends its bittersweet taste as a digestive stimulant.

Michael Moore considers the infused tea "one of our best decongestants" for moist, hypersecretory lung and sinus conditions characterized by productive cough and wheezing. He also explains that the anti-inflammatory flavonoids are useful in chronic gastritis and urethral irritation.[67] Moore finds the woolly species more soluble in water and prefers to use those for tea. For mild bladder and urethra infections, he recommends a tincture of the shiny, more resinous varieties.[68] Due to the resinous nature of the leaves of some species of yerba santa, some herbalists suggest a decoction is needed to release the medicinal components. You'll have to find what works for you. Try putting a teaspoon of crushed, dried leaves in a cup of cold water in a saucepan and slowly bringing it up to a gentle boil. Simmer for 1 minute; turn off the heat and steep for 10 to 15 minutes.

Currently, yerba santa extract is on the FDA's GRAS (Generally Recognized as Safe) list for its traditional use as a flavoring agent to mask the bitterness of active ingredients such as quinine and salicin.

### Phytochemicals/Mechanisms of Action

Yerba santa is a phenolic and resinous plant containing a powerful array of flavonoids. Eriodictyol and homoeriodictyol have shown expectorant, antibacterial, anti-inflammatory, antioxidant, and anticarcinogenic activity. A 2020 study identified eriodictyol as a top candidate for developing a drug to prevent infection by the COVID-19 virus.[69] A 2018 study identified another flavonoid, sterubin, as "a potent neuroprotective and anti-inflammatory compound" with potential for treating Alzheimer's disease.[70] Those three flavonoids also block bitter taste receptors. Hispidulin, another flavonoid, has demonstrated antioxidant, antifungal, anti-inflammatory, antimutagenic, and anticarcinogenic properties.

*Borage family cousins poodle-dog bush (E. parryi), the harmful one, left, and yerba santa (E. crassifolium var. nigrescens), the healing one, side by side.* ANNA SZYMKOWIAK-CHUNG

## Cultivation

Yerba santa is best started by division, separating young plants from a parent plant. To avoid digging in the wild, it's best to get a plant from a native plant nursery and follow their instructions for your climate and soil type.

## Cautions

Beware of the poodle-dog bush, *Eriodictyon parryi*. This yerba santa cousin is a look-alike with a taller, straighter growth habit, often reaching 10 feet in height. Long stalks of pinkish-purple flowers shoot up from clusters of lower leaves that resemble the legs of a groomed poodle as the stalks mature. It's often seen in great abundance in the years following wildfires. It is covered with irritating hairs. Contact with it produces a burning, itchy, painful dermatitis.

## Notes

Gather the current year's mature leaves as soon as they've had enough time in the sun to develop resin. This can vary from location to location but is usually after flowering. Leaves that are picked too young will turn black while drying due to the water content. Give the stickier varieties some breathing room while drying to avoid a gooey mess.

# CACTUS FAMILY (CACTACEAE)

The cactus family is made up of about 125 genera and 1,800 species. Virtually all are found in the Americas. With fleshy stems that can store water, they are generally adapted to deserts and dry climates. Clusters of thorny spines and tiny, detachable, bristly barbs called glochids grow out of specialized branch buds called areoles.

## *Opuntia* genus

All 150 species of *Opuntia*, or prickly-pear, are native to the Americas. The genus name *Opuntia* may be derived from the Papago word *opun* or from the ancient Greek city of Opus, where an edible plant grew that, like prickly-pear, could be propagated by planting its leaves.

*An established patch of* Opuntia littoralis. STEVEN MARK NORRIS

## PRICKLY-PEAR CACTUS
### *Opuntia* spp.

**Other common names:** *Nopal* (Spanish)
**Origin:** Native and non-native
**Range:** Mainly in southern and eastern California from sea level to 5,000 feet elevation
**Habitat:** Dry areas, especially deserts
**Related species in California:** *Cylindropuntia* spp. (cholla)

**Related species globally:** Mission prickly-pear (*O. ficus-indica*) and many others

**Conservation status rankings:**

   **IUCN Red List:** Not listed

   **CNPS Rare Plant Rank:** Not listed, except short-joint beavertail (*O. basilaris* var. *brachyclada*), 1B.2; Bakersfield cactus (*O. basilaris* var. *treleasei*), 1B.1; curved-spine beavertail (*O. curvispina*), 2B.2; brittle prickly-pear (*O. fragilis*), 2B.1

   **NatureServe State Rank:** SNR, except those mentioned above

**Uses:** Blood sugar regulation, lowering cholesterol; externally as a poultice for sunburn

**Parts used:** Pads, flowers, and fruits

**Edibility:** Pads, fruits, and seeds are edible.

## Description

There are fourteen native species and varieties of *Opuntia* in California. One of the two naturalized species is the widely cultivated mission prickly-pear (*O. ficus-indica*). Natural hybridizing is common in this genus. In addition, between 1907 and 1925 the famed horticulturalist Luther Burbank developed over sixty varieties of spineless prickly-pears from hybrids of mission prickly-pear.[71]

The flattened, oblong or round pads are known to botanists as thalli or cladodes and to Spanish speakers as *nopales*. They often resemble paddles or beaver tails and have a waxy, water-repellent, sun-reflecting green skin. Pads and fruits are dotted with bumps called areoles. Areoles sit inside small depressions on

*First-year (edible) pad of prickly-pear cactus (*Opuntia littoralis*) showing young, fleshy, pre-spine leaves next to a flower.* STEVEN MARK NORRIS

the pads, where they produce long woody spines and clusters of tiny glochids (irritating, detachable, barbed spines). They also form glochids, and sometimes spines too, on the fruits. First-year pads have a small, fleshy leaf at the base of each areole that will grow into a needlelike spine on most species. Beavertail prickly-pear (*O. basilaris* var. *basilaris*) and the non-native mission prickly-pear have no spines, only glochids, on the pads and fruits.

The fruits are known as *tunas* in Spanish. They form along the edges of one-year-old pads, beginning as large roselike flowers. Petal color varies among species from shades of yellow and orange to pink and magenta. The ripe fruits are generally dark red-purple, juicy and sweet, with the texture of ripe watermelon and full of mucilaginous seeds. Fruits of some species are golden yellow or even yellowish green when ripe.

## Conservation Status

Other than the threatened species listed above, prickly-pears are common and unthreatened.

## Traditional Uses

Prickly-pear pads, fruits, and seeds have long been consumed as survival foods and health foods by Native Americans, Mexicans, and Mexican-Americans. (See Nyerges's *Foraging California* for edible uses.) The Cahuilla, Chumash, Kumey-aay, Luiseño, Serrano, and Tongva of California and indigenous Mexican Indians drink a juice of the pads or eat them raw or cooked to prevent and control diabetes.

Color variation of prickly-pear cactus flower (*Opuntia littoralis*). JAMES DAVID ADAMS JR.

Several tribes scrape and split the pads to make a wound dressing or poultice that reduces swelling, relieves pain, and is believed to speed healing. Romero reports that the Mahuna band of the Cahuilla are known to have scraped the spines off a pad and cut a plug out of it to insert directly into a wound for rapid healing.[72]

## Modern Uses

From Mexico to South America, preparations of prickly-pear pads and fruits continue to be widely consumed to help regulate blood glucose levels in adult-onset (type 2) diabetes. (See "Recipes" for a nopal smoothie.) The astringent flowers, rich in flavonoids known to be antioxidant and anti-inflammatory, are

*Three buds and a flower emerging from the edge of an* Opuntia littoralis *pad.* KEITH FARRAR

used fresh as a tea or dried and powdered in capsules to treat diarrhea, colitis, and enlarged prostate. The pads are applied externally throughout the Americas as a first-aid treatment for wounds and sunburns.

## Phytochemicals/Mechanisms of Action

Prickly-pear pads and ripe fruits are high in soluble fiber and pectin, a gelatinous polysaccharide that has been shown to lower cholesterol levels and also may help regulate blood sugar. Much research has been completed since two clinical studies by a team of Mexican researchers published in the journals *Diabetes Care* (1988)[73] and *Phytotherapy Research* (1990)[74] documented a strong hypoglycemic effect of prickly-pear pads in the treatment of type 2 diabetes. A decrease in glucose absorption and improved insulin response were observed. Further studies have confirmed the blood sugar–lowering properties. Although the exact mechanisms of action are still unclear, some researchers believe the fiber and pectin content in the pads and fruits may physically prevent absorption of glucose in the intestines.

Describing external use, Michael Moore explains that the mucopolysaccharide gel inside the pads is strongly hydrophilic (water-attracting). Through the process of osmosis, the gel absorbs some of the fluid exuding from wounds when the pads are applied as a dressing. The gel also softens the skin, decreasing the tension against the injury, which relieves the pain.[75]

## Cultivation
Prickly-pears can be propagated from seed or by simply removing a pad, letting the exposed end dry for a few days, and replanting it in sandy soil. There are many spineless varieties to choose from for any sunny yard or garden location if you don't have a designated spiny cactus space.

## Cautions
Care must be taken at all stages of harvesting and processing to avoid the spines and glochids. Leather gloves are recommended in the field and rubber gloves in the kitchen. Salad tongs can be used to hold the pad while harvesting. Collect the youngest pads—best for eating—before they form spines. Cut or burn off the spines on older pads. Glochids on the pads or fruits can be brushed or burned off. Fruits can be twisted off the mature pads with salad tongs or, in a pinch, pierced in the end with a sharp stick and broken off. See "Recipes" for more instructions.

Chumash plant expert Juanita Centeno showed her students how to use a sprig of coyote brush (*Baccharis pilularis*) to remove any glochids embedded in the skin. Look closely at the affected area to see at what angle the glochids entered. The silica-rich, sandpapery coyote brush leaves grab the glochids when carefully brushed across the skin back in the direction from which the glochids attacked. A small lock of hair also will work as a brush.

## Notes
Nutritionally, nopales are high in minerals, especially calcium, magnesium, and potassium, and contain a wide range of amino acids.

The gel from nopales was once used by the Diegueño to lubricate oxcart wheels. Native Californians traditionally applied yucca charcoal tattoos with prickly-pear spines.

# HEATH FAMILY (ERICACEAE)

Worldwide, the Heath family consists of 100 genera made up of 3,000 species, including cranberries and blueberries. The twenty-six genera in California are represented by some very diverse plants, ranging from madrone trees to the large-flowering shrubs azalea and rhododendron to the edible fruits of huckleberry, manzanita, bearberry, and salal, to the non-green pinedrops and snow plant that parasitize soil fungi for their nutrients.

## *Arctostaphylos* genus

Almost all the world's sixty-two species of *Arctostaphylos* are natives of California, and all but one goes by the common name "manzanita." That one exception is *A. uva-ursi*, known as bearberry, uva ursi, or kinnikinnick. Although bearberry is the best known of the genus in herbal medicine, the leaves of all species of *Arctostaphylos* have been used interchangeably by Indigenous and Western herbalists. The genus name *Arctostaphylos* comes from the Ancient Greek *arktos* ("bear") and *staphule* ("bunch of grapes").

## MANZANITA
### *Arctostaphylos manzanita* et al.

**Other common names:** Common manzanita, whiteleaf manzanita

**Origin:** Native

**Range:** Throughout the state at varied elevations

**Habitat:** Varied, often in rocky soils in chaparral, conifer forests

**Related species in California:** Many species of manzanita, including bigberry manzanita (*Arctostaphylos glauca*); Pacific madrone (*Arbutus menziesii*)

**Related species globally:** Strawberry tree (*Arbutus unedo* et al.)

*Bigberry manzanita (*Arctostaphylos glauca*) flowers.* JAMES DAVID ADAMS JR.

**Conservation status rankings:**

> **IUCN Red List:** Most species LC
>
> **CNPS Rare Plant Rank:** Most species not listed. Several species and subspecies of manzanita are considered rare or endangered.
>
> **NatureServe State Status:** Most species SNR

**Uses:** Antibacterial, astringent; for acute urinary tract inflammation

**Parts used:** Leaves

**Edibility:** Berries are edible.

*Bearberry (*Arctostaphylos uva-ursi*).* BEN GRANGEREAU

# BEARBERRY
## *Arctostaphylos uva-ursi*

**Other common names:** Uva ursi, kinnikinnick, bearberry manzanita
**Origin:** Native
**Range:** Mainly close to the central and northern coast, below 300 feet
**Habitat:** Acidic soils in stabilized dunes, rocky outcrops, grassy coastal areas, coastal sage scrub

## Description
Like manzanitas, bearberry is evergreen with peeling reddish-brown bark; alternate, leathery, oblanceolate to ovate leaves, darker green above; and urn-shaped, whitish-pink flowers. Unlike most of its taller manzanita cousins, bearberry is a low-growing plant (under 1½ feet high) that spreads by runners into large mats. Its berries are red, in contrast to the reddish-brown berries of manzanita. Other than a lone colony in the subalpine Eastern Sierra, bearberry is found hugging the central and northern coast. It grows in acidic soils from sea level to 300 feet elevation in rocky outcrops and other coastal settings. Bearberry's range extends to all the northern states in the United States.

Bearberry and the rest of the manzanitas are found throughout California and the western United States, often in chaparral habitat, from the coast to the mountains. Their size can range from ground covers to shrubs to small trees.

*Manzanita bark peels every summer after the berries are ripe, exposing a new green skin that is able to photosynthesize while the plant is in summer dormancy (*Arctostaphylos glauca*).* ROBERT E. MERRITT

## Conservation Status

Bearberry is currently common and unthreatened. On the other hand, there are many species and subspecies of manzanita considered rare or endangered. In addition to the usual reasons (development, grazing, etc.), manzanitas are victims of poaching of their attractive wood. If you are collecting leaves and berries, please access secure populations.

## Traditional Uses

In California, the Karok, Pomo, and Cahuilla drink a tea of *Arctostaphylos* leaves for diarrhea. The Pomo boil the leaves for a cleansing wash for body and head.[76] [77] [78] The Atsugewi boil the leaves to treat cuts and burns.[79] The Pomo boil the bark for diarrhea.[80] [81] The Chumash sometimes use the water in which the berries have been boiled as a wash for poison oak rash.[82] Outside California, an infusion of bearberry leaves is widely used by numerous tribes, including the Cherokee, as a tea for urinary diseases and a mouthwash for cankers and sore gums. The leaves are the basis of an ointment for peeling scalp, rashes, and skin sores.

## Modern Uses

A hot or cold infusion of bearberry leaves is used specifically as a short-term treatment for acute, painful urinary tract infections, often associated with urine that is too alkaline. Slightly acidic urine (below 7.0 pH) inhibits naturally-occurring intestinal flora (bacteria) normally found in the urinary tract. This antimicrobial tea kills the bacteria and relieves the pain and inflammation caused by the bacterial irritation of the urethra.[83] The maximum antibacterial effect should occur about 3 or 4 hours after drinking the tea. Bearberry leaf tea is Commission E approved for this purpose. Manzanita leaves can be substituted in any recipes calling for bearberry.

The tea, when prepared as a decoction, is astringent, making it useful in sitz baths for hemorrhoids and as a wash for cuts, scrapes, and burns. Clinical trials with rats have shown that bearberry may be effective for preventing and treating kidney stones.

## Phytochemicals/Mechanisms of Action

Arbutin, a phenolic glycoside, is the active constituent in *Arcostaphylos* species and other Heath family plants like cranberry. It is concentrated in the leaves. When it reaches the kidneys, arbutin is hydrolyzed and excreted into the urinary tract as hydroquinone, a powerful antiseptic. The urine must be alkaline for this reaction to occur. It will happen naturally if there is already an infection accompanied by alkaline urine, a condition that sometimes results from a diet low in acid-forming proteins and whole grains. To increase the effectiveness of the tea, acidic urine can be temporarily alkalinized with a diet high in fruits and vegetables. To prevent reoccurrence after treatment, the diet should be rebalanced to maintain slightly acidic, naturally antibacterial, urine.

*Bigberry manzanita (*Arctostaphylos glauca*).* ROBERT E. MERRITT

*Bearberry (*Arctostaphylos uva-ursi*) flowers*
*showing typical urn shape of the Heath family*
DIETER WILKEN, COURTESY OF SANTA BARBARA BOTANIC GARDEN

*Bearberries (*Arctostaphylos uva-ursi).
J. R. "BOB" HALLER, COURTESY OF SANTA BARBARA
BOTANIC GARDEN

Another major component of the leaves and berries of bearberry and man-zanita is tannin, known for its cleansing and astringent action. The leaves also contain the antibacterial triterpenoid and flavonoid glycosides such as quercetin and hyperoside, which are reported to have antioxidant and antibacterial activity.

## Cultivation

Many cultivars of manzanita and bearberry are available in native plant nurseries. They prefer full sun and well-drained soil. No fertilizer is required.

## Cautions

The hydroquinone and tannin from the leaves can be irritating and potentially toxic to the kidneys and bladder if used in excess. The standard infusion of the tea should not be used for more than two to three days and not at all by preg-nant women or those with kidney disease. It can be prepared as a cold infusion, soaked for 6 to 12 hours, to lessen the tannin content.

## Notes

The widespread Indigenous use of the fruity, sour berries of manzanita and bearberry for food and drink may outshine the plants' medicinal reputations. The seeds can also be ground and used as flour. (See "Recipes" in this book, and refer to Christopher Nyerges's *Foraging California* for more information.)

For centuries, native people across North America have combined bearberry or manzanita leaves with tobacco and other herbs to make a smoking mixture known as "kinnikinnick." Bearberry is so common an ingredient in these varied mixtures that the plant itself is sometimes called kinnikinnick.

# PEA FAMILY (FABACEAE)

Formerly known as Leguminosae, the Pea or Legume family is the third-largest plant family. There are 730 genera and over 19,000 species. It is commercially important for peas, beans, and peanuts in the human diet as well as alfalfa and clover for livestock. Fabaceae have alternate, compound leaves; flowers with a banner, wings, and keel; and seeds in pods. Pea family plants host important nitrogen-fixing bacteria on their roots.

## *Glycyrrhiza* genus

Most of the twenty species of *Glycyrrhiza* are native to Europe and Asia, including the famous licorice root of commerce, *G. glabra*. Only one species, *G. lepidota*, is native to North America. The name *Glycyrrhiza* derives from the Greek *glukos riza*, meaning "sweet root."

## AMERICAN LICORICE
### *Glycyrrhiza lepidota*

**Other common names:** Wild licorice, sweet root
**Origin:** Native
**Range:** Western-central and southern California and the east side of the southern Sierras to 6,500 feet elevation
**Habitat:** Moist, rich, disturbed soil; streambanks, roadsides
**Related species in California:** None
**Related species globally:** Cultivated licorice (*G. glabra*), Chinese licorice (*G. uralensis*)
**Conservation status rankings:**
    **IUCN Red List:** LC
    **CNPS Rare Plant Rank:** Not listed
    **NatureServe State Rank:** SNR
**Uses:** Demulcent, anti-inflammatory; for coughs, sore throats, stomach ulcers
**Parts used:** Root
**Edibility:** Roots can be chewed, although not as sweet as cultivated licorice.

*American licorice (*Glycyrrhiza lepidota*) flowers.* ROBERT MULLER, COURTESY OF SANTA BARBARA BOTANIC GARDEN

## Description

American licorice (*Glycyrrhiza lepidota*) is found throughout much of southern and western central California and on the east side of the southern Sierras to an altitude of 6,500 feet. Its native range extends to much of the United States. It is a perennial with a long taproot supporting erect, branching stems that reach 2 to 3 feet high. Creeping rhizomes create colonies in rich, moist, disturbed soil, often along streambanks and in river valleys. Its alternating compound leaves have nine to nineteen lanceolate leaflets covered with sticky glands, also found on the stems, that create a slightly hairy appearance. The flowers are white to yellowish green in color, sometimes tinged with purple, appearing in long, thick clusters in the upper leaf axils from June to August. The spiny seedpods distinguish wild licorice from all other members of the Pea family that grow in the western United States.

### Conservation Status
American licorice is common and unthreatened throughout its range.

### Traditional Uses
American licorice has been used by many tribes across the United States. The fresh root is chewed for a "strong throat" for singing. An infusion or decoction is drunk for coughs, chest pains, and sore throats. Externally, an infusion of the roots is applied to swellings.[84]

### Modern Uses
Cultivated licorice root (*G. glabra*) is a worldwide botanical star and one of the most researched of all plants. Our humble American licorice plays second

*American licorice (*Glycyrrhiza lepidota*).* ROBERT MULLER, COURTESY OF SANTA BARBARA BOTANIC GARDEN

*Close view of an American licorice (*Glycyrrhiza lepidota*) flower cluster blooming. Sticky glands on the stem to the left are also visible.* JAMES DAVID ADAMS JR.

fiddle to it because it has a much lower percentage of glycyrrhizin, the main active ingredient. Still, *G. lepidota* is highly recommended by Michael Moore for inflammation of the throat, bronchioles, and lungs, especially in combination with other herbs. Its anti-inflammatory and pain-relieving activity also makes it useful for treating stomach ulcers. The phytosterol content may help with estrogen and adrenal corticosteroid deficiencies. Moore suggests 2 to 3 cups a day of a strong decoction for one week for painful menstrual cramps.

*G. glabra* is Commission E approved for inflamed upper respiratory mucus membranes and for gastric and duodenal ulcers. It is widely used in Chinese and Ayurvedic medicine and Western herbalism for those purposes and also as an expectorant and mild laxative. Chinese herbalists often add it to respiratory and digestive teas in low doses as a supporting herb, believing its sweet flavor can "harmonize" a formula. Once official in the *US Pharmacopoeia* for its medicinal activity,[85] it is still listed as a flavoring in the *National Formulary*.

### Phytochemicals/Mechanisms of Action

Glycyrrhizin, a triterpenoid saponin, makes licorice root sweet. It also is the main ingredient providing the medicinal properties. While American licorice contains some glycyrrhizin (around 0.11 percent by weight), it is a small amount compared to cultivated licorice, which contains about 5–9 percent.[86] That makes cultivated licorice anywhere from forty-five to eighty times sweeter. In fact, American licorice tastes more bitter than sweet. Likewise, cultivated licorice is much more potent medicinally than our wild American licorice.

When ingested, glycyrrhizin in licorice root is converted to glycyrrhetinic acid, the main active constituent. It can increase mucus secretions in the respiratory tract, soothing the throat and making it easier to cough up phlegm. In the digestive tract it increases prostaglandins, which, in turn, reduce stomach acid secretions and increase stomach mucus. Both of these effects show its potential for treating stomach ulcers. Carbenoxolone, a derivative of glycyrrhetinic acid, has been used clinically for years to treat gastric and duodenal ulcers. In a promising 2003 study, glycyrrhizin inhibited replication of the SARS-associated coronavirus.[87]

American licorice has a number of other medicinal compounds. The isoflavonoids glabridin and glabrene are antimicrobial agents against *Staphylococcus*, *Candida*, and other infections. They also act as phytoestrogens and may boost low estrogen production. Other flavonoids such as glepidotin, glabranin, and pinocembrin may provide anti-inflammatory effects. The essential oil contains some eighty compounds, including many terpenoids known to relieve pain.[88]

### Cultivation
If you have a place to sustainably collect American licorice, you can replant root sections with buds into your garden. Seed is also available to purchase. Licorice likes moist, sandy soil and plenty of sun. If it's happy, it will grow for years.

### Cautions
A few brands of black licorice candy contain small amounts of natural licorice extract from *G. glabra* as a flavoring and sweetener. If taken in large quantities, licorice extract is known to increase blood pressure or create heart arrhythmias by temporarily dropping potassium levels. In a widely publicized case in 2020, a 54-year-old man died from cardiac arrest after eating too much black licorice.[89] Fortunately, a decoction of American licorice root would not provide enough glycyrrhizin to create this problem.

### Notes
Prepare American licorice root tea as a strong decoction by putting 1 ounce (by weight) of dried roots in 1 quart (by volume) of water. Bring to a boil and boil for 10 minutes. Strain and add water to bring it back to 1 quart.[90]

The species name of *G. lepidota* means "scaly" in Latin.

The familiar flavor associated with black licorice candy does not come entirely from licorice root. It's there from adding oil of anise seed (*Pimpinella anisum*).

# BEECH FAMILY (FAGACEAE)

The Beech family includes 7 genera and about 900 species, mostly in the Northern Hemisphere. They are trees or shrubs with simple, alternate leaves, often toothed or lobed. Some are evergreen, but most are deciduous. The Beech family produces true botanical nuts, including edible beechnuts, chestnuts, and acorns.

## *Quercus* genus

At least 500 species of *Quercus*, or oak, are found worldwide, mainly in temperate regions. It is one of the most widespread genera of trees in the Northern Hemisphere. Not counting subspecies and hybrids, there are twenty-six species of native *Quercus* in California. Other than California tanbark-oak (*Notholithocarpus densiflorus*), all oaks in California belong to this genus. There are two basic types of oaks: evergreen and deciduous. Some of the evergreens are called "live oaks" because they have green, often spiny, leaves all year. The deciduous species often have lobed leaves.

## OAK
### *Quercus* spp.

**Other common names:** *Encina* (Spanish for "evergreen oaks"), *roble* (Spanish for "deciduous oaks")

**Origin:** Native

**Range:** Widespread throughout California from sea level to 9,600 feet elevation

**Habitat:** Most habitats

**Related species in California:** California tanbark-oak (*Notholithocarpus densiflorus*)

**Related species globally:** 600 *Quercus* species worldwide

**Conservation status rankings:**

    **IUCN Red List:** LC or unlisted, except coastal sage scrub oak (*Quercus dumosa*), EN, and valley oak (*Q. lobata*), NT

*Spring pollen catkins, spiny-edged mature leaves, and new growth on coast live oak*
LANNY KAUFER

    **CNPS Rare Plant Rank:** Several localized species are listed.

    **NatureServe State Rank:** SNR, except coastal sage scrub oak (*Q. dumosa*), S3

**Uses:** Astringent, anti-inflammatory, antibacterial; for sore throat gargle and wash or compress for rashes, wounds, and burns

**Parts used:** Bark, leaves, galls

**Edibility:** Acorns are edible after leaching out tannins and cooking or baking them.

## Description

California's oaks range in size from medium-size shrubs to large trees. The "Champion Oak," a canyon live oak (*Q. chrysolepis*), in San Bernardino County is currently the largest oak in the United States. It has a trunk circumference of roughly 42 feet, stands 100 feet high, and is 100 feet wide. Valley oak (*Q. lobata*) can reach similar size. Coast live oak (*Q. agrifolia*), another large species reaching 80 feet in height, is the most common species in southern California.

Other common widespread species include blue oak (*Q. douglasii*), California black oak (*Q. kelloggii*), interior live oak (*Q. wislizenii*), scrub oak (*Q. berberidifolia*), and Oregon white oak (*Q. garryana*). Despite the variation in size and shape of the trees and their parts, all true oaks share certain characteristics. They have separate male and female parts on the same tree. Male catkins contain pollen, and female buds are clustered in the terminal twigs. The fruit they produce is a nut (acorn), partly enclosed in a cup. All acorns are edible. All species, including tanbark-oak, can be used interchangeably for medicinal purposes.

Oak galls, sometimes called "oak apples" for their appearance, are created when gall wasps deposit eggs into twig tissue. The wasp larvae secrete a chemical similar to the tree's own growth hormone, stimulating the tree to produce a firm but pithy ball around the larvae. The larvae eat their way through the gall as it matures and hardens. Oak galls are generally higher in tannin and more astringent than other parts of oaks.

*Natural growth pattern of coast live oak (*Quercus agrifolia*) canopy, shading the trunk from sun exposure*
LANNY KAUFER

## Conservation Status

Several small populations of localized species and varieties of oaks are listed on the California Native Plant Society's Inventory of Rare and Endangered Plants. The majority, including those mentioned in this chapter, are common and iconic trees of California. That being said, habitat loss and disease are causing population declines that must be monitored over time.

## Traditional Uses

Worldwide, oak bark has been used for centuries as a reliable and readily available astringent, both internally and externally. In California, a tanbark-oak bark infusion is used by the Sinkyone to treat colds and stomachaches. Leaves of blue oak are chewed by the Maidu to relieve sore throats.[91] The Chumash burn the fresh green bark of coast live oak down to charcoal, mix it with water, allow it to sit overnight, and then drink the liquid for indigestion and bowel trouble.[92] The Miwok use a bark decoction of valley oak bark as a cough medicine.[93] [94] The Ohlone use the red inner bark of the coast live oak, placed directly against a tooth, to cure toothache. They and the Chumash chew this bark to tighten loose teeth.[95] [96] A toothbrush is made by chewing on a twig. See the chapter on California bay (*Umbellularia californica*) for Chumash "toothbrush." Pomo suck canyon oak

*Mature coast live oak acorns.* LANNY KAUFER

acorns when they have a cough or sore throat. The tannin soothes their throat and acts as a cough drop.[97] The Ohlone and Yuki use the water from processing coast live oak or valley oak acorns to stop diarrhea.[98] [99]

California tribes use oak bark and galls externally to treat every kind of wound and skin condition. The Diegueño use a coast live oak bark decoction to bathe sores and boils.[100] The Ohlone wash sores, especially on the face, with an infusion of bark from tanbark-oak. The Pomo use it as a skin disinfectant. The Kawaiisu powder the bark from California black oak and interior live oak to treat burns. The Miwok do the same with valley oak and interior live oak bark and sprinkle the dust on running sores and the umbilical cords of newborn babies. Ashes from the burnt bark of valley oak are dusted on sores, cuts, and bruises by the Shasta.[101] Edith Van Allen Murphey writes that an unnamed tribe created a forerunner to penicillin. They covered acorn meal to make it

*Valley oak (*Quercus lobata*).* BEN GRANGEREAU

sweat and mold, then peeled off the skin of the mold and used it to draw out inflammation from boils or bad sores.[102]

Oak galls generally are harvested while still green, as soon as possible after the larvae have exited. They can be used fresh or dried for future use. The Diegueño squeeze out the juice from fresh scrub oak galls for a sore throat gargle. They also boil them and use the decoction as an eyewash.[103] The Atsugewi and Luiseño use scrub oak galls to treat sores and wounds. The Atsugewi dry and pulverize them, mix them with water, and use the solution as an eyewash or gargle for sore throats. They also drink gall tea to treat dysentery, diarrhea, hemorrhoids, and to prevent colds. The Chumash apply the fresh juice of coast live oak galls to sores and wounds. They consider the charred galls a good treatment for hemorrhoids.[104]

## Modern Uses

Just like the Indigenous peoples of North America, modern herbalists continue to make use of the astringent and antiseptic properties of oak bark, leaves, and galls. Washes, compresses, and other external applications are used for inflammatory skin conditions such as poison oak rash. The decoction is used as a tea for diarrhea and as a sore throat gargle. It is used in various forms as a treatment for hemorrhoids. Teas of the galls are also used as gargles. Reflecting these long-standing uses, the German Commission E reported astringent and virustatic activity for oak bark and approved its internal use for nonspecific, acute diarrhea and as a local treatment for mild inflammation of the mouth and throat. They also approved it for external use for inflammatory skin diseases.[105]

## Phytochemicals/Mechanisms of Action

Many plants create unpleasant-tasting tannins to deter insects and browsing herbivores. The hydrolyzable (water-soluble) tannins found in high concentrations in all parts of oak trees, especially galls, are responsible for oak's astringent actions. These tannins are polyphenols that can shrink body tissues by binding with tissue proteins. This binding action results in tightening the tissues, drying up excess secretions, preventing bleeding, and protecting inflamed mucus membranes, such as in eczema and burns.[106]

The bark, leaves and galls of all oaks also contain bioactive compounds such as phenolic acids (gallic and ellagic acids), flavonoids (quercetin, kaempferol, and flavan-3-ol), fatty acids (linoleic acid), and triterpenoids (lupeol). Working together, these compounds have shown strong antibacterial and anti-inflammatory activity in laboratory tests.[107] Quercetin, named for *Quercus* where it was first discovered, is found throughout the plant world and is a known antioxidant and a capillary and blood vessel protectant.

Valley oak leaves showing lobes that give it the scientific name Quercus lobata
LANNY KAUFER

## Cultivation

We need to plant more oaks to replace those lost to development and disease. They do best, however, where they have room to grow naturally without lifting up walkways and cracking house foundations. Oaks can easily be started from sprouted acorns or purchased as seedlings from native plant nurseries.

## Cautions

Excess consumption of tannins, like all astringents, can irritate the stomach and may also inhibit the body's ability to absorb iron from plant food sources.

When collecting from oaks, watch out for poison oak (*Toxicodendron diversilobum*), no relation to oak trees. It is often found growing around coast live oak and other riparian oaks in creek and canyon habitats.

*Valley oak acorns.* BEN GRANGEREAU

## Notes

Cut or strip bark from pruned branches or recently downed trees, never from the trunk of a living tree. See "Sustainable Collecting" in front of this guide for tips on collecting bark.

Acorns are historically the most important food for all California tribes who lived among sufficient numbers of oak trees. They contain good amounts of protein, carbohydrates, and healthy fats, making them an ideal food for year-round daily consumption. The nuts must be leached of tannic and phenolic acids and cooked before eating. See Christopher Nyerges's *Foraging California* for detailed information on preparing them. Historically, Chumash doctors routinely prescribed a diet of thin acorn gruel mixed with clam meat for sick and recovering patients.[108]

*Green oak galls on coast live oak, prior to exiting of larvae.* LANNY KAUFER

# ST. JOHN'S WORT FAMILY (HYPERICACEAE)

The St. John's Wort family includes 37 genera made up of 1,610 species worldwide. Most are found in the tropics.

## *Hypericum* genus

The genus *Hypericum* has over 490 species worldwide. All are known in English as St. John's wort. The genus name *Hypericum* is derived from the Greek *hyper* ("above") and *eikon* ("picture"), referring to the ancient placement of the fresh-picked plant over shrines to ward off evil spirits on Midsummer Day, June 24, known in the Christian era as St. John's Day or the Feast Day of St. John the Baptist. "Wort" is a Middle English word for "plant" or "herb."

California has three native *Hypericum* species, with Scouler's St. John's wort (*H. scouleri*) being by far the most common. Of the several non-natives, klamathweed (*H. perforatum*) is the most common.

### TINKER'S PENNY
#### *Hypericum anagalloides*

**Other common names:** Bog St. John's wort, creeping St. John's wort, pygmy St. John's wort
**Origin:** Native
**Range:** Coastal Northern California and Sierras to 10,500 feet elevation
**Habitat:** Coastal salt marsh; wetlands and meadows in forest and chaparral habitats

### GOLD-WIRE
#### *Hypericum concinnum*

**Other common names:** California St. John's wort
**Origin:** Native
**Range:** Coast range from Napa County to Mendocino County, west side of the Sierras from Maricopa County to Butte County; from 100 to 5,200 feet elevation
**Habitat:** Grassland, chaparral, and woodland slopes; conifer forest

*Canary Island St. John's wort* (Hypericum canariense)*, a non-native species that grows in disturbed soils along the California coast.* STEVE JUNAK

# KLAMATHWEED
## *Hypericum perforatum* subsp. *perforatum*

**Other common names:** Common St. John's wort, European St. John's wort
**Origin:** Non-native
**Range:** Coast range from Santa Cruz County to Mendocino County, Sierras from Amador County to Butte County; to 6,500 feet elevation
**Habitat:** Open, disturbed areas in many plant communities

# SCOULER'S ST. JOHN'S WORT
## *Hypericum scouleri*

**Synonym:** *Hypericum formosum*
**Other common names:** Western St. John's wort
**Origin:** Native
**Range:** All of California, except the Central Valley and southeast deserts, to 9,600 feet elevation
**Habitat:** Wet meadows and streambanks, mainly in forest habitats
**Related species in California:** Several other non-native *Hypericum* species, including Canary Island St. John's wort (*H. canariense*)

*Scouler's St. John's wort* (Hypericum scouleri)*, a California native.* JAMES DAVID ADAMS JR.

**Related species globally:** Common or perforate St. John's wort (*H. perforatum*) and many other *Hypericum* species

**Conservation status rankings:**

    **IUCN Red List:** LC for *H. perforatum*; others not listed

    **CNPS Rare Plant Rank:** Not listed

    **NatureServe State Rank:** *H. perforatum* is SNA; the rest are SNR.

**Uses:** Mild to moderate depression, anxiety; externally for skin inflammations and burns

**Parts used:** Flowering tops

**Edibility:** Roots were once eaten but are not considered edible today.

## Description

Though different in size and growth patterns, all St. John's wort (SJW) species in California have opposite leaves and similar-looking, five-petaled yellow flowers with many yellow stamens. They all have dots (glands) on the leaves. Dark glands contain hypericin, a pigment that stains the fingers red or purple when the leaves are rubbed. Pale or clear glands contain hyperforin. The flowers sometimes have dots as well.

Tinker's penny (*Hypericum anagalloides*) is a small annual or perennial native growing in mats of creeping aboveground stems less than 1 foot high. Its roundish, ⅛- to ½-inch-long leaves have clear glands. There are one to fifteen flowers per stem, with petals less than ⅛ inch long. The plant blooms from May to September.

Gold-wire (*Hypericum concinnum*) is a slightly larger perennial native, standing 5 to 8 inches high with many slender stems. Its linear to lanceolate leaves are ½ to 1½ inches long with dark glands. There are three to nine flowers per stem. The petals are ⅜ to ⅔ inch long with dark glands on the edges. Gold-wire flowers from May to August.

The non-native, fast-spreading klamathweed (*Hypericum perforatum* subsp. *perforatum*) is much larger than the natives, standing 1 to 4 feet tall on many erect stems. Its narrow, oblong leaves are ⅔ to 1 inch long with dark glands on the edges and noticeable, clear glands on the lower surface. It has from twenty-five to as many as one hundred flowers per stem. The petals are ⅓ to ½ inch long with many dark glands. Klamathweed flowers from May to August.

Scouler's SJW (*Hypericum scouleri*) is a perennial native with a few slender, erect stems 7 to 28 inches tall. It has oval leaves, ⅜ to 1¼ inches long, with dark glands on the edges and pale glands on the lower surface. It may have from three to as many as twenty-five flowers per stem. The petals are ¼ to ½ inch long. It blooms from June to September.

## Conservation Status

Native *Hypericum* populations are currently secure. The introduced klamathweed has an aggressive root system and is listed as a noxious, invasive weed by the

California Department of Food and Agriculture and the California Invasive Plant Council. A leaf-eating beetle was introduced in California in 1945 to biologically control it. The effort reduced the klamathweed population by 99 percent, but it's still abundant in some areas, where locals are usually happy to see it removed.

## Traditional Uses

California tribes have traditionally used native species of SJW for external treatments. The Miwok use a decoction of the upper parts of gold-wire as a wash for infected sores.[109] The Paiute and Shoshone soak aching feet in a decoction of Scouler's SJW. They also prepare a poultice from the boiled plant to heal sores and reduce swellings. The Shoshone apply the dried, powdered plant to cuts and wounds.[110] Back east, the Cherokee drink an infusion of common SJW (*H. perforatum*) for fevers, dysentery, and other bowel problems. A decoction is drunk for suppressed menstruation, and the sap is rubbed on sores.

In Europe, where common SJW (*H. perforatum*) is native, the use of the flowering parts to treat neuralgia and heal wounds dates back to Hippocrates and the ancient Greeks. It has been used to treat psychiatric disorders since the 1500s. In traditional European medicine, it has been used up to the present day to treat nerve pain, anxiety, and depression. Common SJW was brought to northeast America by European colonists and soon was growing wild. By the nineteenth century, American Eclectic physicians were prescribing it for hysteria and depression. Externally, they applied it to wounds and bruises.

## Modern Uses

According to the World Health Organization, clinical data supports the use of SJW for "symptomatic treatment of mild and moderate depressive episodes."[111] The flowering parts are German Commission E approved for internal use for "psychovegetative disturbances, depressive moods, anxiety and/or nervous unrest." Oil preparations are approved for digestive problems. Externally, the oil is approved for "treatment and post-therapy of acute and contused injuries, myalgia, and first-degree burns."[112] SJW is one of the best-selling herbal supplements in the United States and Europe.

Michael Moore, David Hoffmann, and other herbalists point out that SJW can be effective taken internally (tincture or infusion) as a sedative and pain reliever and for some cases of mild to moderate depression, but that it is *not* a treatment for severe depression. Moore considers the fresh plant superior to the dried for all preparations and recommends the tincture as more effective than the infusion for internal use. Hoffmann suggests it especially for irritability and anxiety associated with menopause. He also considers it useful for neuralgia, sciatica, and rheumatic pains. For external use, both experts recommend the steeped oil of the fresh flowering parts as an ointment for skin inflammations and, according to Moore, to apply topically for sciatica, low back pain, and carpal tunnel syndrome.[113] [114] (See "Recipes.")

### Phytochemicals/Mechanisms of Action

An analysis of more than twenty-eight controlled clinical trials concluded that SJW works as effectively as standard antidepressants, with much fewer side effects. The main phytochemicals considered responsible for its antidepressant effects are hyperforin and adhyperforin, two of a class of organic compounds called phloroglucinols. Hypericin and pseudohypericin, red pigments found in the dots on the leaves and flowers, also are important medicinal constituents. They are from another group of organic compounds called naphthodianthrones. Bioactive flavonoids (kaempferol, quercetin), mono- and sesquiterpenes, and tannins also are present.

Studies are ongoing to determine the exact roles of these ingredients and their mechanisms of action. Current theories suggest reuptake inhibition of neurotransmitters such as serotonin, noradrenaline, dopamine, and others.[115] [116] [117] [118]

### Cultivation

Native SJW species can be started from seed or from plants, if you can find them, and grown in damp soil until they develop root systems. They can be allowed to spread to prevent slope erosion. Otherwise, you will need a root barrier to contain them. Please do not plant klamathweed. There is plenty growing wild—much to the dismay of ranchers, farmers, and environmentalists.

### Cautions

The safety and efficacy of SJW has been tested in more than 5,000 patients in numerous reports and studies. It is considered safe to use, but it should not be taken with other antidepressant drugs.

### Notes

The upper parts of the native species should be gathered while flowering. The flower buds are the preferred parts of klamathweed.

Historically, the Central Miwok have been known to use the roots of Scouler's St. John's wort as food.[119]

# WALNUT FAMILY (JUGLANDACEAE)

Found worldwide in temperate regions and subtropical mountains, the Walnut family includes nine genera and at least sixty species. Walnuts, pecans, and hickory nuts are commercially important family members.

## *Juglans* genus

The *Juglans* genus includes twenty-one species in North America, South America, and temperate regions of Asia. The genus is represented by two California natives: the southern California black walnut (*J. californica*) and the northern California black walnut (*J. hindsii*), the latter now too rare for ethical collecting. The well-known English walnut of commerce *(J. regia)* is an important crop in central California. The eastern black walnut (*J. nigra*), native to the eastern United States, is sometimes found growing wild in California from previous plantings. The good news for herbal foragers is that all *Juglans* species have similar medicinal properties. The nuts of the native species have much thicker shells and are more intensely flavored than English walnuts.

According to Maud Grieve's *A Modern Herbal*, "It was said that in the 'golden age,' when men lived upon acorns, the gods lived upon Walnuts, and hence the name of *Juglans*, *Jovis glans*, or Jupiter's nuts."[120]

## SOUTHERN CALIFORNIA BLACK WALNUT
### *Juglans californica*

**Origin:** Native

**Range:** Inland canyons and valleys

**Habitat:** Southern oak woodland

**Related species:** Northern California black walnut (*J. hindsii*), English walnut (*J. regia*), eastern black walnut (*J. nigra*)

**Conservation status rankings:**

    **IUCN Red List:** NT

    **CNPS Rare Plant Rank:** 4.2; threatened by development

    **CNPS State Rank:** S4

**Uses:** Astringent, laxative, vermifuge

**Parts used:** Leaves, green husks

**Edibility:** The mature nuts are edible and delicious; high in protein, fats, B vitamins, and minerals.

*New growth and pollen catkins (*Juglans californica*).* LANNY KAUFER

*Southern California black walnut tree (*Juglans californica*) with ripening walnuts.* LANNY KAUFER

## Description

Southern California black walnut is found in the oak woodland habitat of inland valleys from Santa Barbara County south to San Diego County. It is a large deciduous tree ranging from 15 to 40 feet tall with a spread of 10 to 20 feet. The compound leaves are composed of nine to nineteen toothed, pinnate leaflets 6 to 12 inches long. They begin to turn yellow in late summer as the nuts ripen. The trees are monoecious, having both male and female flowers, which appear in early spring before the leaves. The female flowers are spikes in the leaf axils; the male flowers hang in catkins. In late summer and fall, the trees produce thick-shelled, spherical nuts with shallow grooves on the shells. They are surrounded by a smooth, fleshy husk that turns from green to yellow to brown as they ripen. The nuts inside the husks can vary from ¾ inch to 1¼ inches in diameter.

## Conservation Status

Unfortunately, *Juglans californica* and its severely threatened northern cousin, *J. hindsii*, like to live in the rich alluvial soil of California's valleys—the kinds of places perfect for agricultural and housing developments. (Please do not collect from *J. hindsii*.) On the bright side, wherever southern California black walnut is still numerous, it can grow quite large, allowing for some mindful collecting of aboveground parts. Ecologically, it's even better to harvest the equally useful English walnut, *J. regia*, where it is available. Some old, mature specimens of English walnut can still be found in California's backyards and fields where houses replaced commercial orchards.

When harvesting nuts, keep in mind that squirrels and other rodents depend on them. The ones they stash in the ground but don't get back to are potential sprouts for future generations.

## Traditional Uses

Other than the Ohlone, who have been known to make a tea of the leaves for "thin blood,"[121] there are no records of California Indians using local walnut trees medicinally. However, several tribes around the country use the closely related eastern black walnut, *J. nigra*, for a variety of purposes. An infusion of the leaves or green hulls is used as a wash for itchy skin conditions; the same parts are crushed to produce juice to rub on ringworm, a fungal infection. Some use a decoction of the bark as a laxative and to eliminate intestinal parasites.

*Telltale serrated compound leaves and green walnuts of* Juglans californica
STEVEN MARK NORRIS

Globally, the use of walnut leaf for medicine has been recorded for thousands of years. In Ayurvedic medicine, walnut oil is used for tapeworms. Over time, Western herbalists settled on its efficacy for treating skin disorders and intestinal problems, including parasites.

## Modern Uses

The German Commission E approved the use of a decoction of the leaves of *J. regia* as an astringent wash or compress for mild inflammations of the skin and excessive perspiration of the hands and feet.[122]

Modern herbalists continue to use the dried bark in a tincture, powder, or bitter-tasting infusion as a mild laxative and to kill intestinal worms. The green nuts are also an effective vermifuge.[123] Michael Moore recommends the leaves in a fresh tincture or infusion as an astringent and tonic to the ileum and colon, improving mucus membrane absorption of nutrients.[124]

## Phytochemicals/Mechanisms of Action

All parts of walnut trees contain astringent tannins and the bitter glycoside juglone, the active ingredient, which has demonstrated antibacterial, antifungal, and antiparasitic properties. A 1990 study found that juglone extracted from

*Southern California black walnuts (*Juglans californica*) nearing maturity.* JAMES DAVID ADAMS JR.

green walnut hulls showed antifungal activity as effective as commercial anti-fungal products.[125] Another study in 2016 confirmed its antibacterial activity against *Staphylococcus*.[126]

### Cultivation
Black walnut is propagated by planting the nuts. It does best in soils that simulate the rich loam of its native inland valleys. It likes sun but will tolerate some shade. Once mature it requires little care beyond removing suckers and dead wood. The juglone excreted by walnut roots is toxic to other plants, especially those of the Nightshade family (Solanaceae), so take care where you plant it.

### Cautions
Contact with fresh leaves or husks will stain the skin yellow and may even cause dermatitis in some people. There are no known side effects of using walnut internally, but those with nut allergies should exercise caution. Internal use of walnut leaves and husks while pregnant is discouraged.

### Notes
The Chumash and other tribes eat the sweet and oily nuts and then use the carefully-split half-shells as pieces in a game. The shells are filled with asphaltum from natural tar seeps by coastal tribes and decorated with small pieces of abalone shell. In the absence of tar, inland tribes use the pitch of creosote bush (*Larrea tridentata*). The shells are tossed and scored as landing either flat side up or down.

A decoction of walnut parts makes an effective yellow dye. The decocted green parts, especially the hulls, can be used as an insecticide for lawns and gardens.

# MINT FAMILY (LAMIACEAE)

The Mint or Deadnettle family is composed of 236 genera and 7,500 species. It is characterized by square (four-sided) stems, opposite leaves, and whorls of two-lipped flowers. Many species contain aromatic oils. The Mint family includes popular Mediterranean culinary herbs such as basil, sage, rosemary, thyme, oregano, lavender, and, of course, the mints. California's own Mediterranean climate is home to several native medicinal herbs of the Mint family described in this section, including five species of sage (*Salvia*).

## *Clinopodium* genus

Most of the 150 species of *Clinopodium* are native to the Mediterranean region. All are aromatic. Of the three species native to California, only California yerba buena (*C. douglasii*) is common enough to consider collecting aboveground parts for tea.

## CALIFORNIA YERBA BUENA
### *Clinopodium douglasii*

California yerba buena (Clinopodium douglasii) with two-lipped flowers typical of the Mint family. STEVE JUNAK

**Synonyms:** Formerly *Satureja douglasii, Micromeria chamissonis*, and *Micromeria douglasii*

**Other common names:** Indian mint, Douglas' savory, Oregon-tea

**Origin:** Native

**Range:** San Luis Obispo County north to the Oregon border and beyond

**Habitat:** Northern coastal scrub, redwood forest, chaparral, mixed evergreen forest

**Related species in California:** San Diego yerba buena (*Clinopodium chandleri*) and monkey-flower yerba buena (*C. mimuloides*) are both rare. See below.

**Related species globally:** Aromatic species of *Clinopodium, Satureja*, and *Micromeria*

**Conservation status rankings:**

    **IUCN Red List:** Not listed

    **CNPS Rare Plant Rank:** *C. douglasii* not listed; *C. chandleri* is 1B.2; *C. mimuloides* is 4.2.

    **NatureServe State Rank:** SNR

**Uses:** Relieves colds, fevers, gas; soothes stomach; increases menstrual flow

**Parts used:** Leaves and flowers

**Edibility:** Beverage tea and flavoring as one might use spearmint

*A closer view of California yerba buena (*Clinopodium douglasii*) in flower*
DONALD MYRICK, COURTESY OF SANTA BARBARA BOTANIC GARDEN

## Description

California yerba buena (*Clinopodium douglasii*) is a creeping perennial native herb of the Mint family. It prefers shady, moist locations below 3,000 feet elevation in the coast ranges from San Luis Obispo County north to British Columbia. Spreading like strawberries, its slender, four-sided runners put down roots wherever possible, forming low mats in its favored sites. The light green, ovate-triangular, opposite leaves are ½ to 1 inch long with scalloped edges, waxy-shiny above and dull beneath. Delicate, tubular, white to purple-tinged two-lipped flowers with two lobes above and three below emerge singly from the leaf axils on short stems. The entire plant exudes a pungent and refreshing minty aroma.

California yerba buena is not to be confused with its European cousin, spearmint (*Mentha spicata*), a common garden escapee that is also called "yerba buena" by Spanish speakers. Their aromas are similar, but California yerba buena has a unique scent all its own, like a sweet spearmint with a pleasant note of camphor.

## Conservation Status

California yerba buena is common within its chosen habitats. Once found as far south as Ventura, it has moved farther north due to grazing, droughts, and development. There are two rare *Clinopodium* species in California that should not be collected. San Diego yerba buena (*C. chandleri*) is a short, white-flowered yerba buena shrub found only in the San Diego area. Monkey-flower yerba buena (*C. mimuloides*) is another small shrub with orange flowers; it is found in coastal central California.

## Traditional Uses

California yerba buena tea enjoys immense popularity as a beverage as well as a medicinal remedy among Indigenous Californians. Early Oxnard physician C. L. Bard reported in 1894 that the tea was taken by Ventura County–area Chumash for intestinal parasites and to relieve gas, promote menstruation, and reduce fever. The Ohlone drink a decoction of the plant for pinworms and make a warm poultice for toothaches. Cahuilla and Luiseño drink an infusion for colds and fever and to help with insomnia. Mendocino tribes give it to babies to relieve colic.

Several Indigenous groups report using it to "purify the blood," a catch-all term applied to herbs that help the body eliminate toxins and heal various chronic conditions. One of those tribes, the Kashaya Pomo, also drink it for chest colds and "when a person had an upset stomach and was getting thin."[127]

## Modern Uses

Contemporary Chumash and Mexican-Americans value the tea for relaxation, to soothe the stomach, and to treat colic. They also rub the leaves on sore muscles.[128] Michael Moore considers the hot tea effective for inducing sweating for mild fevers but mostly waxes poetic about the flavor.[129] Michael Tierra describes it as an aromatic, warming diaphoretic with carminative and diuretic properties.[130]

## Phytochemicals/Mechanisms of Action

The only documented chemical study on California yerba buena was done in 1908, when it was known as *Micromeria chamissonis*. Researchers found some familiar Mint family constituents: essential oil, resins, a phytosterol, and a considerable amount of glucose. They also identified "a new phenolic substance" they named xanthomicrol and one they called micromerol.[131] Xanthomicrol is now known to be a flavone created by plants to protect against UV radiation. It is currently getting a lot of attention for its antispasmodic, antiplatelet, and anticancer potential. Flavones found in other species of *Clinopodium* are antibacterial, anticonvulsant, and act as central nervous system depressants. Micromerol, now known as ursolic acid, is a triterpenoid reported to have antitumor and antioxidant activity.

Dr. James Duke identifies large amounts of certain aromatic terpenes in *C. douglasii* that are also found in spearmint, pennyroyal, and other mints. These include camphene, camphor, carvone, limonene, menthone, and pulegone.[132]

## Cultivation

Like other mints, California yerba buena can be started from cuttings. Plants are available in nurseries. They prefer cool, moist climates.

## Cautions
California yerba buena and other emmenagogues should be avoided during pregnancy.

## Notes
Jan Timbrook describes one of ethnographer J. P. Harrington's Chumash consultants explaining how a beef head was covered in California yerba buena before being roasted in an earth oven. An Indigenous version of mint jelly, perhaps?

The Ventureño Chumash name for California yerba buena is *'alaqtaha*, which means "both warm and cordial."[133] The city of San Francisco was initially named Yerba Buena for this popular, fragrant plant.

## *Marrubium* genus
The Mediterranean region of Europe and the Middle East is home to most of the world's thirty native species of *Marrubium*. One in particular, horehound (*M. vulgare*) has become a worldwide weed wherever its home climate is found. It has become naturalized in California.

## HOREHOUND
### *Marrubium vulgare*

**Other common names:** White horehound, hoarhound
**Origin:** Non-native
**Range:** Throughout the United States below subalpine elevations
**Habitat:** Disturbed soil, vacant lots, roadsides; generally in dry climates
**Related species in California:** None
**Lookalikes:** Young brickellbush plants (*Brickellia californica*)
**Conservation status rankings:**
    **IUCN Red List:** Not listed
    **CNPS Rare Plant Rank:** Not listed
    **NatureServe State Rank:** SNA
    **Cal-IPC Rating:** Limited
**Uses:** Expectorant, digestive stimulant
**Parts used:** Leaves and flowering tops
**Edibility:** Not edible

*Young horehound plant (*Marrubium vulgare*) surrounded by horehound sprouts.* LANNY KAUFER

## Description
Horehound (*Marrubium vulgare*) is a perennial herb growing up to 2 feet tall with many woolly, white, square stems. The leaves are opposite, 1 to 2 inches long, round-ovate, scalloped, dark green and crinkly above, whitish-gray woolly below. The flowers are small, white, in dense whorls, appearing in the leaf axils inside bristly calyxes that mature to become clingy burs that stick to everything, especially dogs' tails. Though more common below 4,000 feet elevation, horehound can be found growing in disturbed soils at all subalpine elevations.

## Conservation Status
Horehound is a common weed with a minor impact on native species.

## Traditional Uses
Dating back to ancient Egypt and Greece, horehound has a long history of use for coughs and colds as an expectorant, making it easier to expel phlegm. For centuries Europeans have used it for that purpose and also as a bitter digestive tonic, stimulating bile to help digest fats. After settlers introduced horehound in their gardens, several California tribes, including the Ohlone, Diegueño, Kawaiisu, and Yuki, began using a tea of the leaves for coughs and colds.[134]

*Whorls of horehound (*Marrubium vulgare*) flowers in the opposite leaf axils.* JESS STARWOOD

Harvey Wickes Felter, MD, one of the "Eclectic" physicians of the American School of Medicine in the nineteenth and early twentieth centuries, prescribed the hot infusion of horehound as a diaphoretic to induce sweating, the cold infusion as a diuretic to increase urination, and the syrup as an expectorant to help expel phlegm from the lungs.[135]

## Modern Uses *(including parts used)*
Although the FDA no longer approves horehound as a pharmaceutical drug, it is still used today as an ingredient in commercial cough syrups and lozenges. The so-called "horehound candy" sold in old-timey tourist shops is actually a cough drop, not a confection. Expectorant syrups and cough drops are prepared from a decoction of the leaves by contemporary herbalists to make it easier for patients to cough up phlegm. Herbalist Michael Tierra classifies it as a "cooling

expectorant" used for hot, dry phlegm associated with dry coughs, hoarseness, and difficult expectoration.[136]

In 1990 the German Commission E approved horehound for loss of appetite and poor digestion, reporting that marrubinic acid (a derivative of marrubiin) works as a choleretic (bile stimulant). As recently as 2014, the European Committee on Herbal Medicinal Products concluded that, based on its longstanding use, horehound can be used as an expectorant for patients with cough associated with a cold; for treating mild dyspepsia symptoms, such as bloating and flatulence; and for patients with a temporary loss of appetite.

## Phytochemicals/Mechanisms of Action

Horehound contains diterpenes, tannins, the alkaloids betonicine and stachydrine, monoterpene oils, flavonoids, and minerals, especially potassium. The terpenes in horehound, also found in many other Mint family plants, have well-documented anti-inflammatory, analgesic, and antibacterial properties. The main active ingredient in horehound, and the one that gives the herb its bitter taste, is marrubiin, a diterpene lactone. In addition to stimulating bile production, it has been shown to stimulate secretions of the bronchial mucosa, which may explain horehound's expectorant powers.[137]

Several animal studies have shown excellent pharmacological potential for marrubiin and its derivatives, marrubinic acid and marrubenol, in treating gastric ulcers, diabetes, pain, inflammation, and as a cardioprotective agent.[138]

*Pre-flowering horehound plant (*Marrubium vulgare*) showing furry white stems.* LANNY KAUFER

*Horehound about to launch its clingy seeds on the world in July in southern California.* LANNY KAUFER

## Cultivation

Plant it from seed in the early spring in full sun. Horehound is not particular about soil. Harvest it each year to keep it lush and prevent it from seeding. The bristly seeds are notorious hitchhikers, especially on furry dog tails. This can result in unhappy neighbors if you don't harvest your crop.

## Cautions

Horehound is contraindicated in heart disease, high blood pressure, and pregnancy. The fresh juice may cause skin irritation.

## Notes

Harvest the leaves and young flowering tops; use them fresh, or dry them in the shade. Steep an infusion for tea. (See "Recipes" for Horehound Syrup.) To make cough drops, buy a candy thermometer, start with the syrup, and follow a recipe for homemade candy.

Young brickellbush plants (*Brickellia californica*) also have white stems and similarly shaped leaves resembling young, pre-flowering horehound. However, the stems are round and the thin leaves are arrowhead-shaped, not scalloped like horehound. If you see a young brickellbush, there's probably a 6-foot-tall parent nearby.

The original English common name "hoarhound" comes from its hoary (hairy) appearance and its ancient Greek use for treating dog bites. The Latin name *Marrubium* derives from the Hebrew word for "bitter." Horehound is one of the traditional bitter herbs (*maror*) used in the Jewish Passover seder.

## *Mentha* genus

Botanists currently recognize twenty-five true species of mint (*Mentha*) and fifteen hybrids worldwide. All are aromatic with square stems. The most common mints are the peppermint hybrid (*Mentha x piperita*), spearmint (*M. spicata*), and the corn mints or wild mints (*M. arvensis* and *M. canadensis*). Mints can be distinguished from one another by their aromas. Peppermint and corn mint have a similar flavor owing to their high menthol content. Spearmint, on the other hand, is high in carvone. The leaves of mints are used for tea and flavoring; the flowering parts, for making essential oil.

When the Greek god Hades fell in love with a beautiful nymph named Minthe, his jealous wife, Persephone, turned Minthe into a plant. When Hades was unable to bring her back to life, the legend says that he settled for giving that plant a fragrant aroma to remember her by. As you guessed by now, the genus *Mentha* is derived from her name.

### WILD MINT
#### *Mentha arvensis*

**Synonym:** *Mentha arvensis* var. *glabrata*
**Common names:** European field mint, corn mint, brook mint, *poléo* (Spanish)
**Origin:** Non-native
**Range:** Mainly from San Joaquin Valley north to 1,800 feet elevation
**Habitat:** Moist places, fields

*Wild mint (*Mentha arvensis*).* KEIR MORSE

## *Mentha canadensis*

**Synonyms:** *M. arvensis* var. *canadensis*,
*M. arvensis* var. *villosa*
**Common names:** Wild mint, American corn
mint, Canada mint, Japanese peppermint
**Origin:** Native
**Range:** Most of California (excluding deserts)
to 8,000 feet elevation
**Habitat:** Moist areas, streambanks, lakeshores,
fields
**Related species:** peppermint (*Mentha x piperita*)
**Conservation status rankings:**
> **IUCN Red List:** *M. arvensis*, LC; *M.*
> *canadensis*, not listed
> **CNPS Rare Plant Rank:** Neither is listed.
> **NatureServe State Rank:** Both are SNR.

*Wild mint (*Mentha canadensis*).* DONALD MYRICK,
COURTESY OF SANTA BARBARA BOTANIC GARDEN

**Uses:** Calmative, analgesic, diaphoretic, antispasmodic; for anxiety, digestive pain, fevers,
indigestion
**Parts used:** Leaves
**Edibility:** Leaves and flowers are edible as flavorings.

## Description

The reliable Jepson eFlora considers *Mentha canadensis* the only native species of mint in California; the equally reliable CalFlora and other authors and botanists say the genetically similar *M. arvensis* is also native. Still other botanists contend that *M. canadensis* is just a fuzzy variety of *M. arvensis*. Rather than try to settle this ongoing debate about their taxonomy and native or non-native status, we will consider both of California's wild mints very close relatives with nearly equal medicinal properties. Since both are common enough for ethical harvesting, the native/non-native distinction is not so important in this case. As described below, the main visual difference between them is the presence of tiny short hairs on *M. canadensis*. Both species flower from July to October in similar habitats, and both have a pleasant, peppermint-like aroma, making them good substitutes for peppermint (*Mentha x piperita*).

 *M. canadensis* is a native perennial herb growing to 2 feet high from rhizomes in wet soil, often along streambanks. The opposite leaves are light green, ½ to 2 inches long on short petioles, with scalloped to saw-toothed edges. The stems and leaves are covered with tiny short hairs, giving it a fuzzy look. The white to pink or violet flowers are ¼ to 2½ inches long in whorls in the leaf axils.

*M. arvensis* is a naturalized perennial herb growing from rhizomes in wet soil, with branching stems to 2 feet high. The opposite leaves are light green, lanceolate to ovate, saw-toothed, and ¾ to 2¾ inches long. Whorls of two-lipped flowers form in the upper leaf axils with white to pink or violet petals, ¼ inch long, each with four stamens.

## Conservation Status
Both species are common and unthreatened in California.

## Traditional Uses
Several northern California tribes use wild mint for similar purposes. The Maidu use a tea of the leaves and flowers to treat colds, sore throats, toothaches, headaches, fevers, nausea, stomachaches, and intestinal gas. They consider it pain-reducing and tranquilizing. The Modoc use an infusion of wild mint leaves to relieve stomachaches, colds, and coughs. The Miwok drink it for stomachaches and diarrhea. To the east, the Paiute, Shoshone, and Washo use the tea in the same ways. Several tribes use the crushed leaves to poultice swellings and bruises.

Mint has been in wide use worldwide for centuries. It is mentioned in the Egyptian Ebers papyrus, circa 1500 BC, for soothing the stomach. Ayurvedic, Chinese, and Western herbalists have long used mint tea for its calming action on the nerves that affect digestion and as a remedy for coughs, colds, and fever.

## Modern Uses
Modern herbalists like Michael Moore and Gregory Tilford recommend using wild mint as you would peppermint for the antispasmodic effect on smooth muscles of the digestive system to relieve indigestion, gas, colic, and the like.

According to medicinal herb specialist Dr. Fred Siciliano, LAc, OMD, peppermint is classified as a cooling diaphoretic tea that will lower fever, especially from summer heat exposure. Peppermint also promotes good digestion by clearing undigested food that ferments and creates gas. It can be used for gastritis and symptoms of indigestion, food stagnation, or food poisoning.[139]

The German Commission E approved the internal use of peppermint leaf for spastic complaints of the gastrointestinal tract, the gallbladder, and bile ducts.

## Phytochemicals/Mechanisms of Action
Analysis of the aerial parts of *Mentha arvensis* shows an essential oil consisting mainly of two terpene alcohols, menthol and linalool, and a monoterpene, menthone. These aromatic compounds are used in the pharmaceutical, flavor, food, cosmetic, and beverage industries. A 2002 World Health Organization monograph on peppermint found that menthol and menthone are the major constituents of peppermint leaf essential oil.[140]

While peppermint contains 30–55 percent menthol, California's wild mints contain 70–80 percent! One of the world's most-used herbal compounds, menthol has many applications, including as a decongestant, topical analgesic, and ingredient in many dental hygiene products such as toothpaste and mouthwash.

Pharmacological studies of *M. canadensis* have demonstrated antimicrobial, anti-inflammatory, antioxidant, antitumor, gastrointestinal protective, and hepatoprotective activities. Volatile oils, monoterpenoids, polyphenolic acids, flavonoids, and glycosides are believed to contribute to the medicinal benefits of the plant.

## Cultivation
Wild mint can easily be propagated by placing top cuttings or roots with short stems in water, making sure they have at least two pairs of leaves. Adding a green willow stalk to the water will provide natural plant growth hormones. These starts are transferred to damp soil once they put out new roots and leaves. Mint likes shade, but if grown in the sun it will produce more terpenes.

## Cautions
Long-term continuous use of mint tea, especially in winter, can be too cooling for some body types.[141]

## Notes
To make mint tea, pour 1 cup boiling water over 1 teaspoon dried leaves or ⅓ cup fresh leaves; cover and steep for 8–10 minutes.

## *Prunella* genus
Not counting varieties and hybrids, there are just four species of *Prunella* worldwide. They are found in the temperate regions of Europe, Asia, and North America. The name *Prunella* evolved from *Brunella*, which was derived from the German *Bräune*, referring either to a throat disease for which it was used as a cure or to the brown color of the dried flower spikes. The jury is still out on that one.

## SELF-HEAL
### *Prunella vulgaris*

**Other common names:** Heal-all, all-heal
**Origin:** Native
**Range:** Tulare County north to Oregon from 3,000 to 8,000 feet elevation
**Habitat:** Moist places, meadows, woodlands
**Related species in California:** *Prunella vulgaris* subsp. *lanceolata* (lance-leaf self-heal)

*Self-heal (*Prunella vulgaris*) flower.*
JAMES DAVID ADAMS JR.

**Related species globally:** *Prunella vulgaris* subsp. *vulgaris* (common self-heal)

**Conservation status rankings:**

**IUCN Red List:** LC

**CNPS Rare Plant Rank:** Not listed

**NatureServe State Rank:** SNR

**Uses:** Sore throats and mouths, wounds and sores, hemorrhoids

**Parts used:** Leaves, flowering tops

**Edibility:** Young leaves and tops are edible as salad.

## Description

Self-heal (*Prunella vulgaris*) is a creeping herb, less than 1 foot tall when in flower, generally found in small colonies sprouting from perennial rootstocks. It grows in damp canyons and woods at elevations from 3,000 to 8,000 feet.

Self-heal has tender oval to lance-shaped leaves on weak, square stems. Unlike the separated whorls on other Mint family plants, self-heal has dense, terminal clusters of flowers resembling small ears of corn. The two-lipped flowers are bluish purple. Also unlike most mints, self-heal has no odor, although people enjoy the flavor of the flowering tops when eaten fresh or drunk as a tea.

There is one variant of *P. vulgaris* in California, also a native. Lance-leaf self-heal (*P. vulgaris* subsp. *lanceolata*) has narrow leaves and is found at even higher elevations. They can be used interchangeably in herbal recipes.

Self-heal is one of a handful of plants, like elderberry, stinging nettle, chamomile, yarrow, and mugwort, that can be found in temperate zones worldwide and yet are considered natives wherever they grow. One possible explanation for this, suggested by author James D. Adams, is that our distant ancestors recognized their value and brought them on their migrations.

## Conservation Status

Self-heal is a common plant worldwide. There are no conservation concerns.

## Traditional Uses

The Maidu treat burns, bruises, diarrhea, hemorrhages, sore throats, colic, and more with self-heal. Some Indigenous people eat the greens in early spring.[142] Beyond California, various tribes drink an infusion for fevers and wash bruises, sores, cuts, etc., with the tea. They also chew the plant for sore mouths and throats, make a cooling drink with the tops, and use it as a body wash for fevers.[143]

Self-heal, as its name implies, has a long-standing reputation worldwide as a mild, astringent herb for healing wounds and sores of all kinds. It has been applied as a poultice to the skin, gargled for sore mouths and throats, and injected for hemorrhoids. The sixteenth-century English botanist-herbalist John Gerard wrote: "There is not a better Wound herbe in the world."

Ayurveda considers self-heal an all-purpose astringent herb for stopping bleeding, arresting diarrhea, and promoting healing of external tissues.[144] In traditional Chinese medicine self-heal treats conjunctivitis, hypertension, fevers, edema, internal bleeding, and inflammation.

## Modern Uses
Western herbalists use the leaves and flower spikes internally as an infusion and externally as a mild, anti-inflammatory astringent. According to the modern Chinese Pharmacopoeia, self-heal is used for the treatment of a variety of conditions, including sore eyes, vertigo, headache, high blood pressure, and thyroid gland malfunction. It is eaten as a vegetable in southeast China.

## Phytochemicals/Mechanisms of Action
Self-heal's long-standing reputation as a healing herb has generated significant laboratory research. The plant contains phytosterols, anti-inflammatory phenolic acids such as rosmarinic acid, salviaflaside, and caffeic acid, and the antioxidant flavonoid hyperoside. Rosmarinic acid and salviaflaside are of interest due to their wide spectrum of bioactivity, including antioxidant, anti-inflammatory, anticancer, neuroprotective, and immunomodulatory properties. Self-heal also contains ursolic acid and oleanolic acid, triterpenes known to have antioxidant, anti-allergic, anti-inflammatory, and antitumor activity. On another front, the polysaccharide prunellin has shown antiviral activity against HSV and HIV.[145] As with most plants in this book, clinical studies are needed to test out the laboratory evidence.

## Cultivation
Self-heal can be propagated from root cuttings. It needs shade, rich soil, and lots of moisture.

## Cautions
Avoid internal use during pregnancy.

## Notes
Self-heal is best used fresh but can be dried for later use. Treat it like mints when drying, being sure to provide plenty of circulation to prevent molding. A simple infusion is the best way to prepare self-heal for drinking. A compress made with the infusion or a poultice of the fresh plant can be used externally.

# *Salvia* genus
The genus *Salvia* includes over 900 species, making it the largest genus in the Mint family. *Salvia* species are found in the Americas, the Mediterranean, and

central and eastern Asia and have one of the longest histories of medicinal use. The genus name is derived from the Latin *salvus*, meaning "healthy" or "well." Garden sage, *S. officinalis*, is a native of the northern Mediterranean. A popular Latin phrase dating to the Middle Ages translates as "Why should a man die while sage grows in his garden?" Native species in India became staples of Ayurvedic medicine, as did red sage, *S. miltiorrhiza*, in Chinese medicine, where it is known as *dan shen*. The most recent addition to the *Salvia* genus is rosemary, formerly *Rosmarinus officinalis*, now *Salvia rosmarinus*. California's Indigenous people use several local sages for a range of medicinal uses.

As a genus, *Salvia* plants contain many active compounds, including antibiotic diterpenoids, anti-inflammatory compounds, and antianxiety compounds.[146] A number of studies have validated the extensive folk medicine claims for garden sage, the most studied of all sages. KaiserPermanente.org describes sage as "an herb that directly attacks microbes."[147] German Commission E reported antibacterial, fungistatic, virustatic, astringent, and perspiration-inhibiting properties of garden sage. In 1994 they approved its use as a mouthwash or gargle for the treatment of inflammation of the mouth and throat. They also approved its internal use for indigestion and to reduce excessive perspiration. [148] Long known for its ability to inhibit secretions such as sweat, garden sage has been touted as a tea for reducing lactation. As of yet, no studies have confirmed that claim.

*Sage leaves, left to right: hummingbird sage (Salvia spathacea), white sage (S. apiana), black sage (S. mellifera), purple sage, (S. leucophylla), Cleveland sage (S. clevelandii).* BARBARA EISENSTEIN

# WHITE SAGE
## *Salvia apiana*

**Other common names:** Bee sage
**Origin:** Native
**Range:** Northern Santa Barbara County south to Baja California
**Habitat:** Coastal and interior sage scrub, chaparral
**Related species in California:** See other *Salvia* chapters here; also, chia sage (*S. columbariae*).
**Related species globally:** Garden sage (*S. officinalis*) and many others
**Conservation status rankings:**
    **IUCN Red List:** Not listed
    **CNPS Rare Plant Rank:** Not listed
    **NatureServe State Rank:** SNR
    **United Plant Savers:** "Species At-Risk" list

*White sage leaves turn whiter through the summer.* LANNY KAUFER

**Uses:** Antiseptic, decongestant, antiperspirant, astringent, anxiolytic; for colds, coughs, excess perspiration, and anxiety
**Parts used:** Leaves
**Edibility:** Seeds and flowers are edible.

## Description
White sage (*Salvia apiana*) is a native perennial shrub, woody at the base, reaching 3 to 4 feet in height with flowering stalks up to 8 feet. The upper flowering stems are square. Opposite, lanceolate, lightly serrated, 1½- to 3-inch leaves start out green and turn noticeably whiter as they mature. White sage's common name comes not from its leaves but from its white, lavender-tinged flowers. They appear from April to July in open panicles, not the dense whorls of other sages. Two stamens arch out well beyond the flowers. White sage prefers the dry slopes of the coastal and interior sage scrub habitats, giving those plant communities the "sage" in their names. It also extends into the chaparral plant community. It can be found below 5,000 feet from Santa Barbara south to the middle of Baja California. CALTRANS planted a large stand of white sage on the south-facing summit of Cuesta Grade on US 101 in San Luis Obispo County, some distance north of its natural range. It seems to be thriving there.

## Conservation Status
Once abundant, white sage is now severely impacted by overharvesting and illegal collecting in areas accessible by car. It is on United Plant Savers' "Species

*Young white sage plant (*Salvia apiana*), still in the green stage.* LANNY KAUFER

At-Risk" list.[149] Otherwise, populations are stable (for now) throughout its range, although the fragmentation of its habitat by human development is not a good sign for its future. Please exercise the utmost respect if collecting this plant, be vigilant about where you purchase it, and do not burn whole bundles for smudging. One leaf is usually enough. If you purchase white sage, ask the seller for proof of sustainable collecting or wholesale purchase from a farm.

## Traditional Uses

According to Cecilia Garcia, white sage may be the foundation of Chumash healing, as it helps the patient "become calm enough to be rational" and "can help set the spirit back to normal." She believes that "ideally, we should all take white sage every day to help maintain spiritual health when used with prayer."[150] (See "Recipes" for instructions on preparing white sage water.)

The Luiseño and Cahuilla chew or smoke the leaves of white sage as a decongestant. The Diegueño drink a hot tea of the leaves for coughs and as a blood tonic.[151] The Kumeyaay, Cahuilla, Tongva, and Chumash use an infusion of the leaves for chest colds, coughs, flus, and other bronchial problems. The steam may also be inhaled. These tribes, as well as the Ohlone and Kawaiisu, place white sage seeds or those of chia sage (*S. columbariae*) in the eyes to allow the gel that forms to collect foreign particles, making them easier to remove. Some Indigenous groups apply the fresh leaves as a deodorant, mix them with water for a soapless hair and scalp cleanser, steam them in the sweat lodge to purify the air, and burn the leaves as a fumigant. Many native people across the country use white sage as a ceremonial smudge for spiritual purification.

## Modern Uses

Michael Moore considers white sage tincture antibacterial when used in a skin wash against *Staphylococcus* bacteria, in a vaginal douche to fight *Candida* fungal infections, and as a tea and steam inhalation against *Klebsiella* bacteria associated with pneumonia. A 1991 study confirmed that white sage was able to completely inhibit the growth of all three of those organisms in the laboratory. Moore prefers the tincture for external use as the alcohol can better extract the carnosic diterpenes.[152] [153] He also recommends the cold tea of sage species for stopping lactation and the hot tea as a warming diaphoretic in feverish infections accompanied by chills.[154]

*White sage's flowering stalks shoot up as much as 4 feet above the rest of the plant.* ROBERT E. MERRITT

I have found that white sage tincture, 2 dropperfuls in 8 ounces of water, makes an excellent mouthwash and gargle. Spit out the potent solution after gargling; do not swallow it. If necessary, other *Salvia* species can be used in the absence of white sage.

### Phytochemicals/Mechanisms of Action

A 2010 study identified the major constituents in white sage as monoterpenoids, including eucalyptol (cineole), camphor, pinene, carene, camphene, limonene, myrcene, and terpinolene. Monoterpenoids have shown antianxiety, antimicrobial, and pain-relieving activity in numerous studies. Eucalyptol is a well-known antimicrobial and has been reported to be useful for the treatment of bronchial asthma and cough. It may also have an anti-inflammatory effect on bronchial tissues. A 2016 study found that white sage inhibited the growth of *Escherichia coli* bacteria.[155]

Diterpenoids, including carnosol and rosmanol, are known to be present in white sage. They have been reported to have broad anticancer properties in several cell line models, including prostate, breast, and leukemia cancers.[156] Diterpenes, in general, are gaining attention for antimicrobial, anti-inflammatory, neuroprotective, antioxidant, and anticancer properties. Sesquiterpene hydrocarbons, known to be anti-inflammatory and pain-relieving, were also found in white sage.[157]

### Cultivation

White sage can be grown from seed planted in the fall. Plants are available from nurseries. It likes full sun and well-drained soil. Prune dead branches and flowering stalks for a compact look. Bees love it!

### Cautions

Thujone, a monoterpene ketone, is a known toxin in certain plants if ingested in large quantities. Although it is a major constituent in the essential oil of garden sage, it has not shown toxicity in that plant and has not been detected at all in white sage.[158] There's still a chance

*White sage flowers, showing off their purple highlights on a square Mint family stem*
JAMES DAVID ADAMS JR.

it's there, so to be on the safe side, white sage should be ingested as a leaf infusion rather than a tincture or essential oil.[159] Nursing mothers should avoid drinking white sage tea, as it is known to dry up secretions, possibly including breastmilk.

## Notes

One evening, outside the tepee just before a Native American Church ceremony, I witnessed the fire chief pacify an angry, inebriated man who refused to accept that he wasn't allowed to enter the ceremony in his condition. While the man argued with someone at the tepee door, the fire chief began smudging him with white sage. In less than a minute, the man relaxed and walked away.

*Native California bumblebee demonstrates why white sage is also called bee sage.* MARK MOORE

White sage flowers and seeds are edible. Historically, the Chumash peeled and ate the tender young stems in the spring. They lined their acorn granaries with the leaves, possibly to deter insects.[160] *S. apiana*'s species name derives from the Latin *apis* ("bee"), and from that comes its common name, bee sage.

## BLUE SAGE
### *Salvia dorrii*

**Synonym:** *Salvia carnosa*
**Other common names:** Gray ball sage, desert sage, desert purple sage
**Origin:** Native
**Range:** Eastern California to 10,000 feet elevation
**Habitat:** Deserts, dry places

*Notice the characteristic browning, older flowers in this patch of blue sage (*Salvia dorrii*).* ENRIQUE VILLASEÑOR

*Swallowtail butterfly visiting a flowering purple sage plant.* LANNY KAUFER

## PURPLE SAGE
### *Salvia leucophylla*

**Other common names:** Button sage
**Origin:** Native
**Range:** Southern California to 2,500 feet elevation
**Habitat:** Coastal sage scrub, lower chaparral

*Honeybee up to her ears in a black sage flower.* BEN GRANGEREAU

## BLACK SAGE
### *Salvia mellifera*

**Other common names:** None
**Origin:** Native
**Range:** Coastal California to 4,000 feet elevation
**Habitat:** Coastal sage scrub, lower chaparral
**Related species in California:** White sage (*S. apiana*), Cleveland sage (*S. clevelandii*), chia sage (*S. columbariae*), hummingbird sage (*S. spathacea*)
**Related species in Europe, Asia, North Africa:** Garden sage (*S. officinalis*), dan shen (*S. miltiorrhiza*)
**Conservation status rankings:**
    **IUCN Red List:** Not listed
    **CNPS Rare Plant Rank:** Not listed
    **NatureServe State Rank:** SNR
    **United Plant Savers:** Not listed
**Uses:** Colds, coughs, pain relief, anxiety relief
**Parts used:** Leaves
**Edibility:** Seeds are edible, similar to chia seeds. Flowers are edible. Leaves are used for flavoring.

## Description

All three of these common sage species are native, perennial shrubs with similar descriptions and medicinal properties. Three varieties of blue sage (*S. dorrii*) can be found in dry places from 1,500 to 10,000 feet throughout almost all of eastern California and beyond to the Great Basin states. They reach 1 to 3 feet in height and spread. The fleshy, mildly aromatic leaves are ½ inch to 1½ inches long, grayish green, tapered at the base, rounded at the tip, and wider in the mid-

*Whorls of blue sage flowers.* JAMES DAVID ADAMS JR.

dle, like a spoon. They are often folded like a taco shell along the central vein. Thick clusters of blue, purple, or rose-colored flowers appear from May to July and stay on the stalks, turning brown for some time after blooming.

Purple sage (*Salvia leucophylla*) reaches 3 to 4 feet in height and 2 to 4 feet in spread, sending up pinkish-red, square-stemmed flowering stalks to 6 feet high in the spring. It's found in coastal sage scrub habitat below 2,500 feet from San Luis Obispo south to Dana Point. The moderately aromatic leaves are simple, opposite, narrow, lanceolate, and 1 to 2 inches long. They are grayish green when young, turning almost white by the end of the long summer sea-

son. Their surfaces have the typical Mint family wrinkles. The aroma is closer to the garden sage you might find in your cupboard, not as musky and strong as black sage. From April to June, dense whorls of aromatic, pinkish-purple flowers on large spikes are prolific and beautiful, attracting many butterflies as well as bees. It is an iconic native California plant.

Black sage (*S. mellifera*) is the same size as purple sage and occupies roughly the same habitat, but its range extends farther north and south and to higher elevations. It grows from sea level to 4,000 feet from the Bay Area south to the Mexican border. Black sage leaves have a similar shape and texture as purple sage but are dark green above and lighter green below. They typically turn yellow early as

*Young green-leaved purple sage plant (*Salvia leucophylla*).* LANNY KAUFER

Black sage seed heads still on the stalks in the fall, long after they've dried and spilled their contents
LANNY KAUFER

the plant goes into summer dormancy. The leaves are strongly aromatic. Black sage produces whorls of pale lavender-blue flowers on square stems, usually covered with bees. For the last half of the year, the dark brown, dried seed stalks are what you'll notice first.

Cleveland sage (*S. clevelandii*) looks like a cross between purple and black sage and can be used as a substitute for the three species described above. It is found in San Diego County from sea level to 4,500 feet elevation.

## Conservation Status
These three species have secure populations with no conservation concerns. Purple and black sage are common, widespread species in the coastal sage scrub plant community, which draws its name from them.

## Traditional Uses
A decoction of black sage leaves is taken by the Ohlone for coughs and used in baths

Young black sage plant (Salvia mellifera)
LANNY KAUFER

for paralysis. The leaves are heated and held against the ear for pain or wrapped around the neck for sore throat. The fresh leaves are chewed for gas pains.[161] The Mahuna (Cahuilla) of the Palm Springs area consider the strong infusion one of the most valuable treatments for deep, dry, chronic coughs. Small doses are drunk hot during the day, followed by one big dose at bedtime.[162] Delfina Cuero of the Kumeyaay people says the fresh or dried leaves are boiled and the water used for bathing when a person aches due to flu, rheumatism, and arthritis.[163]

In eastern California, the Paiute, Shoshone, and Washo value the tea of blue sage leaves as a remedy for the common cold, taken as a decoction or as a

*Purple sage just before flowering*
STEVEN MARK NORRIS

hot or cold infusion. They also use it to treat pneumonia, influenza, fevers, sore throat, venereal disease, and indigestion. Sometimes the leaves are boiled with juniper twigs or piñon pine resin to make a tea for colds and chest congestion. Along with these teas, a poultice of the leaves may be applied to the head and chest.[164] Cleveland sage, which looks very similar to these three and has similar phytochemistry, can be substituted for any of these sages.

## Modern Uses

Researchers reported in 2019 that a foot soak made with a sun tea of black sage was effective in treating pain throughout the body. Monoterpenoids and diterpenoids in the tea can penetrate the skin of the feet to reach the nervous system, where they are able to stop the pain chemokine cycle.[165] Purple sage can be substituted for black sage, but more must be used because it's not as strong. (See "Recipes" for foot soak instructions.)

*Flowering black sage plant.* LANNY KAUFER

## Phytochemicals/Mechanisms of Action

The powerful aroma of black sage comes from a cocktail of terpenoids that are known to be pain-relieving, anxiety-relieving, and anti-inflammatory. The fifty-plus monoterpenoids include eucalyptol (cineole), camphor, and pinene. Diterpenoids include aethiopinone, carnosic acid, carnosol, rosmanol, salvicanol, and salviol. Ursolic acid, a triterpenoid, is a proven anti-inflammatory compound.

Purple and blue sage, although not studied as much as black and white sage, probably contain many of the same compounds. Their milder aromas may indicate lower concentrations of terpenes. Researchers studying the growth-inhibiting effect of purple sage on nearby plants discovered a similar monoterpene profile to black sage.

The diterpenoids carnosic acid and carnosol mentioned above were first identified and named in blue sage when it was previously known as *S. carnosa*. Their properties are discussed in the section on white sage (*S. apiana*). Other diterpenoid compounds called tanshinones are present

*Honeybee collecting purple sage nectar for sage honey.* KEITH FARRAR

in some *Salvia* species, such as dan shen (*S. miltiorrhiza*) and chia sage (*S. columbariae*), and can help the immune system fight colds and venereal disease.

## Cultivation

Sages can be propagated from seed and stem cuttings. Many varieties of these popular bee and butterfly attractors are available in nurseries.

## Cautions

Black sage has the same considerations as for white sage.

## Notes

In general, sages should be gathered just before or during flowering. They can be used fresh or preserved for future use by drying in a dark, dry place with good air circulation. Due to the medicinal importance of the aromatic terpenes, they should be prepared as a sun tea or infusion in a covered vessel. Try fresh or dried purple sage leaves as a substitute for commercial garden sage in cooking.

Bees love all sages! Sage honey from mixed species is always in demand. Black sage honey is considered the premier California varietal.

Chia seeds come from chia sage, another *Salvia*. California's native chia, *S. columbariae*, is used mainly as a food plant, although medicinal activity has also been reported.[166] Information on its edibility can be found in Christopher Nyerges's *Foraging California*.[167]

*S. mellifera* is derived from the Latin *mel* ("honey") and *fer* ("bearing" or "carrying"). *S. leucophylla* is derived from the Latin *leuco* ("white") and *phyll* ("leaf"). *S. dorrii* is the sage of Zane Grey's novel *Riders of the Purple Sage*. It is named for Nevada plant collector Clarendon Herbert Dorr, 1816–1887. Its earlier name of *S. carnosa* is derived from the Latin *carnosus* ("fleshy"). The origin of black sage's name is a mystery. My theory is that it's because the seed heads turn almost black by the end of California's long Mediterranean-type summer. (See photo.)

# HUMMINGBIRD SAGE
## *Salvia spathacea*

**Other common names:** Crimson sage, scarlet sage, crimson pitcher sage, *diosa* (Spanish)
**Origin:** Native
**Range:** Coastal Monterey County to coastal Orange County, below 2,500 feet elevation
**Habitat:** Oak woodland, riparian zone, coastal-sage scrub, shaded slopes
**Related species in California:** See other *Salvia* species in this section.
**Conservation status rankings:**
    **IUCN Red List:** Not listed
    **CNPS Rare Plant Rank:** Not listed
    **NatureServe State Rank:** SNR
**Uses:** Anxiety, sore throats, chest colds
**Parts used:** Leaves
**Edibility:** Not edible

Leaf of hummingbird sage (Salvia spathacea) compared to its namesake, a pie server spatula. LANNY KAUFER

## Description
Hummingbird sage (*Salvia spathacea*) is that rare sage that likes the shade. It will thrive in sunny locations too, with enough moisture. It's a low-growing, colony plant with perennial rhizomes sending up annual stems as high as 3 feet. There's just a single stalk per plant, but the patches can spread as wide as 4 feet if they're in the rich loam they prefer. Hastate leaves, shaped like a pie server spatula, are 3 to 7

inches long, with the longer ones clustered at the base. They are typically Mint family wrinkled, dark green above, light green and slightly fuzzy underneath. The whole plant is covered with fine, glandular hairs that give it a soft but not woolly texture. When rubbed, the leaves have a pleasantly unique fruity-minty aroma.

Unbranched, square flower stalks bear dense whorls of 1- to 1½-inch-long, dark pinkish-red flowers with stamens extending out some distance. The narrow, tubular flowers bloom from February to June and, due to their length, are accessed primarily by hummingbirds. This sage grows mainly in the coast ranges from Monterey south to Laguna Beach, although a few colonies have been spotted in canyons in Solano County and around Mount Diablo.

*A brilliant profusion of hummingbird sage flower stalks.* TRICIA WARDLAW, COURTESY OF SANTA BARBARA BOTANIC GARDEN

### Conservation Status

Hummingbird sage is a native of California and found in no other state. Fortunately, it is still common within its range and chosen habitats. That being said, such a beautiful plant deserves special consideration, not just for its looks but also for the role it plays in the ecosystem. Its spreading rhizomes, along with those of mugwort, poison oak, and blackberry, help to hold the topsoil together and prevent erosion in our creekside oak forests.

### Traditional Uses

Curiously, there is little record of Indigenous use of this aromatic herb, especially considering that the Spanish around Santa Barbara who learned of it from the Chumash named it *diosa* ("goddess"). According to Jan Timbrook's *Chumash Ethnobotany*, Fernando Librado told anthropologist J. P. Harrington that a tea of hummingbird sage leaves was drunk for lung problems and used as a bath for rheumatism. He also gave an account of its use to cure an illness caused by sorcery. The treatment involved laying the patient on a bed of the leaves and administering the tea while rubbing fresh leaves all over the body. He said the sorcerer died when he learned of the patient's recovery.

In earlier times, the Pomo reportedly chewed the leaves to lessen thirst and for sore throats. The women used a plug of the dried leaf as a bolus for vaginosis.[168]

## Modern Uses

Chumash herbalist Cecilia Garcia taught James Adams and her other students a recipe for a Chumash-Mexican hummingbird sage and chocolate tea for calming anxiety. (See "Recipes.") She also suggests adding hummingbird sage to bitter teas to make them sweeter and more palatable.

Michael Moore recommends an infusion of the tea as a decongestant expectorant for colds. Though not at all bitter like its Mint family cousin horehound, it has a similar action: stimulating secretions to help cough up phlegm. Like most sages, it is probably antimicrobial and can be gargled and drunk for sore throats. Like white sage, it can be made into an air-purifying smudge stick by letting the

*First flower stalk rising from a bed of hummingbird sage leaves.* LANNY KAUFER

leaves wilt for a day, rolling them tightly into a tall cone shape, and drying them wrapped in thread.[169]

## Phytochemicals/Mechanisms of Action

Nothing is known yet about the active constituents in hummingbird sage. (Pharmacologists and researchers, are you listening?) Many other sages, garden sage in particular, have been thoroughly studied, so it's likely that a sage as aromatic and sticky as hummingbird sage has an abundant supply of terpenes, resins, and flavonoids known collectively for their antimicrobial, anti-inflammatory, and antianxiety properties.

## Cultivation

If you have shade in your yard (an oak tree, perhaps?) or live close to the coast where direct sun is not too hot, hummingbird sage is an excellent ground cover. It can be started from seed or by dividing the rhizomes. Plants are readily available in nurseries. Try to mimic the humus-rich soil of its native habitat. It goes into summer dormancy in dry locales so may need cutting back after you've collected some seed, or you can give it summer water to keep it green.

## Cautions

There are no known safety concerns regarding the use of hummingbird sage.

## Notes

Once you find an abundant supply, gather a few of the larger basal leaves just before the plant flowers, while they're still fresh and green. They can be used fresh or dried. Dry and store them whole until just before use to preserve the aromatic components.

Medicinal uses aside, hummingbird sage makes a delicious tea with a sagey, minty, piney, fruity taste like nothing else. It blends well with many herbs, especially other members of the Mint family. To retain its aroma, it should always be prepared as a standard infusion, never boiled, even though it barely colors the water.

Some older texts call it by one of its outdated common names, pitcher sage. This could lead to confusion, as that name

*Hummingbird sage patiently waiting for a hummingbird.* SMITTY WEST

is much more closely allied today with *Lepechinia*, which is not a sage, although it is in the Mint family. Then there's Texas hummingbird sage, a different species (*S. coccinea*) over yonder, also known as scarlet sage. Ah, the corn maze of common names of plants.

## *Scutellaria* genus

Approximately 300 species of *Scutellaria* are found in temperate zones worldwide, including 9 that are native to California. The name *Scutellaria* is derived from the Latin *scutella* ("a small dish"), referring to the shape of the fruiting calyx.

## SKULLCAP
### *Scutellaria californica*

**Other common names:** California skullcap, California white skullcap, scullcap
**Origin:** Native
**Range:** Klamath Ranges, North Coast ranges, southern Sierra Nevada to 7,000 feet elevation
**Habitat:** Open sites, scrub, woodland

*The white, Mint family–shaped flowers of California skullcap (*Scutellaria californica*)*
STEPHEN SHARNOFF

**Common related native species in California:** Bladder-sage (*Scutellaria mexicana*), gray-leaved skullcap (*S. siphocampyloides*), blue tuberous skullcap (*S. tuberosa*)

**Rare related native species in California:** Side-flowering skullcap (*S. lateriflora*), marsh skullcap (*S. galericulata*). **Please do not collect these or other species that are rare in California.**

**Related species globally:** Chinese or baical skullcap (*S. baicalensis*)

**Conservation status rankings:**

    **IUCN Red List:** Not listed

    **CNPS Rare Plant Rank:** Not listed

    **NatureServe State Rank:** SNR

**Uses:** Anxiety, insomnia, nervous irritability, muscle spasms

**Parts used:** Leaves, flowering tops

**Edibility:** Not edible

## Description

California skullcap (*Scutellaria californica*) is found in lower forests, dry stream-beds, and open areas of Northern California to an elevation of 7,000 feet. It grows from creeping rhizomes to reach 6 to 12 inches tall on weak, hairy, square stems. The lanceolate upper leaves clasp the stems; the lower ovate-to-oblong leaves have petioles. In typical Mint family style, the leaves are opposite and the flowers are two-lipped. The flowers are white to pale yellow in color and emerge from the upper leaf axils looking like snapdragon flowers. Although the leaves are not aromatic, the flowers contain terpenes that give them an apple-like scent.

## Conservation Status

Although California skullcap is found only in the Golden State, it is common within its range. There are no conservation concerns. It is featured here because it is one of the few skullcap species with white flowers. While some native blue-flowering skullcaps, such as bladder-sage (*S. mexicana*), gray-leaved skullcap (*S. siphocampyloides*), and blue tuberous skullcap (*S. tuberosa*), are common enough to collect, a few species that are rare in California, like side-flowering skullcap (*S. lateriflora*), also have blue flowers. To avoid picking an endangered plant, be sure to do a thorough study of the local species. Otherwise, it's best to stick to the white-flowered *S. californica*.

## Traditional Uses

The Maidu and Mendocino people use California skullcap to treat chills and fevers. The Miwok use the genetically related gray-leaved skullcap to prepare an eyewash. They also drink a decoction of skullcap tea for coughs and colds. Blue tuberous skullcap was once used as a sedative by an unspecified tribe.[170][171]

Native groups across the country use their local species for various nervous conditions, including menstrual cramping.

In Western herbal medicine, use of side-flowering skullcap as a sedative and anxiety-relieving plant has been recorded over the past few centuries. Skullcap entered the *US Pharmacopoeia* in 1863 as a tranquilizer.[172] From there it was moved to the *National Formulary* in 1916, where it remained until 1947.[173] [174] [175]

## Modern Uses

*Scutellaria* species around the world are highly valued by modern herbalists for calming nervous tension, improving sleep, and treating muscle spasms. Skullcap is used in Ayurvedic medicine for its bitter and cooling properties to treat insomnia, muscle spasms, convulsions, neurosis, nervous headaches, hypertension, and more. It is also credited with improving awareness and perception.[176] It's important to note that with 300 known species of skullcap, one cannot assume that all can be used in the same way. Nonetheless, Michael Moore considers all western US skullcaps to be excellent remedies for "almost any nervous system malfunction of a mild or chronic nature," including insomnia, fear, and nervous headaches.[177]

## Phytochemicals/Mechanisms of Action

Side-flowering skullcap (*S. lateriflora*) is the most common, commercially available species used in Western herbalism. Although it is a rare and endangered native in California, it is common elsewhere in North America. Some research has been done on it and the related Chinese skullcap, along with a few other skullcaps, many of which exhibit similar phytochemistry. Several skullcap species are rich in flavonoid glycoside pigments, primarily scutellarin and baicalin, with demonstrated anti-inflammatory and analgesic properties. Some also contain the amino acids glutamine and gamma-aminobutyric acid (GABA), a plant metabolite that also is the chief inhibitory neurotransmitter in the human brain. In other words, it decreases excitability and activity in the central nervous system.

Studies have shown that baicalin and other flavonoids in side-flowering skullcap bind to the benzodiazepine site of the GABA receptor in the central nervous system.[178] Skullcap appears to act as a tranquilizing, antianxiety substance by the same mechanism of action as benzodiazepine drugs such as diazepam (known commercially as Valium). Though not proven, California skullcap is likely to contain similar flavonoid compounds.

Only one study has been done on California skullcap, looking at the terpenes and volatile compounds that make up its essential oil and provide its aroma. Of the fifty-two compounds identified in that study, beta-caryophyllene, a sesquiterpene, was by far the most common.[179] In an unrelated study, beta-caryophyllene showed strong pain-relieving activity by binding to $CB_2$ receptors in the endo-cannabinoid system.[180]

## Cultivation

Skullcap can be propagated by seed or root divisions. Several species are available in nurseries. Given the medicinal reputation and rare status of side-flowering skullcap in California, it would be nice to see it growing in home gardens.

## Cautions

Because skullcap appears to act like a benzodiazepine, it should not be taken by those using medications such as diazepam, as it may result in an overdose. Avoid using with alcohol or other substances that may cause drowsiness. Skullcap is contraindicated during pregnancy.

## Notes

Clip the leaves and flowering tops in midsummer or whenever they are in full flower, being careful not to uproot them. It is best used fresh to prepare an infusion or tincture, but if drying for future use, as with other delicate, Mint family plants, allow plenty of dry, warmish air and good circulation to avoid molding.

## *Trichostema* genus

All the approximately eighteen species of *Trichostema* are natives of North America, with eleven of those native to California. The name comes from the Latin *trich* ("hair") and the Greek *stēma* ("stamen"), describing the long, hairlike stamens.

## WOOLLY BLUE CURLS
### *Trichostema lanatum*

**Other common names:** *Romero* (Spanish)
**Origin:** Native
**Range:** Southern California to 4,000 feet elevation
**Habitat:** Chaparral and coastal sage scrub
**Related species in California:** Vinegar weed (*T. lanceolatum*), Parish's blue curls (*T. parishii*)

*Flowering stalks of woolly blue curls.*
STEVE JUNAK

**Conservation status rankings:**
   **IUCN Red List:** Not listed
   **CNPS Rare Plant Rank:** CBR
   **NatureServe State Rank:** SNR
**Uses:** Stomachic, disinfectant, pain relief, women's health
**Parts used:** Upper leaves, flowers
**Edibility:** Seasoning

*Woolly blue curls (*Trichostema lanatum*) coming back after fire and flood.* LANNY KAUFER

## Description

Woolly blue curls is one of the most beautiful California native plants. A short-lived perennial shrub of the chaparral and coastal sage scrub communities, it grows to 5 feet tall at elevations up to 4,000 feet in the southern half of the state. It has narrow, pointed leaves, and its flowers are covered with many short hairs, giving it a woolly appearance. Clusters of fuzzy, tubular flowers in shades of pink, blue, and purple form in the upper leaf axils from March to June. Four arching stamens extend out like long hairs the length of the flower from which they emerge. The entire plant has a pleasant minty-piney aroma with a hint of vinegar.

Woolly blue curls' cousin, vinegar weed (*Trichostema lanceolatum*), has a strong vinegar-turpentine scent. This common, purple-flowered annual, less than 2 feet tall, is found in the drier parts of the state in coastal sage scrub, chaparral, and oak woodland habitats. A less common perennial shrub, Parish's blue curls (*T. parishii*), looks similar to woolly blue curls. Its flowers are more purple and not quite as fuzzy. It grows only in the southwestern corner of California and into northwestern Baja California.

## Conservation Status

Woolly blue curls has a limited range but is not currently threatened within that area. Vinegar weed is common throughout much of California. Two less common annual species of *Trichostema* are on the CNPS Rare Plant Index.

## Traditional Uses

Woolly blue curls is revered as great medicine by California Indians. The Concow, Wailaki, and Yuki consider it a panacea. The Diegueño treat colds with the tea.[181] The Cahuilla drink a tea of leaves and flowers for stomach problems.[182] Dr. Cephas Bard, an Oxnard physician, wrote in 1894 that it was a "much extolled aromatic tonic" for the Chumash.[183] Contemporary Chumash still use it as a stomach tea and drink it for nervous conditions and rheumatism. They use the

*Woolly blue curls (*Trichostema lanatum*) in all its glory.* BRYANT BAKER

tea for health issues specific to women, including preparing a sweet-scented douche from the leaves and stems. The leaves are mixed with those of vinegar weed (*T. lanceolata*) and drunk by new mothers to help expel the placenta. The Chumash also consider it a strong disinfectant wash and hair rinse for humans and animals. The Ventureño Chumash name for it, 'akhiye'p, (apostrophes here should be glottal stops) translates simply as "medicine."[184] [185] [186] The Paipai of northern Baja California make a tea from the leaves of Parish's blue curls for menstrual problems.

Vinegar weed is an equally important Native American medicine with similar uses. A simmering tea of the leaves is used by the Maidu as steam therapy for uterine problems. Among the traditional Miwok, the cure was to sit over that steaming decoction. The Miwok also drink a tea of vinegar weed for colds, feverish flus, and headaches. They chew the fresh leaves for toothache and place the leaves around an aching tooth. The Ohlone use the tea for

*Single woolly blue curls flower showing the four stamens.* JAMES DAVID ADAMS JR.

bathing infected sores and treating colds. They also rub ground leaves of vinegar weed on the skin for pain as well as on the face and chest for colds, much in the same way people use Vicks VapoRub today. They also use the leaves, steeped in cold water, for colds.[187] The Kawaiisu take an infusion of the whole plant for colds and stomachaches. The Karok put the leaves in bedding to prevent fleas.

## Modern Uses

Herbalist Michael Moore says an infused tea of the flowering tops of woolly blue curls "will settle stomachache as quickly as chamomile." He also recommends the tea to promote sweating in dry fevers and suggests trying the fresh leaves in marinades, sauces, and salad dressings.[188]

## Phytochemicals/Mechanisms of Action

Little is known about the specific chemistry or pharmacological activity of these *Trichostema* species. Garcia and Adams report that the genus as a whole has a number of aromatic compounds, several of which are pain-relieving monoterpenoids.[189]

*Low-growing vinegar weed (*Trichostema lanceolatum*).* MATT BELOW

A 2016 in vitro laboratory study found that an extract of woolly blue curls inhibited the growth of the Gram-negative bacterium *Escherichia coli*.[190] In 2018 a further study inspired by its Chumash uses found that the extract also had antibacterial activity against Gram-positive bacteria, including *Staphylococcus*. This latest finding would support its Indigenous use as a topical treatment for cuts and sores. The study also showed reduced inflammatory responses associated with rheumatic conditions.[191] What little science we have supports its traditional uses. Woolly blue curls deserves more study!

## Cultivation

Woolly blue curls is a fire follower with a short life span in nature. It's nearly impossible to start from seed and considered difficult to grow even from nursery starts, but it is well worth the effort if you have the right site and do your homework.

## Cautions

Woolly blue curls should not be used when pregnant because it may act as a mild uterine stimulant.

## Notes

The species name of *T. lanatum* derives from the Latin *lana* ("wool").

In a nod to its aromatics and the shape of its leaves, the early Spanish settlers in southern California named woolly blue curls *romero*, the same name given to rosemary (*Salvia rosmarinus*), another Mint family medicinal plant they knew from Europe.

# MYRTLE FAMILY (MYRTACEAE)

Most of the 100 genera and 3,500 species in the Myrtle family are found in Australia or tropical and subtropical America. The family also includes cloves, allspice, guava, and tea tree.

## *Eucalyptus* genus

There are no native Myrtaceae in California but 200–300 species of *Eucalyptus* have been introduced since the 1870s. Blue gum eucalyptus (*E. globulus*), a native of Tasmania and southeastern Australia, has become a common naturalized resident of California and is now found worldwide. It is the most recognizable and most studied of all the species. The genus name *Eucalyptus* means "well-covered," from the Greek *eu* ("well") and *kalyptos* ("covered") and refers to the cap-like membrane over the unopened flower buds.

## EUCALPYTUS
### *Eucalyptus globulus*

*Telltale peeling bark of blue gum eucalyptus (*Eucalyptus globulus*).* LANNY KAUFER

**Other common names:** Blue gum, Tasmanian blue gum, Australian fever tree

**Origin:** Non-native

**Range:** Coastal California from Humboldt County to the Mexican border

**Habitat:** Near highways, agricultural land, disturbed soil, urban areas

**Related species in California:** Over 200 species have been introduced from Australia, including the red ironbark eucalyptus (*E. sideroxylon*) shown on page 188 and many others.

**Related species globally:** Hundreds

**Conservation status rankings:**
　　**IUCN Red List:** LC
　　**CNPS Rare Plant Rank:** Not listed
　　**NatureServe State Rank:** SNA

**Uses:** Decongestant, expectorant, antibacterial

**Parts used:** Young leaves

**Edibility:** Not edible

## Description

Blue gum eucalyptus (*Eucalyptus globulus*), the eucalyptus of commerce, is among the world's largest trees, reaching 200 feet in height. It is the most common and recognizable of the *Eucalyptus* species in California. These fast-growing, aromatic evergreens are easily identified by their leaves; their smooth tan and blue-gray bark that eventually dries to brown and peels off in strips; and the woody, warty seed capsules that form after flowering. The caps of these so-called "buttons" are divided into three to six segments, or valves. The flower buds appear in the axils of the alternate, narrow, sickle-shaped, 6- to 12-inch-long mature leaves before opening in a spray of white stamens. The young leaves, preferred for home remedies, are opposite, rounded, and whitish. They sprout from the younger branches or may pop out anywhere.

*The young, first-year blue gum (*Eucalyptus globulus*) leaves recommended for home use*
LANNY KAUFER

Blue gums are usually surrounded by a dead zone of old bark and leaf litter. They are found throughout coastal California, often concentrated in groves near their original plantings along highways and on the edges of agricultural land, where they were planted as windbreaks, as a possible timber source, or to suck water out of swampy ground.

### Conservation Status
No conservation concerns. In fact, it is often considered an invasive non-native plant.

### Traditional Uses
As with other introduced plants, there is virtually no record of medicinal use by native Californians. Australian aborigines make an infusion of eucalyptus leaves from various species for pains and fevers. They also use a bark decoction of some species to bathe sores and consider the bark charcoal antiseptic.[192] Once eucalyptus was planted globally, its therapeutic uses were integrated into traditional herbal systems, including European, Chinese, and Ayurvedic medicines.

American Eclectic physicians of the nineteenth century used the oil as an external antiseptic and prescribed the tea, taken internally or as a steam inhalation, for bronchial conditions.

### Modern Uses
While the fruits and older leaves are the parts of blue gum used in the manufacture of eucalyptus oil, Michael Moore and other herbalists agree that the young

leaves are best for home use. Moore suggests drinking a hot infusion of several leaves as the best way to take the herb as an antiseptic expectorant for respiratory conditions.[193] The hot tea is also diaphoretic, bringing down fevers by stimulating sweating. Further, when the infusion is drunk slowly or used as a gargle, the tannins have a cleansing, astringent effect on the mucus linings. A stronger infusion also can be used as an antiseptic steam inhalant for sinus or bronchial congestion, just as you would use yerba santa. (See "Recipes" for instructions for herbal steam inhalations.) You can even turn your house into a giant herbal humidifier by letting a pot of tea gently simmer uncovered on the stove.

*Blue gum (*Eucalyptus globulus*) flowers, leaves, and buttons.* LANNY KAUFER

Externally, the strong infusion can be used as a disinfectant wash. If you don't have leaves handy, Michael Tierra advocates mixing 1 ounce eucalyptus oil in 1 pint lukewarm water to make the wash.[194]

The German Commission E approved the internal use of eucalyptus leaf for inflammation of the mucus lining of the respiratory tract. In Germany, eucalyptus leaf is licensed as a standard medicinal tea for bronchitis and inflammation of the throat. The British Herbal Pharmacopoeia reported antiseptic action.[195] Eucalyptus is one of several California plants listed at the Kaiser Permanente website as "herbs that directly attack microbes."[196]

## Phytochemicals/Mechanisms of Action

All *Eucalyptus* species have similar phytochemical profiles, but blue gum is the most thoroughly researched. In California it is the most common species you will likely encounter. Blue gum contains several antimicrobial compounds active against a range of pathogens, including flu viruses. Aromadendrene, a sesquiterpenoid, and

*Red ironbark eucalyptus (*Eucalyptus sideroxylon*), showing furrowed bark, red stems, and pink flowers visited by honeybees* LANNY KAUFER

eucalyptol (cineole), a monoterpene, are the major constituents. Both are well-documented antimicrobials. Also present are other terpenes, phenols, resinoids, and tannins. Blue gum is the preferred species for manufacturing eucalyptus oil due to its high content of eucalyptol. The essential oil shows strong activity against multidrug-resistant species of Gram-positive *Staphylococcus* and Gram-negative *Listeria* and *Haemophilus*, among other pathogens.

*Red ironbark eucalyptus (*Eucalyptus sideroxylon*) flowers and unopened (capped) flower buds.* LANNY KAUFER

Eucalyptus tea and steam inhalant work in a manner similar to horehound by stimulating mucus secretions throughout the respiratory tract. This action helps to expel phlegm. At the same time, as with other aromatic herbs, the gas from internal absorption of the oil contained in the leaves is exhaled from the bloodstream through the lungs, where it inhibits the growth of bacteria.[197]

### Cultivation
Further cultivation of blue gum and other *Eucalyptus* species in California is discouraged due to their flammability and suspected toxic effect on native species. Native plant advocates argue that their size, water consumption, and herbicidal litter give them an unfair advantage over natives competing for space.

### Cautions
Older leaves contain more of the monoterpenes phellandrene and piperitone. These are moderately toxic at higher doses and sometimes cause headaches. The essential oil can cause burning and irritation and must be used with care.

### Notes
Fresh, young Australian eucalyptus leaves are the only food of the koala, one of several marsupials who can tolerate the potentially toxic oil.

In the search for safer weed killers, the aqueous extract of blue gum has shown potential as a pre-emergent bioherbicide.[198]

The UC Santa Cruz Arboretum, where I had a work-study job while earning my biology degree, has the largest collection of eucalyptus outside of Australia.[199] I learned to appreciate the great diversity of species and the subtle differences in their aromas.

Blue gum's species name, *E. globulus*, is Latin for "little button," describing the shape of the seed capsules.

# POPPY FAMILY (PAPAVERACEAE)

The Poppy family includes 200 species spread across 25 to 30 genera. Many poppies, California's natives among them, contain narcotic alkaloids. The most famous poppy is the opium poppy (*Papaver somniferum*), the source of opium, morphine, codeine, and heroin.

## *Eschscholzia* genus

Not counting subspecies, there are thirteen species of *Eschscholzia* in California. All are natives. California poppy (*E. californica*) is the most common. The seven species listed below under "conservation status rankings" are rare and should not be collected. The genus was named for Johann Friedrich von Eschscholtz, a German naturalist who first discovered it for Europeans in 1816 while on a Russian scientific expedition in California.

## CALIFORNIA POPPY
### *Eschscholzia californica*

**Synonyms:** *Eschscholtzia californica*
**Other common names:** California golden poppy, *copa de oro* (Spanish)
**Origin:** Native
**Range:** Throughout California from sea level to 8,200 feet elevation
**Habitat:** Widespread in coastal scrub, sandy streambanks, grasslands, chaparral, and forests
**Related species in California:** Another 12 species of *Eschscholzia*, prickly poppy (*Argemone* spp.), bush poppy (*Dendromecon rigida*), fire poppy (*Papaver californicum*), and Matilija poppy (*Romneya* spp.)
**Related species globally:** Opium poppy (*Papaver somniferum*)

California poppy (Eschscholzia californica) in Antelope Valley Poppy Reserve. NEIL REICHLINE

**Conservation status rankings:**
   **IUCN Red List:** Not listed
   **CNPS Rare Plant Rank:** *E. californica* not ranked. Related Joshua tree poppy (*E. androuxii*), San Benito poppy (*E. hypecoides*), Tejon poppy (*E. lemmonii* subsp. *kernensis*), Red Rock poppy (*E. minutiflora* subsp. *twisselmannii*), Kernville poppy (*E. procera*), island poppy (*E. ramosa*), and diamond-petaled California poppy (*E. rhombipetala*) are considered rare.
   **NatureServe State Rank:** SNR

*California poppies in stages of opening, including some buds still covered in yellow sepals on the right.*
NEIL REICHLINE

**Uses:** Anxiolytic, sedative, antispasmodic, analgesic; for insomnia, nervous tension, anxiety, cramps, and pain
**Parts used:** Entire plant, mainly flowers and leaves
**Edibility:** Leaves rumored to be edible cooked but extremely bitter

## Description

California poppy is usually an annual but sometimes becomes perennial in milder climates. It has alternate, branching stems 8 to 20 inches long with bluish-green leaves finely divided into many narrow segments. The leaf blades are ¾ inch to 2¼ inches long.

The solitary, four-petaled, orange flowers are 2 inches long on 2- to 6-inch-long stems branching from the main stem. They first appear enclosed in a hood of two sepals that falls away when the petals open, leaving a rim around the base of the flower. The fruit is a thin, ribbed capsule (pod) 1 to 3½ inches long and full of tiny black or dark brown seeds. California poppy blooms from February to September. The petals close at night or in cold, cloudy weather. Patches of yellow flowers often indicate soil with high mineral content. In the wild, California poppies can show unexpected variation due to well-intentioned people and organizations randomly planting wildflower seed packets.

## Conservation Status

Other than the seven rare species listed above, California's *Eschscholzia* poppies are common and widespread.

## Traditional Uses

The Ohlone lay the flowers under a child's bed to bring on sleep. Bard (1894) reported that the Chumash used its analgesic properties to treat colic and prepare a "hypnotic extract." Bean and Saubel report that the plant was used by the Cahuilla "to provide a sedative for babies," but with no further details. The Yuki of Mendocino County place the fresh root in a dental cavity to stop toothache pain. They ingest a preparation of the root to treat stomachache and, paradoxically, also use it to induce vomiting. Externally, they make an extract from the root to use as a wash for headaches and to apply to weeping sores. It is said that some unscrupulous gamblers

*California poppy flower.* JAMES DAVID ADAMS JR.

have used it to secretly drug their competition.[200] The Wintu apply the dried, powdered root to the severed umbilical cord to heal the navel more rapidly.[201]

The fluid extract of California poppy appears as early as 1894 in the Parke, Davis & Co. catalogue with high praise: "An excellent soporific [sleep inducer] and analgesic [pain reducer], and above all, harmless. A very useful anodyne [relaxing pain reliever], and a good substitute for opium for administration to children."[202]

## Modern Uses

California poppy is used today by herbalists for its mild sedative, anxiety-relieving, antispasmodic, and pain-relieving properties. It is often combined with other nervine herbs to direct its action into individualized treatments for insomnia, nervous tension, anxiety, cramps, and pain. It is nonaddicting and considered safe for children. A tincture or capsule is often used because the tea is too bitter for most adults, let alone children, to drink.

## Phytochemicals/Mechanisms of Action

Although in the same family, California poppy does *not* contain morphine and codeine, the addictive, opioid alkaloids found in the opium poppy (*Papaver somniferum*). It does, however, have its own set of related isoquinoline alkaloids. Californidine is the primary constituent in the leaves and stems. Eschscholtzine is the main compound in the flowers. Allocryptopine is mainly in the roots. Small amounts of protopine, sanguinarine, and chelerythrine are also found in the plant. These potent alkaloids collectively have shown pain-relieving, sleep-inducing, sedative, antianxiety, and antispasmodic effects.[203] Actually, 15 to 30 percent of all flowering plants create bitter-tasting alkaloids like those found in California poppy to prevent browsing by herbivores. They generally affect the central nervous system (CNS) of any animal that gets past the bitterness to ingest them. It's rare to see signs of browsing on California poppies.

*California poppy seed capsule, center, surrounded by smaller capsules, finely dissected leaves, covered buds, open flowers, and one flower emerging from its hood of sepals.* ROBERT E. MERRITT

## Cultivation

California poppy is drought tolerant and easy to grow from seed collected in the wild. After flowering the first year, it typically will propagate itself by seed and then go into summer dormancy. It may last until the next rainy season in mild climates.

## Cautions

California poppy is considered safe to use as a tea in moderation. As with any plant or drug that contains alkaloids that affect the CNS, excessive use can be dangerous. The tendency to use California poppy as a tincture or in a capsule because of the bitter taste increases the risk of an overdose. Pregnant women should avoid it.

## Notes

The "golden poppy" is the probable source of California's nickname, the Golden State. It became the state flower in 1903. A popular rumor that it has special protection from picking because of its official status is false. It does, however, fall under the same California Penal Code statute 384a that protects all plants on public lands: "A person shall not willfully or negligently cut, destroy, mutilate, or remove plant material that is growing upon public land or upon land that is not his or hers without a written permit from the owner of the land."[204]

# ROSE FAMILY (ROSACEAE)

The Rose family includes over 4,800 species in 91 genera. It takes its name from the type genus *Rosa*, as in *Rosa californica*, one of several medicinal Rose family members native to California. Rosaceae are usually deciduous, have five-petaled flowers, and can take the form of herbs, shrubs, small trees, or vines. Many commercial fruits, nuts, and berries, such as apples, pears, peaches, cherries, apricots, almonds, blackberries, and strawberries, belong to the Rose family. Almonds too.

Rose family plants produce tannins to prevent insects and herbivores from eating the leaves or unripe fruit. Tannins create an astringent, dry mouthfeel when tasted, but they dissipate as the fruit matures. Some Rose family members also produce bitter cyanogenic glycosides as another defense. These toxic compounds are strategically concentrated in the seeds to ensure animals won't bite into them when eating the sweet fruit. And therein lies the folk tale origin of the poison apple Snow White ate.

## *Heteromeles* genus

Toyon, *Heteromeles arbutifolia*, a native of California, is the only species of this genus.

## TOYON
### *Heteromeles arbutifolia*

**Other common names:** California holly, Christmas berry
**Origin:** Native
**Range:** All of western California to 4,000 feet elevation
**Habitat:** Chaparral, oak woodland, mixed evergreen forest
**Related species in California:** None
**Conservation status rankings:**
    IUCN Red List: LC
    CNPS Rare Plant Rank: Not listed
    NatureServe State Rank: SNR
**Uses:** Anti-inflammatory; for Alzheimer's disease, skin wash
**Parts used:** Berries, leaves, and stems
**Edibility:** Ripe berries, dried or cooked, are edible.

Five-petaled Rose family flowers of toyon (Heteromeles arbutifolia). STEVE JUNAK

## Description

Toyon is a native shrub or tree found throughout most of western California in chaparral, oak woodland, and mixed evergreen forest up to 4,000 feet in the

*Toyon bush loaded with ripe berries.* BRYANT BAKER

Sierra foothills. It usually grows 6 to 15 feet tall but is able to reach 30 feet in good conditions. Thick, leathery, oblong-lanceolate leaves are glossy green, 2 to 4 inches long, with serrated edges. The small five-petaled flowers are white, forming large terminal clusters that bloom from June to August. The bright red fruits are composed of mealy, orange flesh surrounding a core of three to six seeds. They are called berries, although technically they are pomes, like miniature apples. They begin to ripen in December and linger on the bushes through the winter, sometimes into early spring.

Crushing a leaf gives off a subtle almond-like scent as the cyanogenic compounds oxidize and release small amounts of hydrogen cyanide and an aromatic compound called benzaldehyde, which is responsible for the odor.

### Conservation Status
Toyon is abundant throughout its range in western California and small areas in southwestern Oregon and northwestern Baja California.

### Traditional Uses
The ripe berries are eaten, almost always cooked or dried, by many California tribes, including the Chumash, Maidu, Miwok, Kumeyaay, Ohlone, Karok, and Luiseño, to name a few. Some consider it a survival food to be eaten during lean times. A few are known to use the plant medicinally. The Maidu and Yuki steep a tea of the mashed flowers for gynecological problems. They also drink a tea of the

*Ripe toyon berries.* STEVE JUNAK

bark and leaves for various aches and pains, including stomachache. The Ohlone use the tea as a blood purifier and to regulate menstruation.[205] Some Kumeyaay today still drink a tea of leaves and stems for colds and whooping cough. They also use a decoction to bathe sores or as a rinse for sores inside the mouth.[206] The Diegueño steep the bark and leaves for a tea to wash infected wounds.[207]

Chumash healer Cecilia Garcia writes: "Toyon berries and elderberries were used to treat senile dementia, now called Alzheimer's disease."[205] A dose of dried toyon berries that fits in the palm of the patient's hand is slowly chewed and swallowed. This reportedly can slow down the progression of the disease.[209] (See "Recipes" for instructions on drying toyon berries.)

## Modern Uses

The tannins in the leaves and bark of many Rose family plants, including toyon, are astringent. They can help healing of sores by shrinking oozy tissue while

*A closer look at a cluster of toyon pomes (apple-like Rose family "berries").* LANNY KAUFER

*Island fox (*Urocyon littoralis*) feasting on toyon berries.* JAMES WAPOTICH

precipitating blood proteins to form a scab. The anti-inflammatory compounds in toyon may also assist with pain at the site.

Native and non-native Californians enjoy snacking on the dried berries or brewing a cider with them.

### Phytochemicals/Mechanisms of Action

In 2016 pharmacologists found a number of anti-inflammatory compounds in toyon berries that may be useful in treating Alzheimer's disease. Icariside, a glycoside, and maslinic acid, a triterpene, protect the blood-brain barrier, inhibit the formation of amyloid plaques, and prevent inflammatory cell infiltration into the brain. Flavonoids such as catechin and kaempferol inhibit the destruction of protective cells in the brain. Betulin, a triterpene, may prevent fat accumulation that can damage the blood-brain barrier. Another triterpene, lupeol acetate, is known to be a potent anti-inflammatory.[210]

### Cultivation

Toyon can be propagated from seeds or cuttings and pruned for shape and size. It makes a handsome shrub that will bring songbirds to the yard and provide

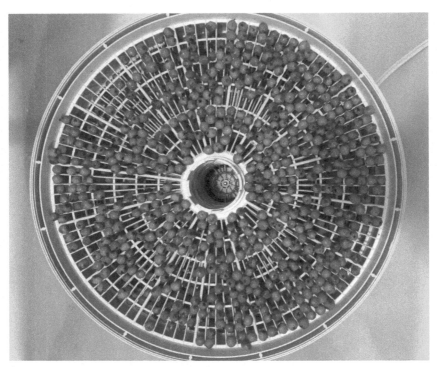

*Culled and washed toyon berries ready for dehydrating.* LANNY KAUFER

you with tasty berries that may protect your brain. See USDA Plant Guide for instructions.[211]

## Cautions
Like other Rose family plants, all parts of toyon may contain small amounts of cyanogenic glycosides, especially the unripe berries. Avoid drinking a decoction of the leaves, and approach an infusion cautiously. The berries should be very ripe and preferably cooked or dried before eating any quantity. See Christopher Nyerges's *Foraging California* for edible uses.

## Notes
Begin tasting the berries for relative sweetness in December, when the tannin content starts to go down. Once harvested and washed they can be sun-dried, although a dehydrator or the pilot or lowest oven setting works best for consistent heat in the winter months. (See "Recipes.")

The Spanish name *toyon* came from the Ohlone *tottcon*. The genus *Heteromeles* translates as "different apple," derived from the Greek *hetero* ("different") and *malus* ("apple"), its Rose family cousin. Like apples, toyon berries are high in pectin, a gelatinous polysaccharide that is beneficial to the intestinal tract. The species name *arbutifolia* (pronounced ar-byoo-tuh-FOE-lee-ah) reflects the similarity of toyon leaves to the foliage of the unrelated, so-called strawberry tree, *Arbutus uneda*, of the Mediterranean. ***Note:*** The phonetic *byoo* sound in "Arbutus" is pronounced as in the word "beauty."

The glossy, green, spiny leaves and red berries of toyon reminded settlers from the eastern United States of the unrelated holly (*Ilex* spp.) of their homelands. They nicknamed it "California holly." The area now known as Lake Hollywood Park in the hills of Los Angeles was dubbed Holly Canyon in the 1800s. The acreage surrounding it was incorporated as the City of Hollywood in 1903 and consolidated with the City of Los Angeles in 1910. By the 1920s, so many toyon branches had been cut for Christmas decorations that the State of California was forced to add section 384b to the California Penal Code, specifically outlawing the harvesting of toyon limbs. An exception is made, however, for harvesting the berries, as long as no limbs or foliage are removed.[212]

## *Prunus* genus

There are over 400 species of *Prunus* worldwide, among which are some widely cultivated fruit crops: apricots, peaches, plums, cherries, and almonds. Including subspecies, California has ten native *Prunus* species. All four described below are commonly known as "wild cherry."

### BITTER CHERRY
#### *Prunus emarginata*

**Other common names:** Western bitter cherry
**Origin:** Native
**Range:** All of California except the Central Valley to 10,000 feet elevation
**Habitat:** Canyons and slopes in chaparral, sagebrush scrub, and coniferous forests

### HOLLYLEAF CHERRY
#### *Prunus ilicifolia* subsp. *ilicifolia*

**Other common names:** *Islay* (Spanish)
**Origin:** Native
**Range:** Coastal central and southern California to 5,200 feet elevation
**Habitat:** North-facing slopes in chaparral, coastal sage scrub, and oak woodland

*Green hollyleaf cherries with characteristic spiny leaves.* ROBERT E. MERRITT

# CATALINA CHERRY
## *Prunus ilicifolia* subsp. *lyonii*

**Other common names:** Island cherry
**Origin:** Native
**Range:** On Channel Islands to 2,000 feet elevation; escaped cultivar elsewhere in southern California
**Habitat:** Slopes and canyons in chaparral and oak woodland

*Ripe Catalina cherries (*Prunus ilicifolias
subsp. lyonii*).* LANNY KAUFER

# WESTERN CHOKECHERRY
## *Prunus virginiana* var. *demissa*

**Other common names:** Common chokecherry
**Origin:** Native
**Range:** All of California except the Central Valley to 10,000 feet elevation
**Habitat:** Slopes and riversides in chaparral, oak woodland, and yellow pine forest
**Related species in California:** Several other native *Prunus* species, including Pacific plum (*P. subcordata*)
**Related species globally:** Many, including black cherry (*P. serotina*) in the eastern United States, and several commercially important stone-fruit trees originally from Asia
**Conservation status rankings:**
    **IUCN Red List:** *P. ilicifolia* spp. not listed; *P. emarginata* and *P. virginiana* are LC.
    **CNPS Rare Plant Rank:** Not listed
    **NatureServe State Rank:** SNR
**Uses:** Sedative, cough suppressant
**Parts used:** Inner bark
**Edibility:** All except bitter cherries are sweet enough to eat fresh when fully ripe, although chokecherries can be tart. *P. ilicifolia* pits can be processed (carefully) for eating.

*Western chokecherry blossoms and finely serrated leaves.* STEVE JUNAK

*Blossoms of hollyleaf cherry (*Prunus ilicifolia *subsp.* ilicifolia*).* DAVID WHITE

## Description

All wild cherry trees have reddish-brown bark on the younger stems, turning gray when mature. They have the typical five-petaled flowers of the Rose fam-

ily and bear stone fruits, or drupes. Bitter cherry and chokecherry live in colder climates and are deciduous; the two southern-dwelling subspecies of *P. ilicifolia* are evergreen. All except bitter cherry have edible fruit. The bark of all *Prunus* species can be used interchangeably for preparing medicinal home remedies.

Bitter cherry (*Prunus emarginata*) can grow to a 50-foot tree farther north, but in California it is often found as a thicket of shrubs. It has dull green, oval, finely-toothed leaves, longer than they are wide, and clusters of three to twelve small, white, almond-scented flowers. The fruit is a small, bitter, red to purple cherry. Hollyleaf cherry (*Prunus ilicifolia* subsp. *ilicifolia*) is a multi-trunked shrub but can grow to a 30-foot tree. It has dark green, glossy, spine-toothed leaves and long clus-

*A hollyleaf cherry branch with inner bark removed. (See "Collecting, Drying, and Storing Tree Bark" in the introduction to this book.)* LANNY KAUFER

ters of small white flowers. The ripe cherries are dark purplish red, ½ to 1 inch in diameter, and mostly pit with a thin layer of sweet fruit. Catalina cherry (*Prunus ilicifolia* subsp. *lyonii*) is a larger version of hollyleaf cherry, sometimes reaching

The author's hand showing the size of ripe hollyleaf cherries. LANNY KAUFER

50 feet, with larger, smooth-edged leaves and sweet, dark purple fruits ¾ to 1 inch in diameter. Western chokecherry (*Prunus virginiana* var. *demissa*) is a shrub or small tree, less than 20 feet tall, with dull green, finely-toothed leaves and long, drooping clusters of eighteen or more flowers. The fruit is a small, reddish-purple cherry, ¼ to ½ inch in diameter, and astringent until fully ripe.

## Conservation Status
All four species are abundant within their ranges.

## Traditional Uses
Native people in California and around the country have a long history of using the inner bark of their local species of wild cherry, mainly for its sedative effect on coughs. Mendocino-area tribes use a tea of chokecherry bark as a general tonic, to stop diarrhea, and to calm the nerves. The Cahuilla, Karok, and Maidu use it to cure colds. The Cahuilla and Diegueño drink an infusion of the bark of hollyleaf cherry for coughs and colds. For coughs in particular, the Diegueño drink a hot tea of the leaves.[213]

Cherokee women have traditionally used an infusion of the inner bark of black cherry (*P. serotina*) to relieve pain in labor and childbirth. The same tea is drunk by the Cherokee, Micmac, Iroquois, and other eastern tribes for coughs, colds, diarrhea, sore throats, fever, and indigestion. Adopted by European settlers and their physicians, wild cherry bark was listed in the *US Pharmacopoeia* from 1820 to 1960 as a cough suppressant and has formed the basis of countless cough syrups and lozenges.[214]

## Modern Uses

Modern herbalists value wild cherry bark as a safe respiratory sedative if used properly. David Hoffmann recommends 1 teaspoon of powdered bark infused in 1 cup of boiling water for 10–15 minutes, drunk three times a day.[215] Michael Moore recommends chokecherry bark for a dry cough with rapid, hectic breathing, asserting that it is completely safe, even for children, if gathered in the fall, prepared as a cold infusion of one part bark soaked overnight in thirty-two parts water, and given in small doses of 2 to 4 ounces, three times a day.[216] Michael Tierra recommends a dose of 2 teaspoons of bark infused in hot or cold water three times a day for coughs. He also uses wild cherry bark as a sedative for the nervous and circulatory systems and for digestive problems such as diarrhea.[217] (See "Recipes" for my Wild Cherry Cough Syrup.)

*Catalina cherry (*Prunus ilicifolia *subsp.* lyonii*) blossoms, leaves, and green cherries.*
SANGEET KHALSA, COURTESY OF SANTA BARBARA BOTANIC GARDEN

## Phytochemicals/Mechanisms of Action

While there are no phytochemical studies yet on hollyleaf or bitter cherry, they contain compounds similar to those found in chokecherry and black cherry, which have both been studied. The primary active ingredients responsible for the sedative effect on the cough reflex are the cyanogenic glycosides prunasin and amygdalin. Also present in cherry bark are benzaldehyde, which provides the almond odor; tannins, which make it astringent; flavonoids known to be antioxidant and anti-inflammatory; minerals such as calcium and potassium; and scopoletin, a coumarin with anti-inflammatory and antianxiety activity.

Once the cold or hot infusion is ingested, the prunasin and other cyanogenic glycosides are converted into hydrocyanic acid (HCN) and excreted rapidly through the lungs without converting to toxic cyanide. In the lungs and bronchioles, the glycosides increase respiration and sedate the nerves that cause the cough reflex.

## Cultivation

With their glossy green leaves, profuse white flowers, and large fruits, hollyleaf and Catalina cherry are popular drought-tolerant landscaping choices. They can

*Western chokecherry (*Prunus virginiana *var.* demissa*) bush in bloom.* LANNY KAUFER

be started from seed or nursery stock and pruned to any shape or size, including an attractive edible and medicinal hedge. Birds and bees love them.

## Cautions
Please note that while woody herbs (barks, roots, etc.) are usually prepared as decoctions, an infusion is recommended for wild cherry bark. An excessive dose or one made from improperly dried or carelessly prepared cherry bark could lead to cyanide poisoning if enough HCN were to make its way through the digestive tract. To be safe, use it under the supervision of a doctor or trained herbalist— and not while pregnant.

## Notes
Cut or strip fresh bark from pruned branches or recently downed trees, never from the trunk of a living tree. See "Collecting, Drying, and Storing Tree Bark" in the front of this guide for tips on processing bark.

At first glance, the spiny-edged leaves of hollyleaf cherry might resemble those of coast live oak (*Quercus agrifolia*). Here's a clue: Hollyleaf cherry leaves are creased down the middle like a taco shell and have wavy edges, while live oak leaves have a dome shape like a bowl turned upside down.

If you have the patience to scrape the small amount of edible fruit off the skins of the ripe cherries, you can experience its sweetness without the slight bitterness of the skins. When I'm outdoors, I just spit out the skins and find the flesh to be delicious. In times past, the pits—dried, cracked, ground, and leached in hot water—were an important food for the Chumash and other tribes. See Christopher Nyerges's *Foraging California* for more on edible uses.[218]

## *Rosa* genus

The genus *Rosa* is divided into four subgenera, including a subgenus also named *Rosa* to which most of California's ten native and three naturalized rose species belong. Our three most common natives are featured below. Fortunately for the forager, all wild roses look basically alike, all can be used interchangeably, and none are endangered in California. Rose family species in general are known as dependable, mild astringents. Rose hips, often from dog rose (*R. canina*), are used in manufacturing natural vitamin C supplements.

## CALIFORNIA WILD ROSE
### *Rosa californica*

**Other common names:** California rose
**Range:** Throughout California below 6,000 feet elevation
**Habitat:** Moist places, canyons, streams

*California wild rose (*Rosa californica*) buds and blossoms.* LANNY KAUFER

## BALD-HIP ROSE
### *Rosa gymnocarpa*

**Other common names:** Wood rose, dwarf rose
**Range:** Central California to the Oregon border below 5,000 feet elevation
**Habitat:** Shaded woods

*Bald-hip rose (*Rosa gymnocarpa*) flower*
KEIR MORSE

# WOODS' ROSE
## *Rosa woodsii*

**Other common names:** Interior rose
**Range:** Interior mountains between 2,000 and 10,000 feet elevation
**Habitat:** Dampish places, shaded forests
**Related species in California:** Several other native and non-native *Rosa* species
**Related species globally:** Dog rose (*R. canina*) and others
**Conservation status rankings:**
  **IUCN Red List:** Not listed
  **CNPS Rare Plant Rank:** Not listed
  **NatureServe State Rank:** SNR

*Woods' rose (*Rosa woodsii*).* KEIR MORSE

**Uses:** Mild astringent for skin wash, eye wash, and diarrhea; diaper rash; colic
**Parts used:** Leaves, flowers, roots, fruit (hips)
**Edibility:** Fresh rose hips are sweet and high in vitamin C.

## Description
All wild roses have prickly stems and alternate, compound leaves, each leaf made up of three to eleven leaflets, most often five to seven. They have five-petaled, five-sepaled, rose-pink flowers that develop into scarlet-red rose hips. The sepals project from the end of the hip, drying as the fruit ripens and eventually falling off. California wild rose (*Rosa californica*) is an erect, branching shrub 3 to 9 feet tall, often forming thickets. The stems have stout, flattened, recurved prickles.

Bald-hip rose (*R. gymnocarpa*) is a small, thin-stemmed shrub growing to about 3 or 4 feet high with slender, straight prickles. Its sepals fall off the hips sooner than other species, hence its common name, bald-hip rose. It's also sometimes called wood rose, but we'll overlook that to avoid confusion with Woods' rose (*R. woodsii*).

Also known as interior rose, Woods' rose is usually an erect shrub 3 to 10 feet tall with slender, straight prickles. It may be solitary or in a briar patch. California wild rose blooms from May to August, the other two species from May to June.

## Conservation Status
Roses are common wild plants worldwide. The same is true in California.

## Traditional Uses
Traditional Chumash used dried, powdered petals of California wild rose as baby powder to prevent and treat chafing and "diaper" rash from being swaddled in a

cradle board. Chumash and other tribes continue to use rose petal tea to treat colic and teething pain in babies and as a wash for sore eyes in children and adults.[219]

Among the native people of eastern California and Nevada, a tea made from leaves of interior rose is a popular beverage, especially as a "spring tonic." A decoction of the roots or inner bark of the stems is drunk for treating colds and diarrhea.[220] Numerous tribes across the country use infusions and decoctions of various parts of their local *Rosa* species as eye and skin washes and as astringent teas for diarrhea, stomach troubles, sore throats, and more.[221]

Chumash healer Cecilia Garcia describes a traditional way to treat a baby for teething pain and colic: Place a few rose petals in a small bowl with a little water and mash them with your finger. Then rub your finger on the baby's gums. For modern times, you can pulverize the petals with a little water in a blender and make ice cubes.[222]

## Modern Uses

Michael Moore recommends steeping five to ten flowers or buds in hot water for 20 minutes for diarrhea. He also uses the flowers as a mild astringent eyewash, suggesting two to three flowers steeped in ½ cup hot water until it reaches body temperature. He notes that isotonic water should be prepared for this eyewash by adding 1 slightly rounded teaspoon of salt to 1 quart of water.

Rose petal tea is German Commission E approved for mild inflammations of the mouth and throat. Ayurvedic medicine echoes the use of rose petals for soothing inflamed surfaces such as sore eyes or sore throat.[223]

*Ripe rosehips of California wild rose (*Rosa californica*) showing the dry sepals that remain on the hips.* LANNY KAUFER

## Phytochemicals/Mechanisms of Action

Rose petals, leaves, and roots contain flavonoids and tannins. Abundant monoterpenes give rose flowers their fragrance as well as their pain-relieving activity. Triterpenes such as arjunic acid are powerful antioxidants. Euscaphic acid, an anti-inflammatory, is found in the leaves and roots. Tannins provide the astringent effects of rose teas and washes.[224]

Rose hips contain pectin, tannins, sugars, flavonoids, and fruit acids and are a rich source of vitamins. They are known for their high content of ascorbic acid (vitamin C), which has antioxidant activity against damaging free radicals, prevents scurvy, stimulates the immune system, and lowers the risk of heart disease. Regular consumption of foods high in vitamin C can shorten the duration of the common cold. Humans are one of the few animals that cannot manufacture their own vitamin C and must get it from their diet.[225] Unfortunately, much of the vitamin C in rose hips is lost in the drying process, so eat them fresh when you have the chance.

### Cultivation

Wild roses can play several roles in a garden, from thickets to hedges to annually pruned, compact bushes. They require much less care than commercial roses and can be started from seeds or transplanted rootstock. A root barrier is required if you want to prevent sprawl.

### Cautions

Unlike the pits of some Rose family fruits like cherries and apricots, rose seeds do not contain toxic cyanogenic glycosides, so it is safe to drink teas, even decoctions,

The "bald hips" that give Rosa gymnocarpa *its common name.* KEIR MORSE

made from whole rose hips. However, the tiny seeds are surrounded by irritating hairs that are best cleaned out before eating fresh rose hips. The official rose hips of commerce are the dried fruit shells with the seeds and hairs removed.

### Notes

Steeped wild rose leaf tea can be drunk as a mildly astringent, caffeine-free substitute for Chinese green tea. The same can be done with the leaves of its Rose family cousins of the *Rubus* genus: raspberry, blackberry, salmonberry, and thimbleberry.

## *Rubus* genus

*Rubus* is an ancient Latin name for blackberry brambles and is derived from *ruber* ("red"). There are at least 250 *Rubus* species worldwide, with 7 native species in California, including the 4 most common ones described here. The closely related raspberry and blackberry are both low-growing shrubs with stout prickles on arching, biennial stems and weaker prickles on the backs of their compound leaves, which are made up of three coarsely-toothed, pinnate leaflets. Their five-petaled flowers are white. In contrast, thimbleberry and salmonberry are tall, erect plants with thornless stems.

## WHITEBARK RASPBERRY
### *Rubus leucodermis*

**Other common names:** Western raspberry, blackcap raspberry
**Origin:** Native
**Range:** Mainly northern California and Sierras from 150 to 7,800 feet elevation
**Habitat:** Slopes and canyons, moist areas, coniferous forests

*Whitebark raspberry (*Rubus leucodermis*)
buds and flowers.* LANNY KAUFER

## THIMBLEBERRY
### *Rubus parviflorus*

**Other common names:** None
**Origin:** Native
**Range:** Coastal central and Northern California, Sierras from 60 to 8,000 feet elevation
**Habitat:** Canyons, moist semi-shaded areas, coniferous forests

*Cluster of ripe and immature thimbleberries
(*Rubus parviflorus*).* JESS STARWOOD

# SALMONBERRY
## *Rubus spectabilis*

**Other common names:** None
**Origin:** Native
**Range:** Coastal Northern California up to 1,600 feet elevation
**Habitat:** Moist areas, streambanks, redwood and mixed evergreen forests

*Salmonberry (*Rubus spectabilis*).* JESS STARWOOD

# CALIFORNIA BLACKBERRY
## *Rubus ursinus*

**Other common names:** Pacific blackberry, Pacific dewberry
**Origin:** Native
**Range:** Throughout western California up to 5,000 feet elevation
**Habitat:** Canyons, streambanks
**Related native species in California:** Waxleaf raspberry (*R. glaucifolius*), roughfruit raspberry (*R. lasiococcus*), wild strawberry (*Fragaria* spp.)
**Related non-native species in California:** Himalayan blackberry (*R. armeniacus*)
**Related species globally:** Many, including European and American raspberries and blackberries

*Vigorous young blackberry (*Rubus ursinus*) shoot showing three leaflets and stout prickles on stem.* LANNY KAUFER

**Conservation status rankings:**
    **IUCN Red List:** Not listed
    **CNPS Rare Plant Rank:** Not ranked, except Cuyamaca raspberry (*R. glaucifolius* var. *ganderi*), 3.1, and snow dwarf bramble (*R. nivalis*), 2B.3
    **NatureServe State Rank:** SNR
**Uses:** Astringent; for sore throat, diarrhea, and uterine muscle toner
**Parts used:** Leaves, roots, berries
**Edibility:** Berries are edible and delicious.

## Description

As the name implies, whitebark raspberry stems (*Rubus leucodermis*) turn white with age. The leaves are green above and white-woolly on the back. The reddish-purple to dark purple fruits, borne on second-year stems, have the typical raspberry shape of a dome with a hollow core, resembling a thimble. Thimbleberry

(*R. parviflorus*) grows 1½ to 8 feet tall with large, five-lobed, coarsely toothed, palmate leaves and white flowers. The fruits are similar to raspberries but smaller, with a wider hollow core inside the "thimble." Salmonberry (*R. spectabilis*) grows from 6 to 13 feet tall with three-lobed compound leaves. It has reddish-pink petals and salmon-orange to red berries, also resembling raspberries. Fruits of California blackberry (*R. ursinus*) have the typical solid blackberry shape and dark purple color. Boysenberry and loganberry are among the commercial hybrids developed from California blackberry.

*Whitebark raspberry, also known as blackcap raspberry.* JESS STARWOOD

The compound leaves of the invasive Himalayan blackberry (*R. armeniacus*) can be distinguished by their five leaflets compared to three on native California blackberry leaves. Himalayan blackberry is common on roadsides and disturbed places, mainly in northern California and throughout the Pacific Northwest. All these *Rubus* plants have edible berries made up of clusters of drupelets. Medicinally, all can be used interchangeably. The leaves of wild strawberry (*Fragaria* species) also can be substituted for *Rubus* leaves.

*Thimbleberry (*Rubus parviflorus*) flowers and immature berry*
STEVE JUNAK

## Conservation Status
These native berries are common and widespread throughout California. Himalayan blackberry is an invasive non-native.

## Traditional Uses
Throughout native North America, including California, an infusion of the leaves of all *Rubus* species has been used as the go-to astringent tea for treating diarrhea and dysentery. A decoction or strong infusion of the roots is used for the same purpose by the Cahuilla, Kashaya Pomo, Maidu, Ohlone, Tolowa, and Yuki. The Karok soak thimbleberry roots in water to drink as an appetizer or digestive tonic. California tribes also use blackberry teas to soothe sore throats and mouths and to treat colds and congestion. The fruit is used to flavor other medicines.

*Flower of California blackberry (*Rubus ursinus*). JAMES DAVID ADAMS JR.*

Chumash and Coast Miwok women use a root tea of California blackberry to ease menstrual pain and cramping.[226] [227] Quinault women of the Northwest drink a decoction of bark to ease labor pains. Farther east, the Cherokee use an infusion of local raspberry leaves for childbirth pains, and the Chippewa infuse roots of Allegheny blackberry to prevent miscarriage.[228]

The Maidu make a poultice of thimbleberry leaves for wounds and burns. The Bear River tribe uses a poultice of ground-up thimbleberry leaves to draw out pus from sores and boils and help healing.[229] The Quinault apply a poultice of salmonberry bark to ease the pain of wounds and aching teeth.[230] In Nevada, dried raspberry stems are pounded to a powder for a dressing on cuts and wounds.[231]

The use of blackberry by the ancient Romans for sore mouths and inflamed bowels has been well documented. American Eclectic physicians of the 1800s prescribed raspberry leaf tea as well as a cordial prepared from blackberry fruit for their mild astringent effect on the bowels. The dried bark of blackberry roots was included as an astringent in the *US Pharmacopoeia* from 1820 to 1916.[232] Raspberry fruit was listed as a flavoring from 1882 to 1905.

## Modern Uses
Michael Moore endorses the traditional uses of the leaf and root teas as well as the fruit for diarrhea and dysentery. He also recommends 2 to 3 cups a day of leaf tea of any *Rubus* species for excessive menstrual bleeding and to increase uterine muscle tone during the last two trimesters of pregnancy.[233] While raspberry

leaf is widely used by herbalists to facilitate labor, and many mothers swear by it, there is not yet any clinical evidence to support this and other traditional uses.

Based on long-standing use and lack of harmful side effects, the German Commission E approved blackberry leaf tea for nonspecific, acute diarrhea and mild inflammation of the mucosa of the oral cavity and throat. The European Union's Committee on Herbal Medicinal Prod-

*California blackberries at different stages of maturity.* KEIR MORSE

ucts approved raspberry leaf preparations for relief of minor spasms associated with menstrual periods, for treatment of mild mouth or throat inflammation, and for treatment of mild diarrhea.[234]

### Phytochemicals/Mechanisms of Action

*Rubus* leaves contain a number of phenolic compounds with astringent properties, including flavonoids, tannins, and ellagitannins. Tannins are known to reduce inflammation, tighten tissues, dry hypersecreting mucus membranes, and prevent or reduce bleeding, including in the uterus. The fruits derive their red and purple colors from other related polyphenols, called anthocyanins and proanthocyanins. These are powerful antioxidants believed to protect the circulatory system from free radical damage.

### Cultivation

Considered difficult to transplant from the wild, native and non-native *Rubus* plants can be purchased in nurseries.

### Cautions

Raspberry, salmonberry, and blackberry species have three-lobed compound leaves similar in shape and size to poison oak (*Toxicodendron diversilobum*) leaves. There are notable differences, including the saw-toothed leaves of *Rubus* species versus the smooth-edged, lobed leaves of poison oak, and prickles on the stems of raspberry and blackberry.

### Notes

On general principles, where it's available and unsprayed, select Himalayan blackberry and leave the natives alone. Leaves are picked before or during flowering, dried, crumbled with gloved hands, and stored for later use.

The genus name of *R. leucoderma* means "white-skinned" in Latin. *R. parviflorus* means "small-flowered." *R. spectabilis* is derived from the same Latin root as the word "spectacular." *R. ursinus* comes from *ursus*, Latin for "bear."

# NIGHTSHADE FAMILY (SOLANACEAE)

Worldwide, the Nightshade family includes 3,000 species spread across 75 genera. Several are familiar foods: potato, tomato, eggplant, bell pepper, chili pepper, and the nutraceutical goji berry. Others, such as petunias, are ornamentals grown for their flowers. Many family members, like datura and belladonna, contain toxic, narcotic alkaloids that are used as pain-relieving medicines or, in the case of tobacco, smoked or chewed recreationally. Because of wild tobacco's central importance to Native American spiritual practices, it is purposely omitted from this book. Please leave wild tobacco stands intact to ensure an ample supply for Indigenous ceremonial use. Grow your own!

## *Datura* genus

All of the approximately thirteen species of *Datura* found worldwide were originally natives of the warmer areas of the Americas. All are poisonous and share a great deal of lore about their spiritual and occult uses. The genus name *Datura* comes from the Sanskit *dhattūra*, meaning "white thorn-apple," referring to the white flowers and spiky fruits.

## SACRED DATURA
### *Datura wrightii*

**Synonym:** *Datura meteloides*
**Other common names:** Western Jimson weed, sacred thornapple, momoy (Chumash), *toloache* (Spanish)
**Origin:** Native
**Range:** Throughout California except the most northerly parts from sea level to 7,200 feet elevation
**Habitat:** Disturbed soil, often sandy or gravelly, in dry, open areas
**Related species in California:** Native desert datura (*D. discolor*) and naturalized jimsonweed, or moonflower (*D. stramonium*)

*Early-season sacred datura (*Datura wrightii*) plant in the author's garden.* LANNY KAUFER

**Related species globally:** Many *Datura* species, including *toloache* (*D. innoxia*), henbane (*Hyoscyamus niger*), belladonna (*Atropa belladonna*), and mandrake (*Mandragora* spp.)
**Conservation status rankings:**
    **IUCN Red List:** Not listed.
    **CNPS Rare Plant Rank:** Not listed
    **NatureServe State Rank:** SNR

**Uses:** Analgesic, for topical pain relief (external use only)
**Parts used:** Leaves and flowers
**Edibility:** All parts are highly toxic to ingest.

## Description

Sacred datura (*Datura wrightii*) is an erect, perennial herb from 1½ to 3 feet tall with widely branching, round, pubescent stems, sometimes tinged reddish purple. The dark green, alternating leaves are ovate to arrowhead shaped, 1½ to 5 inches long, tapering to a point, often with wavy margins. Showy, solitary, night-blooming white flowers uncurl from the leaf axils between April and October and last only one night. They flare out 4 to 8 inches long in a funnel shape, also 4 to 8 inches across, with purple-tinged edges featuring five tendril-like teeth. Nodding, painfully prickly seed capsules are round, 1 to 1½ inches across, and bear many flat, tan seeds, less than ¼ inch in diameter. In colder locations, sacred datura may die

*Closer look at the purplish tinge on stems of sacred datura (*Datura wrightii*).* JESS STARWOOD

back in winter to return again in spring. The leaves smell like peanut butter (yes, really), and the flowers emit a spicy, sweet, and citrusy fragrance reminiscent of the totally unrelated bergamot orange (*Citrus bergamia*). Perhaps they share some aromatic terpenes.

## Conservation Status

Sacred datura is a common plant throughout its range.

## Traditional Uses

Sacred datura and its related species in California and across the country have a long history of medicinal use by Native Americans, primarily as a painkiller and visionary aid. Chumash consultants interviewed by the early twentieth century ethnographer J. P. Harrington said it was one of their people's main medical treatments.

Traditionally, sacred datura was used internally and externally by the Chumash, the Cahuilla, and others for treating the pain of serious injuries and when setting bones. Externally, the Chumash applied crushed leaves as a poultice on hemorrhoids or on aches and pains. The Cahuilla made an ointment with powdered leaves for those purposes and to cure venomous bites. They also steamed the leaves and applied them as a poultice for chest pains or inhaled the vapor for severe bronchial or nasal congestion. The Kawaiisu bathed rheumatic or arthritic limbs in an infusion of mashed or shredded roots.[235] [236] [237] [238] According to Strike, it is used by California Indians "as a tonic, a cathartic, a laxative, a narcotic, a sedative, a hallucinogen, a 'love medicine,' a ceremonial medicine, and a poison."[239]

Sacred datura earned its name from its widespread use among Native Americans as a sacrament in coming-of-age rituals and other ceremonies marking critical life events. Trained shamans use it for divination and other visionary purposes.

## Modern Uses

Poultices and fomentations of fresh datura leaves and flowers are still used today for treating painful joints and swellings. Michael Moore suggests a handful of the fresh or dried plant boiled in a pot of water and added to a hot bath for muscle and joint pain.[240] In *Healing with Medicinal Plants of the West*, Garcia and Adams recommend soaking the hands or feet in a warm sun tea of leaves and flowers for pain relief. (See "Recipes" for instructions.)

*Morning dew on a night-blooming sacred datura flower.* JOSHUA KAPLAN

Small doses of the leaf, root, and extract of sacred datura's closely related cousin *Atropa belladonna* are German Commission E approved for internal use for spasms and colic-like pain in the areas of the gastrointestinal tract and bile ducts. This remedy should not be used without medical supervision.

## Phytochemicals/Mechanisms of Action

All *Datura* species contain powerful tropane alkaloids, varying in amounts among species, individual plants, and within different plant parts. Most notably, scopolamine, hyoscyamine, and atropine are found in high concentrations in the roots of sacred datura and to a lesser degree in the seeds and flowers. The leaves contain large amounts of scopolamine. Applied externally, these alkaloids are able to cross the skin barrier to block muscarinic acetylcholine receptors in the nervous system, resulting in pain relief.

If it enters the bloodstream, scopolamine can cross the blood-brain barrier to the central nervous system, where it can inhibit vomiting, relax bronchial spasms, and dilate the pupils, among other effects. Based on this activity, physicians prescribe scopolamine transdermal patches (known as belladonna patches) for nausea and vomiting associated with motion sickness or postoperative recovery from anesthesia. Gastroenterologists use a safer, altered form of scopolamine to prevent spasms during colonoscopies.

Psychopharmacologists classify *Datura* species as deliriants. Their mix of poisonous, acetylcholine-blocking alkaloids places them in a different class of

Nodding sacred datura seed capsule, still green, with prickles starting to dry out and harden
BRYANT BAKER

Sacred datura flower. JESS STARWOOD

psychoactive plant drugs from nonpoisonous psychedelics or hallucinogens such as peyote (*Lophophora williamsii*) and psilocybin mushrooms, which work on serotonin receptors.

## Cultivation
While many consider it a weed, sacred datura can be a beautiful, fragrant, and exotic garden plant. I started mine from a transplant, but it is easily propagated from seed. In fact, if allowed to reseed, it can rapidly take over your garden.

## Cautions
Despite its long-standing status as a Native American visionary aid or "dream helper," I can't emphasize enough that sacred datura is not a plant for self-experimentation. It should not be ingested in any form unless under the guidance of a trained Indigenous healer. Due to the variability of toxic phytochemicals from plant to plant and the loss of knowledge about how to safely prepare it, everyone should be cautious when considering using this plant. At the least, contact with *Datura* species can cause a rash for those allergic to nightshades. If ingested, larger doses of the compounds in datura can lead to delirium, slowed respiration, increased heart rate, and death. Because scopolamine is very slowly absorbed into the brain, people with slow absorption rates can easily use too much and overdose before they realize it is having an effect.

## Notes
For external use, the leaves and flowers can be harvested in the morning at any point in the flowering season. While best used fresh, they can be dried for future use.

Some archaeologists have long suspected that sacred datura use was somehow involved in the famous cave paintings of the Chumash. A recent DNA study confirmed that quids, or wads, of chewed plant material pushed into cracks in the ceiling of one of these caves were in fact *D. wrightii*. The ceiling features a painting with a striking resemblance to a sacred datura flower about to open.[241]

# NETTLE FAMILY (URTICACEAE)

The Nettle family includes over 2,500 species, including 80 in the genus *Urtica*.

## *Urtica* genus

The stinging nettle genus, *Urtica*, has square stems, opposite leaves, and sting-ing hairs. Three *Urtica* species can be found growing wild in California. They include two native subspecies of giant stinging nettle (*Urtica dioica*) and the invasive, non-native dwarf stinging nettle (*U. urens*). The genus name *Urtica* derives from the Latin *uro* ("to burn").

## GIANT STINGING NETTLE
### *Urtica dioica* subsp.

**Subspecies:** *U. dioica* subsp. *gracilis*: California nettle, American stinging nettle, creek nettle; *U. dioica* subsp. *holosericea*: hoary nettle, creek nettle

**Origin:** Native

**Range:** American stinging nettle found in Northern California only; hoary nettle through-out the state

**Habitat:** Wet places, riparian canyons and creeks

*Leaves of giant stinging nettle (*Urtica dioica subsp. holosericea*) showing trichomes peeking out from stems.* JESS STARWOOD

## DWARF STINGING NETTLE
### *Urtica urens*

**Origin:** Non-native

**Range:** Throughout California

**Habitat:** Disturbed soil, shaded gardens and fields

**Related species in California:** None

**Related species globally:** Several *Urtica dioica* subspecies are found worldwide, including European stinging nettle (*U. dioica* subsp. *dio-ica*). Dwarf stinging nettle (*U. urens*) is native to Europe and naturalized in California.

**Conservation status rankings for U. dioica subspecies:**

> **IUCN Red List:** LC
> **CNPS Rare Plant Rank:** Not listed
> **NatureServe State Rank:** SNR

*Non-native dwarf stinging nettle (*Urtica urens*).* LANNY KAUFER

**Uses:** Mineral supplement, astringent, hemostatic, rubefacient, anti-inflammatory
**Parts used:** Leaves, root
**Edibility:** Leaves edible and highly nutritious

## Description

Our two native California subspecies of giant stinging nettle (*Urtica dioica*) are erect perennial plants. They are often found in wet places with rich soil and can grow to 8 feet tall, with square stems and deeply toothed, dark green leaves 2 to 8 inches long. Equally long clusters of small green flowers bloom in the summer on racemes in the leaf axils. The entire plants, except the flowers, are covered with hollow, stinging hairs called trichomes. There are two subspecies; both are known as giant stinging nettle. American stinging nettle (*U. dioica* subsp. *gracilis*) has oval leaves and is found in Northern California, mostly along the coast. Its range extends north and to much of the United States. Hoary nettle (*U. dioica* subsp. *holosericea*) has lanceolate leaves and is found statewide. In southern California it stays in riparian canyons and other wet places. Both species thrive in soil high in nitrogen.

*Flowering dwarf stinging nettle (*Urtica urens*), past the point for harvesting.* MONIKA SZREK

Dwarf stinging nettle (*U. urens*) is a common, low-growing, annual, non-native weed found statewide below 3,000 feet in shaded yards, gardens, and disturbed soil, especially where there are nitrogen deposits such as manure. The flowering stems generally reach no more than 2 feet high. Its small hairs generally deliver a mild sting compared with giant stinging nettle, although some stingees would disagree. It can be substituted for all nettle uses described below.

## Conservation Status

There are no conservation concerns for either species of *Urtica*.

## Traditional Uses

Giant stinging nettle is widely used by California tribes for food and medicine. Many lightly strike arthritic joints with the stinging branches as a counterirritant. The modern "gate control theory" of pain may explain how the temporary stinging sensation interferes with pain perception. Other Indigenous uses include a leaf tea for colds and internal pain, a root tea to ease menstrual pain or for difficult urination, and a powder of the leaves to stop nosebleeds.

Most native Californians eat young nettle leaves either cooked or raw. The trichomes wilt when cooked, removing the sting. Juanita Centeno, my Chumash teacher, showed me how to eat raw stinging nettles by tightly grasping a young leaf and, while squeezing it, rolling it into a ball between the thumb and first finger and then placing it carefully in between the upper and lower teeth. If done properly, this method crushes the trichomes and renders them harmless.

## Modern Uses

*Midseason patch of giant stinging nettle*
*(Urtica dioica subsp. holosericea)*
LANNY KAUFER

Roy Upton, editor of the *American Herbal Pharmacopoeia*, has published the most complete profile to date on the uses of stinging nettle.[242] He describes its usefulness in lower urinary tract infections and as a nutritional tonic, and he includes recent studies on the use of fresh freeze-dried leaves for treating seasonal allergies. The root is used to reduce symptoms of enlarged prostate gland (benign prostatic hyperplasia, or BPH).

The late herbalists William LeSassier and Michael Moore both recommend nettle tea for internal bleeding, such as in varicose veins, internal hemorrhoids, and excessive menstruation. They also advise drinking the diuretic tea for premenstrual water retention and weight loss. Moore and others praise its ability to increase excretion of uric acid, making it a good choice for treating arthritis, gout, and inflammatory skin conditions, such as the aptly named urticaria (hives).[243] [244]

Pound for pound, nettle leaves rank among the most nutritious foods on the planet, with high quantities of protein, iron, vitamins A and C, and many more vitamins and minerals. Foragers, foodies, and gourmands around the world enjoy eating this superfood juiced, as a steamed vegetable, or blended into soups. Nettle tea makes an excellent broth on which to base a nutritive vegetable soup. (See "Recipes" for an oatstraw and nettle mineral supplement tea.)

## Phytochemicals/Mechanisms of Action

Upton identifies several flavonoids, especially patuletin, as the compounds responsible for the medicinal effects of dried nettle leaves. Acetylcholine and histamine, the active ingredients in the stinging trichomes, show promise in treating allergies when preserved by freeze-drying the fresh leaves.[245] Nettle leaves, fresh or dried, also contain terpenoids, carotenoids, and fatty acids, as well as essential amino acids, chlorophyll, vitamins, tannins, carbohydrates, sterols, and minerals. The roots contain oleanolic acid and sterols. Some of these diverse phytochemicals make nettles active against both Gram-positive and Gram-negative bacteria.[246]

The German Commission E approved drinking nettle leaf tea—along with extra fluid intake—to increase urine flow as part of "irrigation therapy" for inflammation of the lower urinary tract and to prevent and treat kidney stones. Commission E also approved its use as a supportive therapy for arthritis and other rheumatic conditions. One in vitro study showed that nettle leaf extract may have an anti-inflammatory effect on autoimmune diseases like rheumatoid arthritis.[247]

Nettle root is Commission E approved for difficulties in urination resulting in BPH. In treating this condition, the root, decocted as a tea or powdered in capsules, can increase the volume and flow of urine while reducing the residual urine retained in the bladder. Recent clin-

*The needlelike trichomes of American stinging nettle (*Urtica dioica *subsp.* gracilis*) that deliver the sting.* KIM CHISHOLM

ical evidence continues to support its use in treating BPH.[248] [249] On another front, a 2019 study showed that an extract of *U. dioica* inhibited lung cancer cell growth and made the cells more sensitive to the chemotherapy drug cisplatin.[250]

## Cultivation

Stinging nettle plants are hard to find in nurseries, but whole plants or root cuttings can be transplanted to the garden or it can be propagated from seed collected in the fall. A root barrier is recommended to keep it contained. If you have a moist garden with humus-rich soil, chances are that dwarf stinging nettle is already there.

## Cautions

Choose your wild nettle sources carefully, as they like to grow in mining or agricultural runoff, which may be high in the nitrogen that nettle loves but also can be high in heavy metals. Those are poorly processed by the plant and accumulate in the roots over time.

Collect nettle leaves by topping the plants in the spring before they flower. After that point, they develop cystoliths, gritty particles of calcium and silica that can irritate the kidneys.

While it is possible to pick and eat one leaf at a time raw, as described above, unless you have nerves (and skin) of steel, do not attempt to harvest nettles without gloves—you will get stung. The stinging trichomes contain a cocktail of irritating compounds, including histamine and formic acid, which account for the burning rash that results when the tips break off during contact, injecting the irritants into the skin. Formic acid, named for the ant genus *Formica*, is the same chemical responsible for the pain of ant stings. Immersion in cold water and applying the juice of dock leaves (*Rumex* spp.) are common remedies for nettle stings.

*Late season stand of giant stinging nettle (*Urtica dioica *subsp.* holosericea)*, past the point for collecting.* LANNY KAUFER

## Notes

The lactic acid bacteria from fresh nettle leaves can be used as an alternative vegetable "rennet" to replicate the milk curd used in making fresh cheese.[251]

The species name *dioica* means "two houses," as in "dioecious," the botanical term for plants with male and female flowers on separate plants. While this description holds true for the European stinging nettle (*U. dioica* subsp. *dioica*), our native giant nettles and non-native dwarf stinging nettle are "monoecious," with separate male and female flowers on the same plant.

# CALTROP FAMILY (ZYGOPHYLLACEAE)

The Caltrop family includes around 250 species in 27 genera. They are found worldwide in warm, dry regions and often have armed (spiky) seed capsules like the "goatheads" of California's non-native *Tribulus terrestris*. We have one native Californian caltrop, which is, thankfully, unarmed: creosote bush (*Larrea tridentata*).

## *Larrea* genus

The *Larrea* genus consists of five species of evergreen shrubs, all native to the warmer regions of the Americas. The genus was discovered for Europeans in 1800 by a Spanish botanist who named it for another Spanish botanist, Juan Antonio Hernández Pérez de Larrea (1730–1803).

## CREOSOTE BUSH
### *Larrea tridentata*

**Other common names:** Chaparral, *gobernadora* (Spanish)

**Origin:** Native

**Range:** Below 3,300 feet elevation in deserts from Inyo County south to the border

**Habitat:** Alkaline soils in the creosote bush scrub habitat

*Close view of single creosote bush flower with resin visible on entire plant.* JAMES DAVID ADAMS JR.

**Related species in California:** None

**Related species globally:** Chaparral (*L. divaricata*), native to southwestern South America

**Conservation status rankings:**

    **IUCN Red List:** Not listed

    **CNPS Rare Plant Rank:** Not listed

    **NatureServe State Rank:** SNR

**Uses:** Antimicrobial, antifungal, anti-inflammatory; externally for wounds, sores, fungal infections

**Parts used:** Leafy twigs, resin

**Edibility:** Not edible

## Description

Creosote bush (*Larrea tridentata*) is a highly drought-tolerant, evergreen, multibranched woody shrub that can grow up to 12 feet tall but more commonly reaches 5 to 6 feet. It is often equally wide. The older branches are dark reddish brown, while the newer growth is green. The shiny, resinous, opposite, yellowish-green leaves are compound, made up of two leaflets fused at the base. Each

*Creosote bush* (Larrea tridentata). STEVE JUNAK

leaflet is ¼ to ⅔ inch long. They are clustered mainly at the ends of the branches. Five-petaled yellow flowers, ½ to 1 inch wide, appear whenever the plants get enough rain. They mature into fuzzy round capsules less than ½ inch in diameter. Creosote bush's spreading root system creates colonies called clonal rings. One such creosote ring, the "King Clone" in the Mojave Desert, is estimated to be over 11,000 years old, making it one of the oldest living organisms on Earth. Creosote bush does not contain any actual creosote, which is made from coal tar, but it smells like it, hence the name.

## Conservation Status
Creosote bush is a common, often dominant shrub across thousands of square miles of Southwest desert.

## Traditional Uses
Native American tribes of California, Arizona, and Nevada consider creosote bush a powerful healing and cleansing medicine. For internal use, the Cahuilla, Paiute, Shoshone, and Hualapai drink an infusion or decoction of the intensely bitter leaves for colds, lung congestion, and bowel complaints. The Cahuilla, Hualapai, and Pima also inhale the steam for lung congestion and asthma. The Pima drink a decoction of leafy twigs for gas pains or headaches caused by upset stomachs. An infusion is taken for joint pain or rheumatism. They chew and

swallow the plant gum for dysentery and abdominal cramps, and a decoction of the gum is used as a gargle.[252] [253] [254]

For painful joints and limbs, the Diegueño, Kawaiisu, Pima, and Yavapai apply a decoction or heated poultice of the leaves and branches. The Yavapai also use this decoction as a cleansing wash for cuts and sores or sprinkle the dried, powdered leaves on sores. The Pima prepare an infusion of the plant as a wash for impetigo and dandruff and apply a poultice of leaves to scratches, wounds, and sores.[255]

Contemporary Kawaiisu and Tübatulabal make an antibacterial and anti-inflammatory ointment to apply to cuts and burns as well as painful joints, sciatica, or leg and foot cramps. See "Recipes" for Carol Wermuth's Medicinal Ointments (Balms).

## Modern Uses

Creosote bush is best known as "chaparral herb" in the world of herbal commerce. That name is avoided here because of confusion with the California plant community of the same name, a community of which creosote bush is not a part. Creosote bush has been used medicinally across the country and worldwide since settlers of the Desert Southwest first learned of it from Indigenous people. Whatever name you call it, it has a glowing résumé based on its antimicrobial, antifungal, and anti-inflammatory activity. *Larrea tridentata* and its South

*Closer look at creosote bush flowers and fuzzy seed capsules* STEVE JUNAK

American cousin *L. divaricata*, known in Spanish as *chaparral*, are still in use in North American and Mexican herbal practice.

Internally, creosote bush leaf tea is taken for colds, arthritis, and bowel cramps. Externally, it is applied to fungal skin conditions such as athlete's foot, and for bacterial infections. Creosote bush tea is often used as an antiseptic mouthwash and gargle. Unfortunately, as is the case with many of the medicinal herbs in this book, there are no clinical trials that support all these uses. There is only the empirical evidence showing that creosote bush has stood the test of time. That being said, creosote bush and several other plants in this book are listed at KaiserPermanente.org as "herbs that directly attack microbes."[256]

In the 1960s, following an account of a Utah man who cured himself of cancer, the National Cancer Institute studied creosote bush. Due to conflicting results, no official statement was published. There are numerous anecdotal reports of people successfully treating some cancers by drinking an infusion of creosote bush leaves. Such use is beyond the scope of this book.

## Phytochemicals/Mechanisms of Action

Resins make up 20 percent of the leaf mass of creosote bush and provide the phenolic compounds responsible for most of the antioxidant, antimicrobial, antifungal, and anti-inflammatory activity. The key ingredients are polyphenols known as lignans. The main ingredient, nordihydroguaiaretic acid (NGDA), has shown activity against *Salmonella, Streptococcus, Staphylococcus, Pseudomonas*, and other infectious organisms. Creosote bush also contains more than twenty flavonoids, including isorhamnetin, kaempferol, and quercetin, all known to be anti-inflammatory compounds. Volatile oils are also present, containing antimicrobial and pain-relieving terpenes such as calamene, eudesmol, limonene, and pinene.[257]

## Cultivation

Creosote bush roots secrete powerful cytotoxic chemicals to stop competition from other plants. That's not what you need in your garden, is it? Especially when so many thousands of acres of desert are covered with this plant.

## Cautions

In 1993 the American Herbal Products Association (AHPA) and the Food & Drug Administration (FDA) issued warnings about possible liver damage resulting from ingestion of creosote bush products. The AHPA urged distributors to voluntarily suspend sales of the popular herb. The ban was lifted two years later after researchers were unable to find a link.[258] Many herbalists consider it safe as a tea in low doses. The bitterness of the tea is a natural limiting factor in dosage. Still, in light of the eighteen cases of liver toxicity related to creosote bush, any internal use beyond a mild infusion for a short period of time (less than two weeks) should be supervised by a qualified professional. No one with a history of liver disease should ingest it.

NGDA, once widely used as an antioxidant food preservative, has also come under scrutiny over concerns about its effect on the liver. The FDA removed it from the Generally Recognized as Safe (GRAS) list but still allows it in lard and suet to prevent rancidity.

### Notes
The species name *L. tridentata* means "three-toothed" in Latin. This is odd, because the leaves have two leaflets, not three. Its Spanish common name, *gobernadora* ("governess"), derives from its dominion over the desert habitat.

## *Tribulus* genus
The *Tribulus* genus includes about twenty-five species, mostly found in tropical and subtropical regions of the world.

### GOATHEAD
### *Tribulus terrestris*

Thorny, immature goathead (T. terrestris) burs as seen from underside of plant. STEVE JUNAK

**Other common names:** Puncture vine, goat's head, bullhead, little caltrop, *gokshura* (Sanskrit)
**Origin:** Non-native
**Range:** Naturalized throughout warmer regions of the United States
**Habitat:** Dry disturbed areas
**Related species in California:** None
**Conservation status rankings:**
　　**IUCN Red List:** LC
　　**CNPS Rare Plant Rank:** Not listed
　　**NatureServe State Rank:** SNA
**Uses:** Diuretic, anti-inflammatory; reduces cholesterol, excretes uric acid, may improve sexual function
**Parts used:** Whole dried plant, especially fruits (seed capsules)
**Edibility:** Dried, powdered fruits are edible as survival food.

### Description
Thanks to its clingy stickers, this Mediterranean native is an aggressive weed in tropical, subtropical, and temperate zones worldwide. Goathead (*Tribulus terrestris*) is well adapted to dry climates, preferring loose, dry, sandy soil. Yellow flowers bloom June to October, opening in the morning and closing in the

*Goathead (*Tribulus terrestris*) flowers.* STEVE JUNAK

afternoon. Narrow, opposite, hairy compound leaves have six to twelve leaflets. Distinctive spiky fruits, sometimes called burs, are yellow-green when ripe and have several sharp spines, one usually longer than the others. They split into four or five light brown, thorny nutlets when dry.

## Conservation Status

Goathead is an invasive weed. Weevils were introduced to biologically control it in California in 1961. Although goathead can still be found, the effort to eradicate it is considered a success.[259]

## Traditional Uses

Fortunately for California's early inhabitants, who often walked barefoot, there were no puncture vines here until the arrival of Europeans. Goathead, however, has a longtime reputation as a medicinal plant in India and China. In Ayurvedic medicine it's known as *gokshura*. The powdered dried fruits (spiny seed capsules) are combined with other herbs in diuretic formulas for painful urination, urinary tract stones and infections, and prostate problems. It has legendary status in India for treating male sexual dysfunction. It's also used for reducing high cholesterol and hypertension and considered a valuable remedy for helping excretion of uric acid in treating gout, arthritis, and other rheumatic disorders.[260] Chinese herbalists have long used it for heart disease, hypertension, infertility, and impotence.[261]

## Modern Uses

Contemporary herbalist Michael Moore recommends a tea of the whole, dried, powdered plant, including the spiny fruits, for early treatment of elevated blood lipids such as cholesterol and triglycerides that can lead to heart disease. Explaining that uric acid crystals can cause inflammation in the joints, he also uses this herb to reduce uric acid production and as a diuretic to increase its excretion. He recommends small doses, not more than ½ to 1 teaspoon of powdered plant in hot water, taken in the morning and early evening.[262] [263]

Several scientific studies supporting goathead's sterol content and testosterone-boosting abilities in animals led to its inclusion in many over-the-counter products for improving body building results and men's sexual performance. Currently, evidence is conflicting, and more studies are in progress. Stay tuned!

## Phytochemicals/Mechanisms of Action

Goathead contains phytosterols, including diosgenin, a precursor of several hormones. Diosgenin is also found in tropical wild yams (*Dioscorea* spp.). Although more studies are needed, the FDA, the European Food Safety Authority, and Health Canada all conclude that ingesting phytosterols can lower blood cholesterol levels and reduce the risk of heart disease. Goathead leaves and fruits contain several flavonoids, including kaempferol and tribuloside. Kaempferol is a secondary metabolite found in many plants, plant-derived foods, and traditional medicines. It has been shown to have antioxidant and anti-inflammatory activity and may also reduce the risk of cardiovascular and neuroinflammatory diseases.[264]

Several animal studies have shown goathead fruits to be effective in increasing sperm production and enhancing male sexual function. The mechanism of action is still not clear. A 2014 clinical study also found it effective in treating hypoactive sexual desire disorder in women.[265] Studies are ongoing.

## Cultivation

Please do not grow your own goathead plants. Once they escape, your neighbors and every bicyclist for miles around will curse you.

## Cautions

The leaves are toxic to livestock. The fruits can easily puncture the tongues of herbivores or the hands, feet, and bicycle tires of humans. Despite the success of biological control, goathead is still the target of herbicide spraying, so caution is required when harvesting. Be careful not to puncture your skin when collecting the dried seedpods. Keep them contained until you get them home, where you can use whatever electronic or manual tools are at hand to grind them to a powder for immediate or future use.

Goathead is contraindicated in kidney disease, pregnancy, serious cardiovascular disorders, and mild or severe liver disease.

## Notes

A caltrop is an ancient metal device—a forerunner of the modern spike strip—used to deter passage by vehicles, horses, or humans. It has four projecting spikes arranged so that when three of the spikes are on the ground, the fourth points upward to poke a tire, hoof, or foot. *Calcitrapa* and *tribulus* are two Latin words for this device.

In India, flour from the dried seed capsules is made into bread and eaten when other food is scarce.[266]

# RECIPES

## Agua de Manzanita
## (Manzanita/Bearberry Cider)

**Ingredients*:**

½ cup manzanita or bearberry (*Arctostaphylos* spp.) berries, dried and crushed
⅛ cup sugar
4 cups water

**Directions:**

***Note:*** If using bigberry manzanita (*A. glauca*), first crack berries and remove the large seeds. These can be ground to flour for baking or left whole and drilled for necklaces and bracelets.

1. Place ½ cup dried, crushed berries in 4 cups cold water in a covered saucepan. Slowly bring to a boil. Turn off and steep covered for 15–20 minutes.
2. Pour off tea through a strainer, pressing to remove all liquid. (Compost the remaining berries.)
3. Add ⅛ cup sugar. Stir and drink hot, or chill for a cold drink.
4. Refrigerate the remainder. It will keep for 2–3 days.

*The amounts of berries and sugar can be adjusted to your taste.

**Alternative:**

Instead of adding sugar, mix chilled manzanita infusion with equal part apple cider.

To make Agua de Toyon, substitute dried toyon berries (see recipe) for manzanita berries.

## Black Sage Foot Soak

**Ingredients:**

About ¼ pound black sage (*Salvia mellifera*)
About 2 quarts seawater or tapwater

**Directions:**

1. Place black sage leaves and stems in water in a glass jar.*
2. Place jar in the sun for several hours or until the tea is dark green or brown. (Black sage sun tea made with seawater is purple.)
3. Warm the sun tea to body temperature, and soak the feet in the tea for 15–30 minutes.

*Note:* This is very good for arthritis, fibromyalgia, and other aches. (See "Black Sage" chapter for mechanism of action.)

*Purple sage (*S. leucophylla*) or Cleveland sage (*S. clevelandii*) can be substituted for black sage in this recipe. More should be used, as they are not as strong.

—Garcia and Adams, *Healing with Medicinal Plants of the West*

## California Dream Tea

Since mugwort is a very bitter herb and a little goes a long way, it is added separately for a harmonious balance of flavor and medicinal action.

### Ingredients:

1 cup skullcap (*Scutellaria californica*)
1 cup passionflower (*Passiflora* spp.) leaf and flower
½ cup oatstraw (*Avena fatua*)
½ cup pineapple weed (*Matricaria discoidea*) or chamomile (*M. recutita*)
3 leaves mugwort (*Artemisia douglasiana*)
Local raw honey, stevia, or other sweetener, if desired

### Directions:

1. Combine the skullcap, passionflower, oatstraw, and chamomile to create a tea blend. This will be more than a single serving and can be combined and stored to have on hand.
2. Place 1 tablespoon of the combined herbs into a cup (or use a paper or mesh strainer), and pour just-boiled water over the herbs to fill your cup. Allow to steep for 5–7 minutes, covered.
3. Add the mugwort leaves and stir, cover; continue steeping for 3–4 minutes longer.
4. Strain all herbs; sweeten and enjoy before bedtime.

—Recipe by Jess Starwood

## California Poppy Tincture

### Ingredients:

3 ounces dried California poppy (*Eschscholzia californica*) leaf and flower
16 ounces high-proof alcohol (95 percent, such as Everclear, is ideal)

**Directions:**

1. Combine the dried California poppy with the alcohol in a high-speed blender and process roughly. (***Note:*** You can combine them in a jar without blending, but blending helps increase the surface area of the constituents to infuse into the alcohol.)
2. Pour the combined mixture, known as the menstruum, into a glass jar with a tight-fitting lid. Keep this jar in a cool, dark place for 4–6 weeks, shaking occasionally.
3. After this time, the tincture is ready to be strained. Pour the contents through a muslin cloth, and squeeze out any remaining liquid into a clean jar. This is your final tincture. Discard or compost the spent plant material.
4. Seal your jar of California poppy tincture or decant into smaller 1- or 2-ounce bottles; label.

—RECIPE BY JESS STARWOOD

## Candied Wild Fennel Seeds

A tasty post-meal breath freshener and digestive aid or a sweet snack. Inspired by classic Indian *saunf mukhwas*, using the seeds of the invasive wild fennel.

**Ingredients:**

2 tablespoons raw cane sugar
2 tablespoons date sugar
3 tablespoons water
$1/3$ cup dried wild fennel (*Foeniculum vulgare*) seeds

**Directions:**

1. Combine cane and date sugar and water in a small pot; bring to a boil. Stir continuously as the sugar breaks down, turns into a syrup, and bubbles.
2. Reduce heat and add wild fennel seeds. Stir to coat the seeds evenly with the sugar until it crystalizes and dries. Allow to cool.
3. Store in an airtight container. Enjoy as needed after meals.

—RECIPE BY JESS STARWOOD

## Chaparral Cold, Flu, and Fever Tea

***Note:*** This makes more than a single serving; the ingredients can be combined and stored to have on hand.

**Ingredients:**

1 cup dried elderflowers (*Sambucus* spp.)
1 cup black sage (*Salvia mellifera*) leaves
½ cup yarrow (*Achillea millefolium*) flowers and leaves*
½ cup dried elderberries (*Sambucus* spp.)
Local raw honey, stevia, or other sweetener, as needed

**Directions:**

1. Combine all herbs in a glass jar that can be sealed tightly.
2. Place 1 tablespoon of the herbs in a tea sachet or metal strainer, and place in cup. Pour just-boiled water over herbs to fill cup and allow to steep for 10 minutes.
3. Strain and sweeten to taste.

*For a less-bitter and casual everyday chaparral-inspired herbal tea, omit or use less of the yarrow.

—Recipe by Jess Starwood

## Cough Formula Tincture

**Ingredients:**

2 ounces dried wild cherry (*Prunus* spp.) bark
2 ounces dried grindelia (*Grindelia* spp.) flowering tops
2 ounces fresh yerba santa (*Eriodictyon* spp.) leaf (or 1 ounce dried)
½ ounce dried licorice (*Glycyrrhiza glabra*) root
7 fluid ounces vegetable glycerin
4 fluid ounces high-proof alcohol

**Directions:**

1. Chop all herbs coarsely by hand or pulse in a blender along with the glycerin and alcohol.
2. Combine all ingredients in a mason jar and allow to macerate for 4–6 weeks, shaking occasionally.
3. Strain and decant into dropper bottles.

—Recipe by Jess Starwood

## Desert Love Tea Blend

*Note:* This makes more than a single serving; the ingredients can be combined and stored to have on hand.

### Ingredients:

1 cup dried damiana (*Turnera diffusa*) leaf
½ cup dried and crushed prickly-pear (*Opuntia* spp.) fruit
½ cup dried purple sage (*Salvia leucophylla*) leaf
¼ cup dried licorice (*Glycyrrhiza glabra*) root
¼ cup dried ginger (*Zingiber officinale*) root

### Directions:

1. Combine all herbs in a glass jar that can be sealed tightly.
2. Fill a tea sachet or metal strainer with the herb mixture and place in cup. Pour just-boiled water over herbs to fill your cup and allow to steep for 10 minutes.
3. Strain and sweeten to taste.

—RECIPE BY JESS STARWOOD

## Dried Toyon Berries

Between mid-December and the end of January, preferably before too much rain can cause mildew or the birds have gotten them, harvest red ripe toyon berries (*Heteromeles arbutifolia*). Taste for flavor and sweetness before choosing bunches to harvest.

### Directions:

1. Separate berries from stems; rub between hands to remove remaining stems.
2. Wash thoroughly in cold water, discarding any black or otherwise unpalatable berries.
3. Dry berries in a dehydrator, in the sun, or in the oven on pilot light (for gas) or lowest setting (for electric) for several hours or until dry but still slightly chewy. Drying time can vary considerably depending on heat source, probably about 7–8 hours in a dehydrator.
4. Store berries in a paper bag until you're sure they are dry (no residual moisture), then transfer to an airtight jar. Check the jar for moisture for the first few days.
5. Store jar in a cool, dark place. Dried berries will retain flavor and medicinal value for 2 years if stored properly.

*Note:* These berries can be substituted for manzanita berries in the recipe for Agua de Manzanita.

### Elderberry Glycerite Recipe

This glycerite is an excellent tool to use at the first sign of a cold or flu. It also makes a good cough syrup.

**Ingredients:**

2 ounces dried elderberries (*Sambucus* spp.), pulsed in blender or dedicated coffee mill
10 ounces glycerin–distilled water mixture (7.5 ounces glycerin plus 2.5 ounces distilled water)

**Directions:**

1. Weigh and then grind the elderberries in either a coffee mill or blender. Smaller particles are better, as they create more surface for the glycerin (or alcohol if you are making an alcohol extract) to pull from. The result will be a moderately coarse powder.
2. Place the powder in a glass jar.
3. Measure the glycerin and water into a separate glass container. Stir until well mixed.
4. Add liquid to the powdered elderberries. Stir carefully until well mixed.
5. Use a clean paper towel to wipe the rim of the jar if any of the mixture has gotten on it. Cover with wax paper and then screw the lid on tightly. Label with name of preparation, date, and ingredients.
6. Place jar in a spot where you will notice it. Keep it cool and out of direct sunlight. Shake 1–2 times a day for 2–4 weeks. (This is a good time to direct positive thoughts to your blend.)
7. Strain. Because this is a pretty viscous solution, I find it easier to use two strainers to filter it. First use a medium-weave strainer and then strain again with a fine-weave strainer.
8. Bottle in a dark glass bottle. Label well.

—Recipe by Carol Wade

### Elderberry Immune Syrup

**Ingredients:**

16 ounces spring water
1 cup dried elderberries (*Sambucus* spp.)
½ cup dried elderflowers (*Sambucus* spp.)

2 tablespoons dried ginger (*Zingiber officinale*) root
4 ounces brandy
1 lemon, juiced
16 ounces honey, preferably raw and local

**Directions:**

1. Heat water in a sturdy pot just to boiling. Add ginger (and any other immune-boosting root herbs such as astragalus or echinacea); allow to simmer for 10–15 minutes.
2. Turn off heat. Add elderberries and elderflowers; cover with a lid and let cool to room temperature.
3. Add brandy; allow to infuse for 8 hours.
4. Strain out herbs, reserving liquid. If possible, use a fruit press or a fine mesh cloth to squeeze all remaining liquid from the herbs.
5. Add lemon juice and enough honey to equal the final amount of liquid.

*This elderberry syrup is shelf-stable for 6 months but should be refrigerated if exposed to air after bottling. ***Dosage:*** 1–3 teaspoons per day during cold/flu season as a preventative; ½ teaspoon hourly during acute illness.

—RECIPE BY JESS STARWOOD

## Herbal Steam Inhalation

Steam inhalation is a widely used home treatment for congestion in the upper respiratory tract. Inhaling warm water vapor can loosen phlegm and relieve inflammation and swelling. You may feel your nasal passages and sinuses open up immediately, allowing for normal breathing.

Teas of yerba santa (*Eriodictyon* spp.), eucalyptus, cedars (*Calocedrus decurrens* or *Thuja plicata*), creosote bush (*Larrea tridentata*), junipers, pines, white and other sages (*Salvia* spp.), sagebrushes (*Artemisia* spp.), and other aromatic and antibacterial herbs can be used in place of plain water in steam inhalation therapy for upper respiratory conditions, including colds, flus, bronchitis, sinus infections, and allergies causing sinus congestion. They may even help combat an infection.

Sages and sagebrushes should always be prepared as standard infusions for steaming in proportions of 1 teaspoon to 1 cup boiled water for 10–15 minutes. The other more-resinous herbs can be infused for 20 minutes or more or lightly decocted to release the aromatic steam. (See individual plant chapters for more information on their preparations.) You can experiment to find the proportions and method that provide the best steaming result for you.

**Directions:**

1. Have a bath towel on hand.
2. Carefully remove the pan from the stove and place on a pot holder on a table or countertop. Lift the lid to allow the first blast of steam to escape without scalding your face.
3. Lean over the pan, and drape the towel over your head and shoulders and around the pan.
4. Inhale deeply, preferably through your nose, if possible. Continue slow deep breathing for 15 minutes, or until there is no more steam.

*Note:* The liquid can be reheated for use throughout the day. Fresh tea should be made the next day, if needed.

*Caution:* Be very careful handling the container of hot liquid to avoid burning or scalding.

## Horehound Cough Syrup

**Ingredients:**

1 ounce dried or 3 ounces fresh horehound (*Marrubium vulgare*) leaves, with flowers if available
1 pint water
2 cups granulated organic sugar

**Directions:**

1. Prepare a strong infusion by pouring just-boiled water over horehound in a lidded vessel. Steep, covered, for 30 minutes.
2. Strain liquid into a glass or stainless-steel saucepan. Compost the herb.
3. Add sugar and heat, uncovered, over a low flame, stirring occasionally, until the sugar is dissolved and liquid is a syrupy consistency. Add more sugar to thicken, if needed.
4. The syrup can be stored in the refrigerator in a mason jar or stoppered bottle for quite some time. Take 1 teaspoon as needed for coughs.

*Note:* This is an expectorant syrup to help move phlegm out of the lungs. See the Wild Cherry Cough Syrup recipe for a sedative syrup to calm the cough reflex.

## Hummingbird Sage Chocolate Tea for Anxiety

**Ingredients:**

2 leaves hummingbird sage (*Salvia spathacea*), fresh or dried
2 wedges Ibarra Mexican chocolate
1 cup (8 ounces) water*

**Directions:**

1. Place chocolate in cold water and bring just to boiling in a covered saucepan.
2. Turn off heat and whisk mixture to dissolve remaining sugar.
3. Add hummingbird sage leaves; steep, covered, for 10 minutes.

* Milk can be used in place of water.

—Recipe by James D. Adams Jr., adapted from Garcia and Adams, *Healing with Medicinal Plants of the West*

## Medicinal Ointments (Balms)

This recipe can be used with creosote bush (*Larrea tridentata*), cedar (*Calocedrus decurrens* or *Thuja plicata*), grindelia (*Grindelia* spp.), juniper (*Juniperus* spp.), mugwort (*Artemisia douglasiana*), pine (*Pinus* spp.), and other aromatic herbs.

*Note:* Always make an offering before gathering.

1. Gather plants to be used; any poulticing herb can be made into an ointment.
2. Dry plants well; if you don't, ointments will mold.
3. Crumble or chop dried plants and pack into a 1-quart jar, leaving at least 1 inch of space at the top.
4. Fill jar with extra virgin olive oil to within ½ inch of top, making sure to cover all plant material. Seal tightly with lid; label with ingredients, and date.
5. Steep in olive oil for 3 weeks, shaking jar each day and marking on calendar when finished.
6. Strain plant material and oil through cheesecloth, strainer, or jelly bag, and measure infused oil in ounces.
7. Place infused oil in a slow cooker, divide ounces of oil by 4 or 5 (according to texture of ointment desired). Measure one-fourth or one-fifth of amount in beeswax and add to oil in slow cooker (example: 24 ounces of oil needs 6 ounces of beeswax).
8. Place slow cooker on low. Heat until beeswax is completely melted, stirring occasionally; pour into jars. (Jars need not be sterilized if they are new or washed well.)
9. Wipe rims of jars with a paper towel; seal tightly. When cool, clean jars with alcohol and label.

*Note:* Ointments have a shelf life of about 1 year.

I dedicate my learning and knowledge to my teacher and mentor, Rose Barneche, Kawaiisu.

—RECIPE BY CAROL WERMUTH

### Milky Oats Tincture

Harvest oat seeds when they are in the "milky" stage of development. This means that when the seed is gently squeezed, it exudes a white liquid.

**Ingredients:**

8 ounces fresh milky oat seed (*Avena fatua*)
16 fluid ounces high-proof alcohol (95 percent, such as Everclear, is ideal)

**Directions:**

1. Combine the milky oats with the alcohol in a high-speed blender; process roughly. (***Note:*** You can combine them in a jar without blending, but blending helps to increase the surface area of the constituents to infuse into the alcohol.)
2. Pour the combined mixture, known as the menstruum, into a glass jar with a tight-fitting lid. Keep this jar in a cool, dark place for 4–6 weeks, shaking occasionally.
3. After this time, the tincture is ready to be strained. Pour the contents through a muslin cloth and squeeze out any remaining liquid into a clean jar. This is your final tincture. Discard or compost the spent plant material.
4. Seal your jar of milky oat tincture or decant into smaller 1- or 2-ounce bottles; label.

—RECIPE BY JESS STARWOOD

### Nopal (Prickly-Pear) Cactus Smoothie

(***Note:*** "Nopal" is pronounced no-PAHL.)

**Ingredients:**

1 nopal (prickly-pear) cactus (*Opuntia* spp.) pad, cleaned, rinsed, and diced
1 orange, peeled and diced

1 green apple, diced
2 kale leaves, diced
2 celery stalks, diced
⅓ bunch parsley, diced
⅓ bunch mint, diced
2 cups chilled water
1 cup ice
1 slice lime

*Optional:* Small piece fresh ginger, finely diced, to taste

**Directions:**

1. Place diced nopal pad in blender with water; blend.
2. Add diced apple and orange; blend.
3. Add diced kale, celery, and parsley; blend.
4. Add finely diced ginger, if desired.
5. Add additional water to taste if the smoothie is too thick for you. Serve chilled with ice. Use lime to taste. **Do not add sugar.**

If you're not accustomed to a lot of fiber in your normal diet, this drink may have a laxative effect. Start with ½ cup 3 times a day at first and increase to 1½ cups 2 times a day. Enjoy!

**Important Tips**

Use kitchen tongs to hold the nopal pad while harvesting and processing.

Place the cactus pad on a paper plate for trimming. Using a sharp knife (preferably serrated), trim off the top and bottom. Trim the edge around the pad. Scrape off the spines, areoles, and glochids by running your knife from top to bottom until completely clean. Turn the cactus pad over and do the same on the other side. (**Note:** Some people use a potato peeler. I have tried it; it works. However, as with many things in life, it comes down to preference.)

Rinse the cactus pad. Ensure all glochids are removed. You may skip this step by buying bags of prepared, precut pads. However, inspect carefully to ensure freshness.

—Recipe by Enrique Villaseñor

## Oatstraw and Nettle Leaf Mineral Supplement Tea

This herb blend is high in essential, biologically available minerals such as calcium, silicon, iron, and magnesium, among many others.

**Ingredients:**

1 heaping tablespoon dried, finely cut, or ground, green wild oats (*Avena fatua*) stems and flowering tops *
1 heaping tablespoon crumbled stinging nettle (*Urtica* spp.) leaf
24 ounces water, boiled
1-quart mason jar

**Directions:**

*If using your own harvested and hand-cut oatstraw, run it quickly through a blender or dedicated coffee grinder to expose more surface area for infusing.

1. Pour just-boiled water over herbs in mason jar; secure lid tightly. Steep 20–30 minutes, swirling ingredients a couple times.
2. Strain herbs, and return tea to jar. Compost herbs.
3. Refrigerate tea and drink freely, warmed up or cold, throughout the day.

### Pinyon Pine Salve

**Ingredients:**

2–3 ounces pinyon pine (*Pinus monophylla*) resin
8 fluid ounces jojoba oil
1–1½ ounces beeswax granules
1 ounce shea butter

**Directions:**

1. Combine the pinyon pine resin with the oil in a canning jar, and set on a cheesecloth in a nonreactive pot filled with 2–3 inches of water.
2. Heat the water to a low simmer, but do not allow the water to boil. This will dissolve the resin to combine with the oil, a process that may take a few hours. Keep an eye on the level of the water; add more as it evaporates.
3. Once the resin and oil are combined, sift out any debris that may have been stuck in the resin (pine needles, bark, dirt). While it is still warm, and keeping it in the water bath, add the beeswax and shea butter. Stir until melted.
4. Test the consistency of the salve by dipping a spoon into the liquid and briefly placing it in the freezer to cool quickly. If the mixture is too hard, add more jojoba oil. If the mixture is liquid and runny even when cooled, add more beeswax. Adjust to desired consistency.
5. Pour into salve tins or desired containers and allow to cool.

*Note:* Other pine resins can be substituted for pinyon, though the pinyon contributes a nice scent.

—Recipe by Jess Starwood

## Poison Oak Liniment

*Caution: For External Use Only*

**Indications:** Poison oak rash, contact dermatitis, weeping eczema, hot-itchy-damp rashes, insect bites

**Avoid:** Skin around eyes, sensitive tissues

**Ingredients:**

1 ounce dried or 3 ounces fresh of each of the following herbs (can combine dried with fresh, depending on seasonal availability):
    Gumplant (*Grindelia camporum* or *G. hirsutula*) leaves and flowers
    Yarrow (*Achillea millefolium*) leaves and flowers
    Southern California black walnut (*Juglans californica*) green husks
    Mugwort or sagebrush Artemisia (any species of mugwort or sagebrush) leaves
10 fluid ounces 40 percent (80 proof) alcohol, such as vodka
¼ fluid ounce myrrh tincture
½ teaspoon menthol crystals or 10 drops peppermint essential oil

**Directions:**

1. Grind herbs coarsely (dedicated coffee grinder or by hand with pruning shears).
2. Fill clean 1-quart mason jar almost to the top, leaving at least 1 inch for alcohol to cover herbs.
3. Cover with alcohol. Shake well to cover all herb material.
4. Store out of direct light and heat (i.e., a cupboard) for 4 weeks. Shake daily to coat herbs in alcohol.
5. Strain liquid through cheesecloth or muslin; discard or compost herbs.
6. Add myrrh tincture and menthol crystals or peppermint essential oil. Shake well.
7. Store in a dark glass bottle and label: "External Use Only."

*To use:* Apply liniment with cotton cosmetic pads to affected areas, every 4 hours for 1–4 days, to dry and cool rash-affected skin.

—Recipe by Amanda McQuade Crawford

## Rejuvenating Herbal Bath Soak

**Ingredients:**

4 cups water
¼ cup dried coastal sagebrush (*Artemisia californica*) leaves
¼ cup dried mugwort (*Artemisia douglasiana*) leaves
3 tablespoons dried white sage leaves (*Salvia apiana*)
1 cup Epsom salts
6 drops organic lavender essential oil

**Directions:**

1. In a small pot, bring water to a boil; turn off heat.
2. Add dried herbs; cover and let steep for 30 minutes.
3. Strain herbs using a tea strainer. Compost herbs in the garden.
4. Fill tub with hot water. Add Epsom salts, strained herbal tea infusion, and lavender essential oil.
5. Breathe in 10 deep, peaceful breaths, and enjoy your rejuvenating body soak.

—RECIPE BY LAURA PASETTA

## Sacred Datura Soak

**Ingredients:**

7 leaves sacred datura (*Datura wrightii*)
2 quarts seawater or tap water

**Directions:**

1. Place sacred datura leaves in seawater or tap water. (If the flowers are available, put in 7 flowers as well.) Place this in the sun for 2 or 3 days, until the sun tea turns brown.
2. Warm the sun tea to body temperature and use to soak hands and/or feet.

Scopolamine from the sun tea crosses the skin, inhibits muscarinic receptors, and is a powerful pain reliever. This is a useful recipe for people who are sore from working too hard or who suffer from arthritis pain. Scopolamine is not an NSAID, so it does not cause ulcers. It is not an opioid, and it's not addictive. ***Caution:*** If ingested, scopolamine is toxic at high doses and causes respiratory depression. Do *not* drink the sun tea.

—GARCIA AND ADAMS, *HEALING WITH MEDICINAL PLANTS OF THE WEST*

# Sagebrush Liniment

**Ingredients:**

Handful (about ½ pound) coastal sagebrush (*Artemisia californica*) leaves and stems
70 percent isopropyl alcohol or tequila to cover
1 or more crushed or diced avocado seeds (depending on their size) to provide
    a natural oil source
1 leaf white sage (*Salvia apiana*)

**0Directions:**

1. Place avocado seed and white sage leaf at bottom of a 1-quart canning jar.
   Pack coastal sagebrush into the jar. Cover with isopropyl alcohol or tequila.
2. Allow mixture to extract for 6 weeks in the dark.
3. Strain liquid from plant material and store in a brown bottle with a warning
   label.

**To use:** The solution can be applied directly to the skin or transferred to a spray
bottle and sprayed on the skin to relieve pain, swelling, and muscle cramps.

*Caution:* **Do *not* drink this preparation—it contains thujone, which can be
toxic to the kidneys when taken internally. It can be made with any clear
70% alcohol but preparing it with isopropyl alcohol will be a deterrent to
accidental ingestion.**

—JAMES D. ADAMS JR. (ADAPTED FROM GARCIA AND ADAMS,
*HEALING WITH MEDICINAL PLANTS OF THE WEST*)

# St. John's Wort Infused Topical Oil

**Ingredients:**

1 part St. John's wort (*Hypericum* spp.) flowers and buds
2 parts jojoba oil

**Directions:**

1. Fill a clean 1-quart jar with the flowers, almost to the top.
2. Pour enough of the jojoba oil over the flowers to cover them. Stir well, making
   sure the flowers are submerged under the oil. (Anything that ends up sticking
   out of the oil during the infusion process is subject to mold and spoiling.)
3. Seal with a tight-fitting lid; place in a cool, dark place for 2 weeks. Check on it
   frequently to shake and make sure no plant matter is sticking up out of the oil.

4. After 2 weeks, strain the oil from the flowers; reserve. Compost or discard the plant material.
5. Seal your jar of oil, or decant into smaller bottles for use. If oil is kept in a cool, dark place, it should be good for 6–8 months.

—Recipe by Jess Starwood

## Soothing Yerba Mansa Sore Throat Gargle

**Ingredients:**

2 cups water
1 tablespoon dried and chopped yerba mansa (*Anemopsis californica*) root
2 tablespoons dried calendula (*Calendula officinalis*) flowers
1 tablespoon dried plantain (*Plantago* spp.) leaf
½ teaspoon dried and chopped licorice root (*Glycyrrhiza glabra*)

**Directions:**

1. Combine yerba mansa root* and water in a saucepan. Cover and bring to a boil. Reduce heat and simmer for 20 minutes, covered.
2. Remove from heat and add rest of ingredients. Allow to steep, covered, for 20 minutes.
3. Strain mixture. (The strained herb matter can be composted.)

**To use:** Use cooled liquid/tea as a gargle 2–3 times a day. This gargle can also be used for aphthous stomatitis mouth ulcers (canker sores).

*For excellent directions for drying yerba mansa root, see the monograph of yerba mansa in Michael Moore's *Medicinal Plants of the Desert and Canyon West*.

—Recipe by Carol Wade

## Spring Sinus Herbal Infusion

This recipe makes more than a single serving; the herbs can be combined and stored to have on hand.

**Ingredients:**

2 cups dried stinging nettle (*Urtica dioica*) leaf
1 cup dried elder (*Sambucus* spp.) flower

1 cup dried ephedra (*Ephedra* spp.) stems
¼ cup dried licorice (*Glycyrrhiza glabra*) root
Spring water

**Directions:**

1. Combine all herbs into a glass jar that can be sealed tightly.
2. Bring a pot of spring water to boil while you combine ½ cup of the herb mixture in a pint jar. Pour the just-boiled water over the herbs to fill the jar; cover and allow to steep for 30 minutes.
3. Strain mixture into your teacup. Any extra can be reserved in the refrigerator, but it should be consumed within 24 hours.

—Recipe by Jess Starwood

## Toyon Persimmon Bars

**Ingredients:**

1½ cups flour (sprouted wheat or all purpose)
1 teaspoon ground cinnamon
1 teaspoon ground nutmeg
½ teaspoon ground cloves
½ teaspoon salt
1½ cups persimmon pulp
1 teaspoon baking soda
1 egg
⅓ cup brown sugar
½ cup oil (avocado, coconut, or extra virgin olive oil will work)
½ to 1 cup dried and rehydrated toyon berries (plump the dried berries in a bowl of water for 10 minutes, strain off water)
1 cup nuts (black or English walnuts, or chopped, leached, and roasted acorns)

**Directions:**

1. Lightly grease a 9 in. x 13 in. glass pan or a 10 in. x 15 in. jelly roll pan.
2. Preheat oven to 350 degrees.
3. Combine flour, cinnamon, nutmeg, cloves, and salt in a mixing bowl.
4. Stir together persimmon pulp and baking soda in mixing bowl.
5. Stir together egg, brown sugar, oil, and toyon berries in mixing bowl.
6. Fold in nuts.

7. Spread batter in prepared pan and bake in preheated oven for 20 minutes. Remove from oven and insert a toothpick in the middle. If it comes out dry, it's done. If not, return to oven and test again every 5 minutes until toothpick is dry. Length of time may be a little longer with the 9 in. x 13 in. pan because it will not be spread as thin as a jelly roll pan.
8. Once out of oven, cut into 1- or 2-inch squares.

*Note:* If you want the bars to be sweeter, combine ¼ cup powdered sugar and 2 tablespoons lemon juice and spread the baked, slightly cooled bars with this glaze before cutting into squares:

—Recipe by Helen Sweany

## Usnea Antibacterial Double Extraction

Extraction of the medicinal constituents of lichens requires a two-step process, as they are mutualistic organisms composed of both an alga and a fungus. In order to extract the medicinal polysaccharides from the fungal component, it needs to be heated in water for a length of time; the constituents of the alga are alcohol soluble.

### Ingredients:

5 ounces usnea lichen (*Usnea* spp.)
12 ounces spring water
12 ounces organic high-proof cane alcohol (95 proof)

### Directions:

1. Chop and grind usnea as finely as possible. Some strands of the interior "cord" structure will remain.
2. Combine herb with spring water in a slow cooker or in the oven at the lowest setting, covered, for 8–12 hours. Remove from heat, and allow to cool completely.
3. Combine the water-and-herb mixture in a glass mason jar with the organic cane alcohol; seal with a lid and shake well. Allow to macerate for 4–6 weeks.
4. Strain and decant into dropper bottles.

—Recipe by Jess Starwood

## White Sage Water

The best way to use white sage is to put it in the water a patient drinks. Simply put an entire leaf in the water bottle the patient drinks from. Water bottles typically contain about 1 liter of water. Allow the leaf to flavor the water over the next 30 minutes or so before allowing the patient to drink the water. The leaf can be reused for 4 refillings of the bottle. The water may develop a slight sage flavor and smell. Use the leaf for only 1 day. After 1 day the leaf will start to degrade. Another way to use white sage is to put ½ leaf in the mouth and suck on it. The leaf will fill the mouth with sage flavor and soothe the throat.

—James D. Adams Jr. and Cecilia Garcia.
"Traditional Chumash Healing." *Wilderness Way*,
vol. 12, issue 4. abeduspress.com/files
/WildernessWay12_4_2006aGeneral.pdf

## Wild Cherry Cough Syrup

**Ingredients:**

1 ounce dried and powdered or finely cut wild cherry (*Prunus* spp.) bark
1 pint water
2 cups granulated organic sugar

**Directions:**

1. Prepare an infusion by pouring just-boiled water over wild cherry bark in a lidded vessel. Steep covered for 15 minutes.
2. Strain liquid into a glass or stainless-steel saucepan. (Compost or discard the herb.) Add sugar and heat, uncovered, over a very low flame, stirring occasionally, until the sugar is dissolved and liquid is a syrupy consistency. Add more sugar to thicken, if needed.
3. Store syrup in the refrigerator in a mason jar or stoppered bottle. It will keep for quite some time.

**To use:** Take 1 teaspoon as needed for coughs.

*Note:* This is a cough suppressant syrup intended to sedate the cough reflex. See Horehound Cough Syrup recipe for an expectorant syrup to help remove phlegm from the lungs and bronchioles.

# ENDNOTES

## Introduction
1. Lanny Kaufer, "Lanny's Teachers (R.I.P)," HerbWalks.com.
2. Kaufer, "Lanny's Teachers (R.I.P)."

## A Brief History of Medicinal Herbs in America
1. Karen Hardy et al. (2012), "Neanderthal medics? Evidence for food, cooking, and medicinal plants entrapped in dental calculus," in *Die Naturwissenschaften*, vol. 99(8): 617–26.
2. Thomas P. Duffy, "The Flexner Report—100 Years Later," in *The Yale Journal of Biology and Medicine*, 84(3): 269–76.
3. Paul C. Mangelsdorf, "Introduction," in *Plants in the Development of Modern Medicine*, ed. Tony Swain (Cambridge, MA: Harvard University Press, 1972).
4. Roy Upton (ed.) et al., *American Herbal Pharmacopoeia: Botanical Pharma-cognosy—Microscopic Characterization of Botanical Medicines* (Boca Raton, FL: CRC Press, 2011).

## Sustainable Collecting
1. California Native Plant Society, "Inventory of Rare and Endangered Plants of California" (2021). Online edition, v8–03 0.39.
2. California Penal Code, "Crimes Against the Public Health and Safety." California penal code section 384a.
3. Jacque Tahuka Nunez, personal communication.

## Native Plant Conservation
1. International Union for Conservation of Nature and Natural Resources, "The IUCN Red List of Threatened Species," 2020–3.
2. California Native Plant Society, "Inventory of Rare and Endangered Plants of California."
3. NatureServe, "Explorer."
4. United Plant Savers, "Species At-Risk" list.

## Preparing Herbal Home Remedies
1. Michael Moore, *Herbal Tinctures in Clinical Practice*, third edition (1996), Southwest School of Botanical Medicine.

## How to Use This Guide
1. University of California, Berkeley, "The Jepson Herbarium."
2. Peter Ommundsen, "Pronunciation of Biological Latin" (Salt Spring Island, BC: Cape West Publishing).

3. Daniel E. Moerman, *Native American Medicinal Plants: An Ethnobotanical Dictionary* (Portland, OR: Timber Press, 2009).

4. Native American Ethnobotany Database.

5. Michael Moore, 1989, 2003, 1993.

6. Cecilia Garcia & James D. Adams, Jr., *Healing with Medicinal Plants of the West: Cultural and Scientific Basis for Their Use*, third edition revised (La Crescenta, CA: Abedus Press, 2016).

7. California Native Plant Society, "CalScape."

## LICHENS

1. Moerman, 2009.

2. American Botanical Council, Herbal Medicine: Expanded Commission E Monographs.

3. Christopher Hobbs, *Usnea: The Herbal Antibiotic* (Capitola, CA: Botanica Press, 1986).

4. Kaiser Permanente, "St. John's Wort," Kaiser Foundation Health Plan of Washington (2015).

5. American Botanical Council. Herbal Medicine: Expanded Commission E Monographs.

6. Bhaskar Behera et al. (2009), "Optimization of Culture Conditions for Lichen *Usnea ghattensis* G. Awasthi to Increase Biomass and Antioxidant Metabolite Production," *Food Technology and Biotechnology*, 47.

## GYMNOSPERMS

1. Victor K. Chesnut, *Plants Used by the Indians of Mendocino County, California* (US Government Printing Office, 1902).

2. Wendy Applequist & Daniel Moerman, "Yarrow (*Achillea millefolium* L.): A Neglected Panacea? A Review of Ethnobotany, Bioactivity, and Biomedical Research." *Economic Botany* (2011), 65:209–25.

3. Percy Train et al., *Medicinal Uses of Plants by Indian Tribes of Nevada*, revised edition (US Department of Agriculture, 1957).

4. S. A. Barrett & E. W. Gifford, "Miwok Material Culture," in *Bulletin of the Public Museum of the City of Milwaukee*, vol. 2, no. 4 (1933).

5. Applequist & Moerman (2011).

6. Michael Moore, *Medicinal Plants of the Pacific West* (Santa Fe, NM: Red Crane Books, 1993).

7. Sheeba Veluthoor et al., "Composition of the heartwood essential oil of incense cedar (*Calocedrus decurrens* Torr.)," *Holzforschung* 65 (2011).

8. Robert Adams et al., "The Leaf Essential Oils of the Genus *Calocedrus*," *Journal of Essential Oil Research*, 18(6) (October 2006): 654–58.

9. Anna Lis et al., "Chemical Composition of the Essential Oils From Twigs, Leaves, and Cones of *Thuja Plicata* and Its Cultivar Varieties 'Fastigiata,' 'Kornik,' and 'Zebrina,'" *Natural Product Communications* (July 2019).

10. Malini A. Prasad et al. "Leveraging phytochemicals: the plant phylogeny predicts sources of novel antibacterial compounds." *Future Science OA*, vol. 5, 7, FSO407 (25 July 2019).

11. Sandra S. Strike, *Ethnobotany of the California Indians, vol. 2: Aboriginal uses of California's indigenous plants* (Champaign, IL: Koeltz Scientific Books, 1994).

12. Thomas R. Garth, *Atsugewi Ethnography*, "Anthropological Records" 14(2):140–41, 140 (1953).

13. Cephas L. Bard, "A Contribution to the History of Medicine in Southern California," *Journal of California and Great Basin Anthropology*, vol. 26, no. 1 (2006), 95–108.

14. John Bruno Romero, *The Botanical Lore of the California Indians* (New York: Vantage Press, 1954), accessed at Project Gutenberg.

15. Barbara R. Bocek, "Ethnobotany of Costanoan Indians, California, Based on Collections by John P. Harrington," *Economic Botany* 38, no. 2 (1984), 240–55.

16. Train et al., 1957.

17. Applequist & Moerman, 2011.

18. Michael Moore, *Medicinal Plants of the Mountain West* (Santa Fe, NM: Museum of New Mexico Press, 2003).

19. Stephen H. Buhner, *Herbal Antibiotics*, second edition (North Adams, MA: Storey Publishing, 2012).

20. Buhner, 2012.

21. Wilson R. Tavares & Ana M. L. Seca, "The Current Status of the Pharmaceutical Potential of *Juniperus* L. Metabolites," *Medicines*, vol. 5, 3:81 (Basel, Switzerland, July 31, 2018).

22. Ibrahim Tumen et al., "Topical Wound-Healing Effects and Phytochemical Composition of Heartwood Essential Oils of *Juniperus virginiana* L., *Juniperus occidentalis* Hook., and *Juniperus ashei* J. Buchholz," *Journal of Medicinal Food* (January 2013), 48–55.

23. Strike, 1994.

24. L. Hinton, "Notes on La Huerta Diegueño Ethnobotany," *The Journal of California Anthropology*, 2(2) (1975).

25. Carol Wermuth, personal communication.

26. James D. Adams Jr. & Cecilia Garcia, "Women's health among the Chumash." Evidence-based complementary and alternative medicine: eCaliforniaM, vol. 3:1 (2006): 125–31.

27. Steven J. Crouthamel, *Luiseño Ethnobotany* (San Marcos, CA: Palomar College, 2009).

28. Wermuth, personal communication.

29. Train et al., 1957.

30. Adams & Garcia, 2006.

31. Moore, *Medicinal Plants of the Mountain West*, 2003.

32. Michael Cottingham, *Medicinal Uses of Mormon Tea*, Wild Medicine School (November 17, 2020), YouTube video, 4:28.

33. Daphne E. González-Juárez et al., "A Review of the Ephedra genus: Distribution, Ecology, Ethnobotany, Phytochemistry and Pharmacological Properties," *Molecules*, vol. 25, 14, 3283 (Basel, Switzerland: July 20, 2020).

34. Venkata S. Pullela et al., "Isolation of Lignans and Biological Activity Studies of *Ephedra viridis*," *Planta medica* 71 (2005): 789–91.

35. S. Caveney et al., "New observations on the secondary chemistry of world *Ephedra* (Ephedraceae)," *Am. J. Bot.*, 88 (2001), 1199–1208.

36. Bahare Salehi et al., "Therapeutic Potential of α- and β-Pinene: A Miracle Gift of Nature," *Biomolecules* 9(11) (2019), 738.

37. Valeria Radulescu et al. (2013). "Determination of ascorbic acid in shoots from different coniferous species by HPLC," *Farmacia* 61, 1158–66.

## MAGNOLIIDS

1. Barbara R. Bocek, "Ethnobotany of Costanoan Indians, California, Based on Collections by John P. Harrington," *Economic Botany* 38, no. 2 (1984), 240–55.

2. Sara M. Schenck & Edward W. Gifford, *Karok Ethnobotany* (Berkeley, CA: University of California Anthropological Records, 1952), vol. 13(6), 383.

3. Juanita Centeno, personal communication

4. Garcia & Adams, *Healing with Medicinal Plants of the West*, 2016.

5. J. D. Adams & Cecilia Garcia, "Chumash Treatments for Arthritis, Part 2," *Wilderness Way* 15(2) (2009).

6. Moore, *Medicinal Plants of the Mountain West* (2003).

7. Nurhayat Tabanca et al., "Comparative investigation of *Umbellularia californica* and *Laurus nobilis* leaf essential oils and identification of constituents active against *Aedes aegypti*," *Journal of Agricultural and Food Chemistry*, vol. 61, 50 (2013), 12283–91.

8. Richard B. Hemmes, Arlene Alvarado & Benjamin L. Hart, "Use of California bay foliage by wood rats for possible fumigation of nest-borne ectoparasites," *Behavioral Ecology*, vol. 13, no. 3 (May 2002), 381–85.

9. Jan Timbrook, "Virtuous Herbs: Plants in Chumash Medicine," *J. Ethnobiol* 7(2) (Winter 1987), 171–80.

10. Jan Timbrook, *Chumash Ethnobotany* (Santa Barbara, CA: Santa Barbara Museum of Natural History, 2007).

11. Lowell John Bean & Katherine Siva Saubel, *Temalpakh: Cahuilla Indian Knowledge and Usage of Plants* (Banning, CA: Malki Museum, 1972).

12. Erminie Wheeler-Voegelin, *Tübatulabal Ethnography* (Berkeley, CA: University of California Press, 1938).

13. Moerman, 2009.

14. Train et al., 1957.

15. Bocek, 1984.

16. Wermuth, personal communication.

17. Timbrook, 1987.

18. J. D. Adams & Cecilia Garcia, "Chumash treatments for broken bones and sprains."

19. Margarita Artschwager Kay, *Healing with Plants in the American and Mexican West* (Tucson, AZ: University of Arizona Press, 1998).

20. Michael Moore, *Medicinal Plants of the Desert and Canyon West* (Santa Fe, NM: Museum of New Mexico Press, 1989).

21. Keng Hong Tan & Ritsuo Nishida, "Methyl eugenol: its occurrence, distribution, and role in nature, especially in relation to insect behavior and pollination," *Journal of Insect Science* (online), vol. 12 (2012), 56.

22. A. L. Medina-Holguín et al., "Chemotypic variation of essential oils in the medicinal plant, *Anemopsis californica*," *Phytochemistry* 69(4) (February 2008), 919–27, PMID: 18177907; PMCID: PMC2330197.

23. Andrea L. Medina et al., "Composition and Antimicrobial Activity of Anemopsis Californica Leaf Oil," *Journal of Agricultural and Food Chemistry* 53, no. 22 (2005), 8694–98.

24. Wermuth, personal communication.

25. Moore, *Medicinal Plants of the Desert and Canyon West*, 1989.

## MONOCOTS

1. Moore, *Medicinal Plants of the Desert and Canyon West*, 1989.

2. Anne Whitehead et al., "Cholesterol-lowering effects of oat β-glucan: a meta-analysis of randomized controlled trials," *The American Journal of Clinical Nutrition*, vol. 100, no. 6 (December 2014), 1413–21.

## EUDICOTS

1. Mrs. M. A Grieve, *Modern Herbal* (New York: Dover Publications, 1971).

2. James D. Adams, personal communication.

3. Andrzej Sidor & Anna Gramza-Michalowska, "Advanced research on the antioxidant and health benefit of elderberry (*Sambucus nigra*) in food—a review," *Journal of Functional Foods*, vol. 18, part B (October 2015), 941–58.

4. Thorne Research, "*Sambucus nigra* (elderberry) monograph," *Altern Med Rev.* 10(1) (March 2005), 51–54.

5. Nancy J. Selfridge, "Black Elderberry Supplementation for Upper Respiratory Infection Symptoms," *Integrative Medicine Alert* (May 1, 2020).

6. Joanna Harnett et al., "The effects of *Sambucus nigra* berry on acute respiratory viral infections: A rapid review of clinical studies," *Advances in Integrative Medicine*, vol. 7, 4 (2020), 240–46.

7. Jessie Hawkins et al., "Black elderberry (*Sambucus nigra*) supplementation effectively treats upper respiratory symptoms: A meta-analysis of randomized, controlled clinical trials," *Complement Ther Med.* 42 (February 2019), 361–65.

8. Evelin Tiralongo et al., "Elderberry Supplementation Reduces Cold Duration and Symptoms in Air-Travellers: A Randomized, Double-Blind Placebo-Controlled Clinical Trial," *Nutrients*, vol. 8, 4 (24 March 2016), 182.

9. Mateja Senica et al., "The Higher the Better? Differences in Phenolics and Cyanogenic Glycosides in *Sambucus nigra* Leaves, Flowers and Berries from Different Altitudes," *J Sci Food Agric.* 97 (8) (June 2017), 2623–32.

10. California Invasive Plant Council, "*Foeniculum vulgare*" (Cal IPC, n.d.).

11. James D. Adams, personal communication.

12. Karen Hardy et al., "Neanderthal medics?" 2012.

13. Mrs. R. F. Bingham, "Medicinal Plants Growing Wild in Santa Barbara and Vicinity," *Bulletin of the Santa Barbara Society of Natural History*, vol. 1, no. 2 (October 1890).

14. Upton, *American Herbal Pharmacopoeia: Botanical Pharmacognosy—Microscopic Characterization of Botanical Medicines*, 2011.

15. David Hoffmann, *The New Holistic Herbal*, third edition (Rockport, MA: Element Inc., 1991).

16. David Frawley & Vasant Lad, *The Yoga of Herbs: An Ayurvedic Guide to Herbal Medicine* (Santa Fe, NM: Lotus Press, 1986).

17. R. F. Chandler et al., "Ethnobotany and Phytochemistry of Yarrow, *Achillea Millefolium*, Compositae," *Economic Botany*, vol. 36, no. 2 (1982), 203–23, JSTOR.

18. Garcia & Adams, *Healing with Medicinal Plants of the West*, 2016.

19. Applequist & Moerman, 2011.

20. Juanita Centeno, personal communication.

21. Moerman, *Native American Medicinal Plants*, 2009.

22. Incayawar, "Tongva Medicinal Plants," 2010.

23. L. Hinton, "Notes on La Huerta Diegueño Ethnobotany," 1975.

24. David P. Barrows, *The Ethno-botany of the Coahuilla Indians of Southern California* (Chicago: University of Chicago Press, 1900).

25. Moerman, *Native American Medicinal Plants*, 2009.

26. Incayawar, "Tongva Medicinal Plants," 2010.

27. Juanita Centeno, personal communication.

28. Garcia & Adams, *Healing with Medicinal Plants of the West*, 2016.

29. Moore, *Medicinal Plants of the Mountain West*, 2003.

30. Fontaine, "Chemical composition and antinociceptive activity," 2013.

31. Perri, et al., "Naturally occurring sesquiterpene lactones," 2019.

32. Lanny Kaufer, "Chinese researcher," HerbWalks.com.

33. Garcia & Adams, 2016.

34. William LeSassier, personal communication.

35. Garcia & Adams, 2016.

36. Bianca Ivanescu et al., "Sesquiterpene Lactones from Artemisia Genus: Biological Activities and Methods of Analysis," *Journal of Analytical Methods in Chemistry*, vol. 2015 (2015).

37. Moerman, *Native American Medicinal Plants*, 2009.

38. T. J. Lyle, *Physio-Medical Therapeutics, Materia Medica and Pharmacy* (Salem, OH: J. M. Lyle & Bros., 1897).

39. *Pharmacopoeia of the United States of America*, eighth decennial revision (1905).

40. Garcia & Adams, 2016.

41. Carol Wermuth, personal communication.

42. S. J. Dentali & J. J. Hoffmann, "Potential Anti-infective Agents from *Eriodictyon angustifolium* and *Salvia apiana*," *International Journal of Pharmacognosy*, 30:3 (1992), 223–31.

43. Michael Tierra, "Wild Cherry, One of the Great North American Herbs," Michael's blog, East West School of Herbology.

44. Michael Moore, *Medicinal Plants—In The Field With Michael Moore, 4*, Michael Cottingham (December 8, 2011), YouTube video, 9:58.

45. Don Canavan & Eric Yarnell, "Successful Treatment of Poison Oak Dermatitis Treated with *Grindelia* spp.," *Journal of Alternative and Complementary Medicine* 11 (2005), 709–10.

46. Andrew Pengelly, *The Constituents of Medicinal Plants* (Crows Nest, Australia: Allen & Unwin, 2004).

47. European Medicines Agency. "Community herbal monograph on *Grindelia robusta* Nutt., *Grindelia squarrosa* (Pursh) Dunal, *Grindelia humilis* Hook. et Arn., *Grindelia camporum* Greene, herba" (2012).

48. Karen Hardy et al., 2012.

49. Strike, 1994.

50. Bard, "A Contribution to the History of Medicine in Southern California," 2006.

51. Moore, *Medicinal Plants of the Desert and Canyon West*, 1989.

52. H. Viola et al., "Apigenin, a component of *Matricaria recutita* flowers, is a central benzodiazepine receptors-ligand with anxiolytic effects," *Planta Med.* 61(3) (1995), 213–16.

53. D. L. McKay & J. B. Blumberg, "A review of the bioactivity and potential health benefits of chamomile tea (*Matricaria recutita* L.)," *Phytother Res.* 20(7) (2006), 519–30.

54. Garcia & Adams, 2016.

55. J. D. Adams & Cecilia Garcia, "Chumash treatments to aid weight loss."

56. Moore, *Medicinal Plants of the Pacific West*, 1993.

57. Hoffmann, *The New Holistic Herbal*, 1991.

58. Moerman, *Native American Medicinal Plants*, 2009.

59. Eric Yarnell, ND, & Lauren Russel, ND. "Solidago: An Inflammation Modulator," *Naturopathic Doctor News & Review* (April 11, 2018).

60. California Native Plant Society, "CalScape."

61. Bean & Saubel, "Temalpakh: Cahuilla Indian Knowledge," 1972.

62. Hinton, 1975.

63. Michael Wilken-Robertson, *Kumeyaay Ethnobotany: Shared Heritage of the Californias* (San Diego, CA: Sunbelt Publications, 2018).

64. *Dispensatory of the United States of America*, 1877.

65. *Pharmacopoeia of the United States of America*, eighth decennial revision (1905).

66. Timbrook, *Chumash Ethnobotany*, 2007.

67. Moore, *Medicinal Plants of the Pacific West*, 1993.

68. Moore, *Medicinal Plants of the Mountain West*, 2003.

69. Nicholas Smith & Jeremy C. Smith, "Repurposing Therapeutics for COVID-19: Supercomputer-based Docking to the Sars-cov-2 Viral Spike Protein and Viral Spike Protein-human ACE2 Interface," *ChemRxiv* (2020).

70. Wolfgang Fischer et al., "Old age-associated phenotypic screening for Alzheimer's disease drug candidates identifies sterubin as a potent neuroprotective compound from *Yerba santa,*" *Redox Biology,* vol. 21 (2019).

71. Luther Burbank Home & Gardens, "Spineless Cactus," lutherburbank.org /about-us/specialty-gardens/spineless-cactus Opuntia.

72. Romero, *The Botanical Lore of the California Indians,* 1954.

73. Alberto C. Frati-Munari et al., "Hypoglycemic Effect of *Opuntia streptacantha* Lemaire in NIDDM," *Diabetes Care* 11 (1) (January 1988), 63–66.

74. A. C. Frati, E. Jiménez & C. R. Ariza, "Hypoglycemic effect of *Opuntia ficus indica* in non-insulin-dependent *diabetes mellitus* patients," *Phytother. Res.* 4 (1990), 195–97.

75. Moore, *Medicinal Plants of the Desert and Canyon West,* 1989.

76. Marc Baker, "The ethnobotany of the Yurok, Tolowa, and Karok Indians of Northwest California" (1981).

77. Bean & Saubel, "Temalpakh: Cahuilla Indian Knowledge," 1972.

78. Chesnut, *Plants Used by the Indians of Mendocino County,* 1902.

79. Garth, "Atsugewi Ethnography, Anthropological Records," 1953.

80. E. W. Gifford, "Ethnographic Notes on the Southwestern Pomo," Anthropological Records, University of California, Berkeley, vol. 25 (1967), 14.

81. Jennie Goodrich, Claudia Lawson & Vana Parrish Lawson, *Kashaya Pomo Plants* (Los Angeles: American Indian Studies Center, University of California, 1980).

82. Timbrook, *Chumash Ethnobotany,* 2007.

83. Moore, *Medicinal Plants of the Pacific West,* 1993.

84. Moerman, 2009.

85. *Pharmacopoeia of the United States of America,* ninth decennial revision (1916).

86. Hiroaki Hayashi et al., "Phylogenetic Relationship of *Glycyrrhiza lepidota,* American Licorice, in Genus *Glycyrrhiza* Based on rbcL Sequences and Chemical Constituents," *Biological & Pharmaceutical Bulletin* 28 (2005), 161–64.

87. J. Cinatl et al., "Glycyrrhizin, an active component of liquorice roots, and replication of SARS-associated coronavirus," *Lancet* (London, England), vol. 361, 9374 (2003), 2045–46.

88. Lester Mitscher et al., "Antimicrobial agents from higher plants: Prenylated flavonoids and other phenols from *Glycyrrhiza lepidota,*" *Phytochemistry* 22 (1983), 573–76.

89. Maggie O'Neill, "A 54-Year-Old Man Died From Eating Too Much Black Licorice—Here's How That Can Happen," MSN (September 24, 2020).

90. Moore, *Medicinal Plants of the Mountain West,* 2003.

91. Strike, 1994.

92. Timbrook, 2007.

93. Barrett, "Miwok Material Culture," 1933.

94. Gifford, "Ethnographic Notes on the Southwestern Pomo," 1967.

95. Bocek, 1984.

96. Timbrook, 2007.

97. Strike, 1994.

98. Bocek, 1984.

99. Chesnut, 1902.

100. Ken Hedges & Christina Beresford, *Santa Ysabel Ethnobotany* (San Diego, CA: San Diego Museum of Man, 1986).

101. George R. Mead, *The Ethnobotany of the California Indians* (La Grande, OR: E-Cat Worlds, 2003).

102. Edith Van Allen Murphey, *Indian Uses of Native Plants* (Ukiah, CA: Mendocino County Historical Society, 1987).

103. Hedges & Beresford, 1986.

104. Timbrook, 2007.

105. American Botanical Council. Complete German Commission E Monographs.

106. Pengelly, *The Constituents of Medicinal Plants*, 2004.

107. Mehdi Taib et al., "Medicinal Uses, Phytochemistry, and Pharmacological Activities of *Quercus* Species," Evidence-based complementary and alternative medicine: eCaliforniaM, vol. 2020, 1920683 (July 31, 2020).

108. Phillip L. Walker & Travis Hudson, *Chumash Healing: Changing Health and Medical Practices in an American Indian Society* (Banning, CA: Malki Museum Press, 1993).

109. Barrett & Gifford, "Miwok Material Culture," 1993.

110. Train et al., 1957.

111. World Health Organization. WHO monographs on selected medicinal plants, vol. 1–4.

112. American Botanical Council. Complete German Commission E Monographs.

113. Moore, *Medicinal Plants of the Mountain West*, 2003.

114. Hoffmann, *The New Holistic Herbal*, 1991.

115. World Health Organization. WHO monographs on selected medicinal plants, vol. 2.

116. American Botanical Council. Herbal Medicine: Expanded Commission E Monographs.

117. J. Sarris, E. McIntyre & D. A. Camfield, "Plant-Based Medicines for Anxiety Disorders, Part 2: A Review of Clinical Studies with Supporting Preclinical Evidence," *CNS Drugs* 27 (2013), 301–19.

118. Cornelius Schüle, Thomas Baghai, N. Sauer & Grefor Laakmann, "Endocrinological Effects of High-Dose *Hypericum perforatum* Extract WS 5570 in Healthy Subjects," *Neuropsychobiology* 49 (2004), 58–63.

119. U. P. Hedrick, *Sturtevant's Edible Plants of the World* (Mineola, NY: Dover Publications, 1972).

120. Mrs. M. A Grieve, *Modern Herbal* (New York: Dover Publications, 1971).

121. Bocek, 1984.

122. American Botanical Council. Herbal Medicine: Expanded Commission E Monographs.

123. Michael Tierra, *Planetary Herbology* (Santa Fe, NM: Lotus Press, 1988).

124. Moore, *Medicinal Plants of the Pacific West*, 1993.

125. A. M. Clark, T. M. Jurgens & C. D. Hufford, "Antimicrobial activity of juglone," *Phytother. Res.* 4 (1990), 11–14.

126. Jiayi Wang et al., "Antibacterial Activity of Juglone against *Staphylococcus aureus*: From Apparent to Proteomic," *International Journal of Molecular Sciences* 17, Nr. 6 (June 18, 2016), 965.

127. Schenck & Gifford, *Karok Ethnobotany*, 1952.

128. Timbrook, 2007.

129. Moore, *Medicinal Plants of the Pacific West*, 1993.

130. Tierra, 1988.

131. Frederick B. Power & Arthur H. Salway, "Chemical Examination of *Micromeria chamissonis* (Yerba Buena)," *The Journal of the American Chemical Society*, vol. 30, no. 2 (February 1908), as reprinted in the Internet Archive.

132. US Department of Agriculture, Agricultural Research Service. Dr. Duke's Phytochemical and Ethnobotanical Databases.

133. Timbrook, 2007.

134. Moerman, 2009, 301.

135. Michael Moore, Plant monographs extracted from *The Eclectic Materia Medica, Pharmacology and Therapeutics* by Harvey Wickes Felter, M.D. (1922)

136. Tierra, 1988.

137. American Botanical Council. Herbal Medicine: Expanded Commission E Monographs.

138. Olugbenga K. Popoola et al., "Marrubiin," *Molecules*, 18(8) (2013), 9049–60.

139. Fred Siciliano, personal communication.

140. World Health Organization. WHO monographs on selected medicinal plants, vol. 2.

141. Fred Siciliano, personal communication.

142. Strike, 1994.

143. Moerman, *Native American Medicinal Plants*, 2009.

144. Frawley & Lad, *The Yoga of Herbs*, 1986.

145. Ge Meng et al., "Research progress on the chemistry and pharmacology of *Prunella vulgaris* species," *Open Access Library Journal* 1, no. 3 (2014), 1–19.

146. James D. Adams & Cecilia Garcia. "Traditional Chumash Healing," *Wilderness Way* 12(4) 2006.

147. Kaiser Foundation Health Plan of Washington. https://wa.kaiserpermanente.org/kbase/topic.jhtml?docId=hn-2158004

148. American Botanical Council. Herbal Medicine: Expanded Commission E Monographs. https://herbalgram.org/resources/expanded-commission-e/.

149. United Plant Savers, "Species At-Risk" List.

150. Adams and Garcia, 2006.

151. Hinton, "Notes on La Huerta Diegueño Ethnobotany," 1975.

152. Moore, *Medicinal Plants of the Pacific West*, 1993.

153. Dentali & Hoffmann, "Potential Anti-infective Agents from *Eriodictyon angustifolium*," 1992.

154. Moore, *Medicinal Plants of the Desert and Canyon West*, 1989.

155. Brittany J. Allison et al., "Antibacterial activity of fractions from three Chumash medicinal plant extracts and in vitro inhibition of the enzyme enoyl reductase by the flavonoid jaceosidin" (*Natural Product Research*, 2016).

156. J. J. Johnson, "Carnosol: A promising anti-cancer and anti-inflammatory agent," *Cancer Letters*, 305(1) (2011), 1–7.

157. Gary R. Takeoka et al., "Volatile Constituents of the Aerial Parts of *Salvia apiana* Jepson," *Journal of Essential Oil Research*: 22 (2010).

158. Pengelly, *The Constituents of Medicinal Plants*, 2004.

159. Timbrook, 2007.

160. James D. Adams, personal communication.

161. Bocek, 1984.

162. Romero, 1954.

163. Florence Connolly Shipek, *Delfina Cuero: Her Autobiography: An Account of Her Last Years and Her Ethnobotanic Contributions* (Menlo Park, CA: Ballena Press, 1991).

164. Train et al., 1957.

165. James David Adams et al., "*Salvia mellifera*—How Does It Alleviate Chronic Pain?" *Medicines*, vol. 6, 1 18 (Basel, Switzerland, January 24, 2019).

166. Garcia & Adams, 2016.

167. Christopher Nyerges, *Foraging California*, second edition (Lanham, MD: The Rowman and Littlefield Publishing Group, 2019).

168. Moore, *Medicinal Plants of the Pacific West*, 1993.

169. Moore, *Medicinal Plants of the Pacific West*, 1993.

170. Strike, 1994.

171. Barrett & Gifford, *Miwok Material Culture*, 1933.

172. *Pharmacopoeia of the United States of America*, eighth decennial revision (1905).

173. *National Formulary*, fourth edition (1916).

174. *National Formulary*, fourth edition (1916).

175. Michael Castleman, *The New Healing Herbs* (Emmaus, PA: Rodale Press, 2009).

176. Frawley & Lad, 1986.

177. Moore, *Medicinal Plants of the Mountain West*, 2003.

178. R. Awad et al., "Phytochemical and biological analysis of Skullcap (*Scutellaria lateriflora* L.): A medicinal plant with anxiolytic properties," *The Free Library* (November 1, 2003), accessed May 15, 2020.

179. Gary R. Takeoka et al., "Headspace Volatiles of *Scutellaria californica* A. Gray Flowers," *Journal of Essential Oil Research* (February 2008).

180. Klaudyna Fidyt et al., "β-caryophyllene and β-caryophyllene oxide-natural compounds of anticancer and analgesic properties," *Cancer Medicine*, vol. 5,10 (2016): 3007–17.

181. Strike, 1994.

182. Lowell John Bean & and Katherine Siva Saubel, *Temalpakh: Cahuilla Indian Knowledge and Usage of Plants* (Banning, CA: Malki Museum, 1972).

183. Bard, "A Contribution to the History of Medicine in Southern California," 2006).

184. Adams & Garcia, "Women's health among the Chumash," 2006.

185. Timbrook, 2007.

186. Strike, 1994.

187. Bocek, 1984.

188. Moore, *Medicinal Plants of the Mountain West*, 2003.

189. Garcia & Adams, *Healing with Medicinal Plants of the West*, 2016.

190. Brittany J. Allison et al., "Antibacterial activity of fractions from three Chumash medicinal plant extracts and in vitro inhibition of the enzyme enoyl reductase by the flavonoid jaceosidin," *Natural Product Research* (2016).

191. Matthew C. Fleming et al., "Immunomodulatory and Antibacterial Properties of the Chumash Medicinal Plant *Trichostema lanatum*," *Medicines* 5(2) (2018), 25.

192. Deni Bown, *New Encyclopedia of Herbs and Their Uses*, revised edition (New York: DK Publishing, 2001).

193. Moore, *Medicinal Plants of the Desert and Canyon West*, 1989.

194. Tierra, 1988.

195. American Botanical Council. Herbal Medicine: Expanded Commission E Monographs.

196. Kaiser Permanente, "Eucalyptus" (2015).

197. Moore, *Medicinal Plants of the Desert and Canyon West*, 1989.

198. Carolina Puig et al., "Unravelling the bioherbicide potential of *Eucalyptus globulus* Labill: Biochemistry and effects of its aqueous extract," *PLOS ONE* (2018), 13, e0192872.

199. Tim Stephens, "UCSC Arboretum holds the most eucalyptus species anywhere outside of Australia," *UC Santa Cruz News* (September 25, 2007).

200. Chesnut, 1902.

201. Hedrick, *Sturtevant's Edible Plants of the World*, 1972.

202. Parke, Davis & Company, "Descriptive catalogue of the laboratory products of Parke, Davis & Company. Materia medica, therapeutics, formulae, approximate prices" (1894).

203. Franca Tomè, Maria Laura Colombo & Luisa Caldirol. "A Comparative Investigation on Alkaloid Composition in Different Populations of *Eschscholtzia californica* Cham," *Phytochem. Anal.* 10 (1999) 264–67.

204. California Penal Code. Crimes Against the Public Health and Safety, Cal. Penal Code § 384a et seq.

205. Strike, 1994.

206. Michael Wilken-Robertson, *Kumeyaay Ethnobotany: Shared Heritage of the Californias* (San Diego, CA: Sunbelt Publications, 2018).

207. Hinton, 1975.

208. Garcia & Adams, *Healing with Medicinal Plants of the West*, 2016.

209. Xiaogang Wang et al., "*Heteromeles Arbutifolia*, a Traditional Treatment for Alzheimer's Disease, Phytochemistry and Safety," *Medicines* 3 (2016), 17.

210. Ibid.

211. US Department of Agriculture, Natural Resources Conservation Service, "Plant Guide for Toyon."

212. California Penal Code. Crimes Against the Public Health and Safety, Cal. Penal Code § 384b et seq.

213. Hinton, 1975.

214. *Pharmacopoeia of the United States of America*, ninth decennial revision (1916).

215. David Hoffmann, *The New Holistic Herbal*, third edition (Rockport, MA: Element Inc., 1991).

216. Moore, *Medicinal Plants of the Pacific West*, 1993.

217. Tierra, "Wild Cherry, One of the Great North American Herbs."

218. Nyerges, 2019.

219. Timbrook, 2007.

220. Train et al., 1957.

221. Moerman, 2009.

222. J. D. Adams & Cecilia Garcia, "Chumash Baby and Child Therapies—Teething and Ear Ache," *Wilderness Way* 14(1) (2008).

223. Frawley & Lad, 1986.

224. Yasuyuki Hashidoko, "Phytochemistry of *Rosa rugosa*," *Phytochemistry* 43 (1996) 535–49.

225. Linus Pauling Institute, "Vitamin C" (Oregon State University Micronutrient Information Center, n.d.).

226. Adams & Garcia, "Women's health among the Chumash," 2006.

227. Strike, 1994.

228. Moerman, *Native American Medicinal Plants*, 2009.

229. Strike, 1994.

230. Moerman, 2009.

231. Train et al., 1957.

232. *Pharmacopoeia of the United States of America*, eighth decennial revision (1905).

233. Moore, *Medicinal Plants of the Mountain West*, 2003.

234. European Medicines Agency, "Raspberry leaf: Summary for the public" (2017).

235. Strike, 1994.

236. Timbrook, 2007.

237. Bean & Saubel, 1972.

238. George R. Mead, *The Ethnobotany of the California Indians* (La Grande, OR: E-Cat Worlds, 2003).

239. Strike, 1994.

240. Moore, *Medicinal Plants of the Mountain West*, 2003.

241. David W. Robinson et al., "Datura quids at Pinwheel Cave, California, provide unambiguous confirmation of the ingestion of hallucinogens at a rock art site," *PNAS* 117 (49) (December 8, 2020), 31026–37; first published November 23, 2020.

242. R. Upton, "Stinging nettles leaf (*Urtica dioica* L.): Extraordinary vegetable medicine," *J Herbal Med* (2013).

243. LeSassier, personal communication.

244. Moore, *Medicinal Plants of the Pacific West*, 1993.

245. Roy Upton (ed.) et al., *American Herbal Pharmacopoeia: Botanical Pharmacognosy—Microscopic Characterization of Botanical Medicines* (Boca Raton, FL: CRC Press, 2011).

246. Dorota Kregiel et al., "*Urtica* spp.: Ordinary Plants with Extraordinary Properties," *Molecules*, vol. 23, 7 (Basel, Switzerland, July 9, 2018), 1664.

247. S. Klingelhoefer, B. Obertreis, S. Quast & B. Behnke, "Antirheumatic Effect of IDS 23, a Stinging Nettle Leaf Extract, on in Vitro Expression of T Helper Cytokines," *The Journal of Rheumatology* (US National Library of Medicine, 1999).

248. Upton, "Stinging nettles leaf (*Urtica dioica* L.): Extraordinary vegetable medicine," 2013.

249. American Botanical Council. Complete German Commission E Monographs.

250. Brigida D'Abrosca et al., "*Urtica dioica* L. inhibits proliferation and enhances cisplatin cytotoxicity in NSCLC cells via Endoplasmic Reticulum-stress mediated apoptosis," *Scientific Reports*, vol. 9, 1 (March 21, 2019), 4986.

251. Camilia Fiol, Diego Prado, María Mora & J. Iñaki Alava. "Nettle Cheese: Using Nettle Leaves (*Urtica dioica*) to Coagulate Milk in the Fresh Cheese Making Process," *International Journal of Gastronomy and Food Science* (Elsevier, May 28, 2016).

252. Moerman, 2009.

253. Bean & Saubel, 1972.

254. Barrows, *The Ethno-botany of the Coahuilla Indians of Southern California*, 1900.

255. Moerman, 2009.

256. Kaiser Permanente, "Chaparral," Kaiser Foundation Health Plan of Washington (2015).

257. Joanne Barnes, Linda A. Anderson & J. D. Phillipson, *Herbal Medicines*, third edition (London: Pharmaceutical Press, 2007).

258. Mark Blumenthal, "Herb Industry and FDA Issue Chaparral Warning: Experts Unable to Explain Possible Links to Five Cases of Hepatitis" (reprinted from *HerbalGram* magazine).

259. University of California, Riverside, "Detailed Case Histories of Salient Worldwide Biological Pest Control Projects (Puncture Vine)."

260. Frawley & Lad, 1986.

261. Joe Hing Kwok Chu, *Chinese Herbal Medicine Dictionary*.

262. Moore, *Medicinal Plants of the Desert and Canyon West*, 1989.

263. Moore, *Medicinal Plants of the Pacific West*, 1993.

264. Seung-Hee Kim & Kyung-Chul Choi, "Anti-cancer Effect and Underlying Mechanism(s) of Kaempferol, a Phytoestrogen, on the Regulation of Apoptosis in Diverse Cancer Cell Models," *Toxicological Research*, vol. 29, 4 (2013), 229–34.

265. Elham Akhtari et al., "*Tribulus terrestris* for treatment of sexual dysfunction in women: randomized double-blind placebo—controlled study," *Daru: Journal of Faculty of Pharmacy*, vol. 22, 1 (Tehran University of Medical Sciences, April 28, 2014), 40.

266. Ikhlas A. Khan & Ehab A. Abourashed, *Leung's Encyclopedia of Common Natural Ingredients Used in Food, Drugs, and Cosmetics*, third edition (Hoboken, NJ: John Wiley & Sons, 2010).

# BIBLIOGRAPHY

*A Barefoot Doctor's Manual* (Washington, DC: National Institutes of Health, 1974).

Adams, J. D., and Cecilia Garcia (2008). "Chumash Baby and Child Therapies—Teething and Ear Ache." *Wilderness Way* 14(1). abeduspress.com/files/wildernessway14_1_25.2008Child.pdf.

——— (2009). "Chumash Treatments for Arthritis, Part 2." *Wilderness Way* 15(2). abeduspress.com/files/WildernessWay15_2_2009arthritis2.pdf.

———. "Chumash Treatments for Broken Bones and Sprains." abeduspress.com/files/Chumash_treatmets_for_broken_bones_and_sprains.pdf.

———. "Chumash Treatments to aid Weight Loss." abeduspress.com/files/Chumash_treatments_to_aid_weight_loss.pdf.

———. "Traditional Chumash Healing" (2006). *Wilderness Way* 12(4). abeduspress.com/files/Wildernessway12_4_2006aGeneral.pdf.

——— (2006). *Wilderness Way* articles. abeduspress.com/WildernessWay.html.

Adams, James D. Jr, and Cecilia Garcia. "Women's health among the Chumash." Evidence-based complementary and alternative medicine: eCaliforniaM, vol. 3, 1: 125–31. ncbi.nlm.nih.gov/pmc/articles/PMC1375244/.

Adams, James David, et al. "*Salvia mellifera*—How Does It Alleviate Chronic Pain?" *Medicines*, vol. 6, 1 18. Basel, Switzerland, January 24, 2019. ncbi.nlm.nih.gov/pmc/articles/PMC6473501/.

Adams, Robert, Sanko Nguyen, Chang-Fu Hsieh, and Guan Kaiyun. "The Leaf Essential Oils of the Genus *Calocedrus*." *Journal of Essential Oil Research*. October 2006, 18(6): 654–58. researchgate.net/publication/254247259_The_Leaf_Essential_Oils_of_the_Genus_Calocedrus.

Akhtari, Elham, et al. "*Tribulus terrestris* for treatment of sexual dysfunction in women: randomized double-blind placebo—controlled study." *Daru: Journal of Faculty of Pharmacy*, vol. 22, 1 40. Tehran University of Medical Sciences, April 28, 2014. ncbi.nlm.nih.gov/pmc/articles/PMC4045980/.

Allison, Brittany J., et al. (2016). "Antibacterial activity of fractions from three Chumash medicinal plant extracts and in vitro inhibition of the enzyme enoyl reductase by the flavonoid jaceosidin." *Natural Product Research*. pubmed.ncbi.nlm.nih.gov/27482826/.

American Botanical Council. Complete German Commission E Monographs. herbalgram.org/resources/commission-e-monographs/.

———. Herbal Medicine: Expanded Commission E Monographs. herbalgram.org/resources/expanded-commission-e/.

Applequist, Wendy, and Daniel Moerman. (2011). "Yarrow (*Achillea millefolium* L.): A Neglected Panacea? A Review of Ethnobotany, Bioactivity, and Biomedical Research." *Economic Botany* 65: 209–25. link.springer.com/article/10.1007/s12231-011-9154-3.

Awad, R., et al. "Phytochemical and biological analysis of Skullcap (*Scutellaria lateriflora* L.): a medicinal plant with anxiolytic properties." The Free Library, November 1,

2003. May 15, 2020. thefreelibrary.com/Phytochemical+and+biological+analysis +of+Skullcap+(Scutellaria...-a0112687600.

Awang, Dennis V. C. *Tyler's Herbs of Choice : The Therapeutic Use of Phytomedicinals*, third edition. Boca Raton, FL: CRC Press, 2009.

Baker, Marc (1981). "The ethnobotany of the Yurok, Tolowa, and Karok Indians of northwest California." 10.13140/RG.2.2.12690.66240. researchgate.net/publica tion/34885874_The_Ethnobotany_of_the_Yurok_Tolowa_and_Karok_Indians _of_Northwest_California#fullTextFileContent.

Bard, Cephas L. "A Contribution to the History of Medicine in Southern California." *Journal of California and Great Basin Anthropology*, vol. 26, no. 1 (2006), 95–108. escholarship.org/uc/item/72p336fw.

Barnes, Joanne, Linda A. Anderson, and J. D. Phillipson. *Herbal Medicines*, third edition. London: Pharmaceutical Press, 2007.

Barrett, S. A., and E. W. Gifford (1933). "Miwok Material Culture." *Bulletin of the Public Museum of the City of Milwaukee*, vol. 2, no. 4. yosemite.ca.us/library/miwok_mate rial_culture/miwok_material_culture.pdf.

Barrows, David P. *The Ethno-botany of the Coahuilla Indians of Southern California*. Chicago: University of Chicago Press, 1900. biodiversitylibrary.org/bibliography /19178#/summary Cahuilla.

Bean, Lowell John, and Katherine Siva Saubel. *Temalpakh: Cahuilla Indian Knowledge and Usage of Plants*. Banning, CA: Malki Museum, 1972.

Behera, Bhaskar, Neeraj Verma, Anjali Sonone, and Urmila Makhija (2009). "Usnea, Optimization of Culture Conditions for Lichen *Usnea ghattensis* G. Awasthi to Increase Biomass and Antioxidant Metabolite Production." *Food Technology and Biotechnology* 47. ftb.com.hr/66-volume-47-issue-no-1/228-optimization-of-cul ture-conditions-for-lichen-usnea-ghattensis-g-awasthi-to-increase-biomass-and -antioxidant-metabolite-production.

Bingham, Mrs. R. F. "Medicinal Plants Growing Wild in Santa Barbara and Vicinity." *Bulletin of the Santa Barbara Society of Natural History*, vol. 1, no. 2, October 1890. archive.org/stream/bulletinofsanta121890sant/bulletinofsanta121890sant_djvu.txt

Bissett, Norman G., editor. *Herbal Drugs and Phytopharmaceuticals*. Boca Raton, FL: CRC Press, 1994.

Blumenthal, Mark. "Herb Industry and FDA Issue Chaparral Warning: Experts Unable to Explain Possible Links to Five Cases of Hepatitis." Reprinted from *HerbalGram* magazine. encognitive.com/node/14728.

Bocek, Barbara R. (1984). "Ethnobotany of Costanoan Indians, California, Based on Collections by John P. Harrington." *Economic Botany* 38, no. 2, 240–55. jstor.org /stable/4254616?seq=1.

Bown, Deni. *New Encyclopedia of Herbs and Their Uses*, revised edition. New York: DK Publishing, 2001.

Buhner, Stephen H. *Herbal Antibiotics*, second edition. North Adams, MA: Storey Publishing, 2012.

California Invasive Plant Council. "*Foeniculum vulgare*," Cal IPC. cal-ipc.org/plants /profile/foeniculum-vulgare-profile/.

California Native Plant Society. CalScape website: calscape.org.

———. "Inventory of Rare and Endangered Plants of California." Online edition, v8-03 0.38. rareplants.cnps.org .

California Penal Code. "Crimes Against the Public Health and Safety." California penal code section 384a. leginfo.legislature.ca.gov/faces/codes_displaySection.xhtml?sectionNum=384a.&lawCode=PEN.

———. "Crimes Against the Public Health and Safety." California Penal Code §384b et seq. leginfo.legislature.ca.gov/faces/codes_displaySection.xhtml?sectionNum=384b.&lawCode=PEN.

Canavan, Don, and Eric Yarnell (2005). "Successful Treatment of Poison Oak Dermatitis Treated with *Grindelia* spp. (Gumweed)." *Journal of Alternative and Complementary Medicine*, vol. 11: 709–10. pubmed.ncbi.nlm.nih.gov/16131296/.

Castleman, Michael. *The New Healing Herbs*. Emmaus, PA: Rodale Press, 2009.

Caveney, S., et al. (2001). "New observations on the secondary chemistry of world *Ephedra* (Ephedraceae)." *Am. J. Bot.* 88: 1199–1208. bsapubs.onlinelibrary.wiley.com/doi/full/10.2307/3558330.

Chandler, R. F., et al. (1982). "Ethnobotany and Phytochemistry of Yarrow, *Achillea millefolium*, Compositae." *Economic Botany*, vol. 36, no. 2: 203–223. JSTOR, jstor.org/stable/4254376. Accessed September 14, 2020.

Chesnut, Victor K. *Plants Used by the Indians of Mendocino County, California*. US Government Printing Office, 1902. books.google.com/books/about/Plants_Used_by_the_Indians_of_Mendocino.html?id=vLkUAAAAYAAJ.

Chevallier, Andrew. *Encyclopedia of Herbal Medicine*, third edition. (New York: DK Publishing, 2016).

Chu, Joe Hing Kwok. Chinese Herbal Medicine Dictionary. alternativehealing.org/chinese_herbs_dictionary.htm.

Cinatl, J., et al. (2003). "Glycyrrhizin, an active component of liquorice roots, and replication of SARS-associated coronavirus." *Lancet*, vol. 361,9374: 2045–46. ncbi.nlm.nih.gov/pmc/articles/PMC7112442/.

Clark, A. M., T. M. Jurgens, and C. D. Hufford (1990). "Antimicrobial activity of juglone." *Phytother. Res.* 4: 11–14. onlinelibrary.wiley.com/doi/abs/10.1002/ptr.2650040104.

Coombes, Allen J. *The Dictionary of Plant Names*. Portland, OR: Timber Press, 1985.

Cottingham, Michael. *Medicinal Uses of Mormon Tea*. Wild Medicine School, November 17, 2020. YouTube video, 4:28. youtu.be/onTBhnl7cbw.

Crouthamel, Steven J. (2009). "Luiseño Ethnobotany." Palomar College. San Marcos, CA. palomar.edu/users/scrouthamel/luisenob.htm.

D'Abrosca, Brigida, et al. "*Urtica dioica* L. inhibits proliferation and enhances cisplatin cytotoxicity in NSCLC cells via Endoplasmic Reticulum-stress mediated apoptosis." *Scientific Reports* vol. 9:1, 4986. March 21, 2019. ncbi.nlm.nih.gov/pmc/articles/PMC6428841/.

Dentali, S. J., and J. J. Hoffmann (1992). "Potential Anti-infective Agents from *Eriodictyon angustifolium* and *Salvia apiana*." *International Journal of Pharmacognosy*, 30:3, 223–31. tandfonline.com/doi/abs/10.3109/13880209209054003.

DerMarderosian, Ara, and John A. Beutler, co-editors. *The Review of Natural Products*, seventh edition. St. Louis, MO: Wolters Kluwer Health, 2012.

*Dispensatory of the United States of America*, eighteenth edition. 1877, 518. google.com /books/reader?id=QS9OAQAAIAAJ&pg=GBS.PP18.

Duffy, Thomas P., "The Flexner Report—100 Years Later." *The Yale Journal of Biology and Medicine*, 84(3): 269–76. ncbi.nlm.nih.gov/pmc/articles/PMC3178858/.

Duke, James A. *Handbook of Medicinal Herbs*, second edition. Boca Raton, FL: CRC Press, 2002.

European Medicines Agency (2017). "Raspberry leaf: Summary for the public." ema .europa.eu/en/medicines/herbal/rubi-idaei-folium#overview-section.

——— (2012). "Community herbal monograph on *Grindelia robusta* Nutt., *Grindelia squarrosa* (Pursh) Dunal, *Grindelia humilis* Hook. et Arn., *Grindelia camporum* Greene, herba." ema.europa.eu/en/documents/herbal-monograph/final-community -herbal-monograph-grindelia-robusta-nutt-grindelia-squarrosa-pursh-dunal-grinde lia_en.pdf

Fidyt, Klaudyna, et al. (2016). "β-caryophyllene and β-caryophyllene oxide-natural compounds of anticancer and analgesic properties." *Cancer Medicine*, vol. 5,10: 3007–17. ncbi.nlm.nih.gov/pmc/articles/PMC5083753/.

Fiol, Camila, Diego Prado, María Mora, and J. Iñaki Alava. "Nettle Cheese: Using Nettle Leaves (*Urtica dioica*) to Coagulate Milk in the Fresh Cheese Making Process." *International Journal of Gastronomy and Food Science*. Elsevier, May 28, 2016. sci encedirect.com/science/article/pii/S1878450X16300178.

Fischer, Wolfgang, et al. (2019). "Old age-associated phenotypic screening for Alzheimer's disease drug candidates identifies sterubin as a potent neuroprotective compound from yerba santa." *Redox Biology*, vol. 21. sciencedirect.com/science/article /pii/S2213231718311996.

Fleming, Matthew C., et al. (2018). "Immunomodulatory and Antibacterial Properties of the Chumash Medicinal Plant *Trichostema lanatum*." *Medicines*, 5(2): 25. doi .org/10.3390/medicines5020025.

Fontaine P., et al. (2013). "Chemical composition and antinociceptive activity of California sagebrush (*Artemisia californica*)." *J. Pharmacognosy Phytother*, 5(1): 1–11. academic journals.org/journal/JPP/article-full-text-pdf/4DFE9165344.

Foster, Steven, and Christopher Hobbs. *A Field Guide to Western Medicinal Plants and Herbs*. New York: Houghton Mifflin Company, 2002.

Frati, A.C., E. Jiménez, and C. R. Ariza (1990). "Hypoglycemic effect of *Opuntia ficus-indica* in non insulin-dependent diabetes mellitus patients." *Phytother. Res.*, 4: 195–97. onlinelibrary.wiley.com/doi/10.1002/ptr.2650040507.

Frati-Munari, Alberto C., Blanca E Gordillo, Perla Altamirano, and C. Raúl Ariza. "Hypoglycemic Effect of *Opuntia streptacantha* Lemaire in NIDDM." *Diabetes Care*, January 1988, 11 (1): 63–66. care.diabetesjournals.org/content/11/1/63.

Frawley, David, and Vasant Lad. *The Yoga of Herbs: An Ayurvedic Guide to Herbal Medicine*. Santa Fe, NM: Lotus Press, 1986.

Garcia, Cecilia, and James D. Adams. *Healing with Medicinal Plants of the West: Cultural and Scientific Basis for Their Use*, third edition, revised. La Crescenta, CA: Abedus Press, 2016.

Garth, Thomas R. (1953). "Atsugewi Ethnography." *Anthropological Records* 14(2):140–41, 140. digicoll.lib.berkeley.edu/record/84175?ln=en.

Gifford, E. W. (1967). "Ethnographic Notes on the Southwestern Pomo." *Anthropological Records*, vol. 25: 14. University of California, Berkeley. digicoll.lib.berkeley.edu/record/84242?ln=en.

Glatt, Levi. *Medicinal Herbs of Santa Cruz County.* Santa Cruz, CA: Forest Academy Press, 2017.

Gledhill, David. *The Names of Plants*, third edition. Cambridge, UK: Cambridge University Press, 2002.

González-Juárez, Daphne E., et al. "A Review of the *Ephedra* genus: Distribution, Ecology, Ethnobotany, Phytochemistry and Pharmacological Properties." *Molecules* (Basel, Switzerland), vol. 25,14, July 20, 2020: 3283. ncbi.nlm.nih.gov/pmc/articles/PMC7397145/.

Goodrich, Jennie, Claudia Lawson, and Vana Parrish Lawson. *Kashaya Pomo Plants.* Los Angeles: American Indian Studies Center, University of California, 1980.

Grieve, Mrs. M. *A Modern Herbal.* New York: Dover Publications, 1971. botanical.com/botanical/mgmh/mgmh.html.

Hardy, Karen, et al. (2012). "Neanderthal medics? Evidence for food, cooking, and medicinal plants entrapped in dental calculus." *Die Naturwissenschaften*, vol. 99,8: 617–26. pubmed.ncbi.nlm.nih.gov/22806252/.

Harnett, Joanna, et al. (2020). "The effects of *Sambucus nigra* berry on acute respiratory viral infections: A rapid review of clinical studies." *Advances in Integrative Medicine*, vol. 7,4: 240–46. ncbi.nlm.nih.gov/pmc/articles/PMC7443157/.

Hashidoko, Yasuyuki (1996). "Phytochemistry of *Rosa rugosa*." *Phytochemistry* 43: 535–49. 10.1016/0031-9422(96)00287-7. sciencedirect.com/science/article/abs/pii/0031942296002877.

Hawkins, Jessie, et al. "Black elderberry (*Sambucus nigra*) supplementation effectively treats upper respiratory symptoms: A meta-analysis of randomized, controlled clinical trials." *Complement Ther Med.*, February 2019, 42: 361–65. ncbi.nlm.nih.gov/pubmed/30670267.

Hayashi, Hiroaki, et al. (2005). "Phylogenetic Relationship of *Glycyrrhiza lepidota*, American Licorice, in Genus *Glycyrrhiza* Based on rbcL Sequences and Chemical Constituents." *Biological & Pharmaceutical Bulletin* 28: 161–64. bpb.pharm.or.jp/bpb/200501/b01_0161.pdf.

Hedges, Ken, and Christina Beresford. *Santa Ysabel Ethnobotany.* San Diego, CA: San Diego Museum of Man, 1986.

Hedrick, U. P. *Sturtevant's Edible Plants of the World.* Mineola, NY: Dover Publications, 1972.

Hemmes, Richard B., Arlene Alvarado, and Benjamin L. Hart. "Use of California bay foliage by wood rats for possible fumigation of nest-borne ectoparasites." *Behavioral Ecology*, vol. 13, no. 3, May 2002: 381–85. academic.oup.com/beheco/article/13/3/381/221893.

HerbWalks.com. "Chinese researcher wins Nobel Prize for malaria drug derived from 'Sweet Annie.'" herbwalks.com/2015/10/07/chinese-researcher-wins-nobel-prize-for-malaria-drug-derived-from-herbal-medicine/.

Hinton, L. (1975). "Notes on La Huerta Diegueño Ethnobotany." *The Journal of California Anthropology* 2(2). Retrieved from escholarship.org/uc/item/71h7710r. escholarship.org/uc/item/71h7710r.

Hobbs, Christopher. *Usnea: The Herbal Antibiotic*. Capitola, CA: Botanica Press, 1986. christopherhobbs.com/wp-website/wp-content/uploads/2015/01/Usnea-booklet-text.pdf.

Hoffmann, David. *The New Holistic Herbal*, third edition. Rockport, MA: Element Inc., 1991.

Incayawar, Mario, MD (2010). "Tongva Medicinal Plants." runajambi.net/tongva/.

International Union for Conservation of Nature and Natural Resources (2020–3). "The IUCN Red List of Threatened Species." IUCN Red List. iucnredlist.org.

Ivanescu, Bianca, et al. (2015). "Sesquiterpene Lactones from *Artemisia* Genus: Biological Activities and Methods of Analysis." *Journal of Analytical Methods in Chemistry*, vol. 2015. ncbi.nlm.nih.gov/pmc/articles/PMC4606394/.

Jepson Flora Project (editors) (2020). "Jepson eFlora." ucjeps.berkeley.edu/eflora/.

Johnson J. J. (2011). "Carnosol: a promising anti-cancer and anti-inflammatory agent." *Cancer Letters*, 305(1): 1–7. ncbi.nlm.nih.gov/pmc/articles/PMC3070765/.

Kaiser Permanente (2015). "Chaparral." Kaiser Foundation Health Plan of Washington. wa.kaiserpermanente.org/kbase/topic.jhtml?docId=hn-2067001.

——— (2015). "Eucalyptus." Kaiser Foundation Health Plan of Washington. wa.kaiserpermanente.org/kbase/topic.jhtml?docId=hn-2086009.

——— (2015). "Sage." Kaiser Foundation Health Plan of Washington. wa.kaiserpermanente.org/kbase/topic.jhtml?docId=hn-2158004.

——— (2015). "St. John's Wort." Kaiser Foundation Health Plan of Washington. wa.kaiserpermanente.org/kbase/topic.jhtml?docId=hn-2168009.

——— (2015). "Usnea." Kaiser Foundation Health Plan of Washington. wa.kaiserpermanente.org/kbase/topic.jhtml?docId=hn-2177002.

Kay, Margarita Artschwager. *Healing with Plants in the American and Mexican West*. Tucson, AZ: University of Arizona Press, 1998.

Khan, Ikhlas A., and Ehab A. Abourashed. *Leung's Encyclopedia of Common Natural Ingredients Used in Food, Drugs, and Cosmetics*, third edition. Hoboken, NJ: John Wiley & Sons, 2010.

Kim, Seung-Hee, and Kyung-Chul Choi (2013). "Anti-cancer Effect and Underlying Mechanism(s) of Kaempferol, a Phytoestrogen, on the Regulation of Apoptosis in Diverse Cancer Cell Models." *Toxicological Research*, vol. 29,4: 229–34. ncbi.nlm.nih.gov/pmc/articles/PMC3936174/.

Klingelhoefer S., B. Obertreis, S. Quast, and B. Behnke (1999). "Antirheumatic Effect of IDS 23, a Stinging Nettle Leaf Extract, on in Vitro Expression of T Helper Cytokines." *The Journal of Rheumatology*. US National Library of Medicine. ncbi.nlm.nih.gov/pubmed/10606356.

Knishinsky, Ran. *Prickly Pear Cactus Medicine: Treatments for Diabetes, Cholesterol, and the Immune System*. Rochester, VT: Healing Arts Press, 2004.

Kregiel, Dorota, et al. "*Urtica* spp.: Ordinary Plants with Extraordinary Properties." *Molecules* (Basel, Switzerland), vol. 23,7, July 9, 2018: 1664. ncbi.nlm.nih.gov/pmc /articles/PMC6100552/.

Largo, Donna, Daniel F. McCarthy, and Marcia Roper. *Medicinal Plants Used by Native American Tribes in Southern California*. Banning, CA: Malki-Ballena Press, 2009.

Linus Pauling Institute. "Vitamin C." Oregon State University Micronutrient Information Center. lpi.oregonstate.edu/mic/vitamins/vitamin-C.

Lis, Anna, Agata Swaczyna, Agnieszka Krajewska, and Karolina Mellor. "Chemical Composition of the Essential Oils From Twigs, Leaves, and Cones of *Thuja plicata* and Its Cultivar Varieties 'Fastigiata,' 'Kornik,' and 'Zebrina.'" *Natural Product Communications*, July 2019. journals.sagepub.com/doi/epub/10.1177/1934578X19862904.

Luther Burbank Home & Gardens. "Spineless Cactus." lutherburbank.org/about-us /specialty-gardens/spineless-cactus.

Lyle, T. J. *Physio-Medical Therapeutics, Materia Medica and Pharmacy*. Salem, OH: J. M. Lyle & Bros., 1897 [Public domain; accessed online at Internet Archive]. archive .org/details/physiomedicalthe00lyle/mode/2up.

Mangelsdorf, Paul C. "Introduction." *Plants in the Development of Modern Medicine*, Tony Swain, editor. Cambridge, MA: Harvard University Press, 1972.

McKay, D. L., and J. B. Blumberg (2006). "A review of the bioactivity and potential health benefits of chamomile tea (*Matricaria recutita* L.)." *Phytother Res.* 20(7): 519–30. pubmed.ncbi.nlm.nih.gov/16628544/.

Mead, George R. *The Ethnobotany of the California Indians*. La Grande, OR: E-Cat Worlds, 2003.

Medina, Andrea L., et al. (2005). "Composition and Antimicrobial Activity of *Anemopsis californica* Leaf Oil." *Journal of Agricultural and Food Chemistry* 53, no. 22: 8694–98. academia.edu/6364511/Composition_and_Antimicrobial_Activity_of_Anemopsis _californica_Leaf_Oil.

Medina-Holguín, A.L., et al. "Chemotypic variation of essential oils in the medicinal plant, *Anemopsis californica*." *Phytochemistry* 69(4), February 2008: 919–27. euro pepmc.org/article/PMC/2330197.

Meng, Ge, et al. (2014). "Research progress on the chemistry and pharmacology of *Prunella vulgaris* species." *Open Access Library Journal* 1, no. 3: 1–19. dx.doi.org /10.4236/oalib.1100558.

Mitscher, Lester, et al. (1983). "Antimicrobial agents from higher plants: Prenylated flavonoids and other phenols from *Glycyrrhiza lepidota*." *Phytochemistry* 22: 573–76. sciencedirect.com/science/article/abs/pii/0031942283830490..

Moerman, Daniel E. *Native American Medicinal Plants: An Ethnobotanical Dictionary*. Portland, OR: Timber Press, 2009.

Moore, Michael. "Medicinal Plants." *In The Field With Michael Moore—4*. Michael Cottingham, December 8, 2011. YouTube video, 9:58. youtube.com/watch?v =RAQHzxPrqKs (*Grindelia*).

―――. *Herbal Tinctures in Clinical Practice*, third edition. Bisbee, AZ: Southwest School of Botanical Medicine, 1996. swsbm.com/ManualsMM/MansMM.html. swsbm .com/ManualsMM/MansMM.html.

―――. *Medicinal Plants of the Desert and Canyon West*. Santa Fe, NM: Museum of New Mexico Press, 1989.

―――. *Medicinal Plants of the Mountain West*. Santa Fe, NM: Museum of New Mexico Press, 2003.

―――. *Medicinal Plants of the Pacific West*. Santa Fe, NM: Red Crane Books, 1993.

―――. Plant monographs extracted from *The Eclectic Materia Medica, Pharmacology and Therapeutics* by Harvey Wickes Felter, MD (1922). swsbm.com/FelterMM/Fel ters.html.

Mowrey, Daniel B. *The Scientific Validation of Herbal Medicine*. Los Angeles: Keats Publishing, 1986.

Murphey, Edith Van Allen. *Indian Uses of Native Plants*. Ukiah, CA: Mendocino County Historical Society, 1987.

*National Formulary*, fourth edition, 1916. google.com/books/reader?id=mb8qAAAAYA AJ&hl=en&pg=GBS.PP4.

Native American Ethnobotany Database. naeb.brit.org.

NatureServe. "Explorer." explorer.natureserve.org.

Nyerges, Christopher. *Foraging California*, second edition. Lanham, MD: The Rowman and Littlefield Publishing Group, 2019.

Ommundsen, Peter. "Pronunciation of Biological Latin." Salt Spring Island, BC: Cape West Publishing. capewest.ca/pron.html.

O'Neill, Maggie. "A 54-Year-Old Man Died from Eating Too Much Black Licorice— Here's How That Can Happen." MSN, September 24, 2020. a.msn.com/05/en-us /BB19onJX?ocid=se.

Parke, Davis & Company (1894). *Descriptive catalogue of the laboratory products of Parke, Davis & Company. Materia medica, therapeutics, formulae, approximate prices.* archive.org/details/descriptivecatal00park/page/68/mode/2up.

Pengelly, Andrew. *The Constituents of Medicinal Plants*. Crows Nest, Australia: Allen & Unwin, 2004.

Perri, Filomena, et al. "Naturally occurring sesquiterpene lactones and their semi-synthetic derivatives modulate PGE2 levels by decreasing COX2 activity and expression." *Heliyon* 5(3), March 2019: e01366. Published online, March 27, 2019. ncbi .nlm.nih.gov/pmc/articles/PMC6441754/.

*Pharmacopoeia of the United States of America*, eighth decennial revision, 1905. google .com/books/reader?id=5nh66efDQnAC&hl=en&pg=GBS.PP8.

*Pharmacopoeia of the United States of America*, ninth decennial revision, 1916. google .com/books/reader?id=qVZAAQAAMAAJ&pg=GBS.PP1.

Popoola, Olugbenga K., et al. (2013). "Marrubiin." *Molecules* 18(8): 9049–60. mdpi .com/1420-3049/18/8/9049/htm.

Power, Frederick B., and Arthur H. Salway. "Chemical Examination of *Micromeria chamissonis* (Yerba Buena)." *The Journal of the American Chemical Society*, vol.

30., no. 2. February 1908. (as reprinted in *Internet Archive*). archive.org/details /b30613188.

Prasad, Malini A., et al. "Leveraging phytochemicals: the plant phylogeny predicts sources of novel antibacterial compounds." *Future Science OA*, vol. 5,7. FSO407, July 25, 2019. ncbi.nlm.nih.gov/pmc/articles/PMC6695524/.

Puig, Carolina, et al. (2018). "Unravelling the bioherbicide potential of Eucalyptus globulus Labill: Biochemistry and effects of its aqueous extract." *PLOS ONE*. 13. e0192872. journals.plos.org/plosone/article?id=10.1371/journal.pone.0192872

Pullela, Venkata S., et al. (2005). "Isolation of Lignans and Biological Activity Studies of *Ephedra viridis*." *Planta Medica* 71: 789–91. pubmed.ncbi.nlm.nih.gov/16142651/.

Radulescu, Valeria, et al. (2013). "Determination of ascorbic acid in shoots from different coniferous species by HPLC." *Farmacia* 61: 1158–66. farmaciajournal.com /wp-content/uploads/2013-06-art-12-radulescu-1158-1166.pdf.

Robinson, David W., et al. "Datura quids at Pinwheel Cave, California, provide unambiguous confirmation of the ingestion of hallucinogens at a rock art site." *PNAS*, 117 (49), December 8, 2020: 31026–37. First published November 23, 2020. pnas .org/content/117/49/31026.

Romero, John Bruno. *The Botanical Lore of the California Indians*. New York: Vantage Press, 1954. gutenberg.org/files/55009/55009-h/55009-h.htm.

Safford, William E. "Daturas of the Old World and New: An Account of Their Narcotic Properties and Their Use in Oracular and Initiatory Ceremonies" (published in the *Smithsonian Report* for 1920). Washington, DC: Government Printing Office, 1922. books.google.com/books/about/Daturas_of_the_Old_World_and _New.html?id=OtoaAAAAYAAJ.

Salehi, Bahare, et al. (2019). "Therapeutic Potential of α- and β-Pinene: A Miracle Gift of Nature." *Biomolecules* 9(11): 738. mdpi.com/2218-273X/9/11/738#cite.

Sarris, J., E. McIntyre, and D. A. Camfield (2013). "Plant-Based Medicines for Anxiety Disorders, Part 2: A Review of Clinical Studies with Supporting Preclinical Evidence." *CNS Drugs* 27: 301–19. pubmed.ncbi.nlm.nih.gov/23653088/.

Schenck, Sara M., and Edward W. Gifford. *Karok Ethnobotany*. Berkeley, CA: University of California Anthropological Records, vol. 13(6), 1952: 377–92. dotycoyote.com /pdfs/sources/schenck_karok_ethnobotony.pdf.

Schüle, Cornelius, Thomas Baghai, N. Sauer, and Gregor Laakmann (2004). "Endocrinological Effects of High-Dose *Hypericum perforatum* Extract WS 5570 in Healthy Subjects." *Neuropsychobiology* 49: 58–63. epub.ub.uni-muenchen.de/16535 /1/10_1159_000076411.pdf.

Selfridge, Nancy J. "Black Elderberry Supplementation for Upper Respiratory Infection Symptoms." *Integrative Medicine Alert*, May 1, 2020. reliasmedia.com /articles/146146-black-elderberry-supplementation-for-upper-respiratory-infection -symptoms.

Senica, Mateja, et al. "The Higher the Better? Differences in Phenolics and Cyanogenic Glycosides in *Sambucus nigra* Leaves, Flowers and Berries from Different Altitudes." *J Sci Food Agric.*, 97(8), June 2017: 2623–32. pubmed.ncbi.nlm.nih.gov/27734518/.

Shipek, Florence Connolly. *Delfina Cuero: Her Autobiography: An Account of Her Last Years and Her Ethnobotanic Contributions.* Menlo Park, CA: Ballena Press, 1991.

Sidor, Andrzej, and Anna Gramza-Michalowska. "Advanced research on the antioxidant and health benefit of elderberry (*Sambucus nigra*) in food—a review." *Journal of Functional Foods*, volume 18, part B. October 2015: 941–58. sciencedirect.com /science/article/pii/S1756464614002400.

Smith, Micholas, and Jeremy C. Smith (2020). "Repurposing Therapeutics for COVID-19: Supercomputer-based Docking to the Sars-cov-2 Viral Spike Protein and Viral Spike Protein-human ACE2 Interface." *ChemRxiv.* europepmc.org/article/PPR /PPR116961

Stephens, Tim. "UCSC Arboretum holds the most eucalyptus species anywhere outside of Australia." *UC Santa Cruz News,* September 25, 2007. news.ucsc.edu /2007/09/1591.html.

Strike, Sandra S. *Ethnobotany of the California Indians, Volume 2: Aboriginal uses of California's indigenous plants.* Champaign, IL: Koeltz Scientific Books, 1994.

Tabanca, Nurhayat, et al. (2013). "Comparative investigation of *Umbellularia californica* and *Laurus nobilis* leaf essential oils and identification of constituents active against *Aedes aegypti.*" *Journal of Agricultural and Food Chemistry*, vol. 61(50): 12283–91. pubmed.ncbi.nlm.nih.gov/24266426/.

Tadd, Brown. *Brown Tadd—Miwok: One Miwok's View of Native Food Preparations and the Medicinal Uses of Plants.* Tollhouse, CA: Three Forests Interpretive Association, 1988.

Taib, Mehdi, et al. "Medicinal Uses, Phytochemistry, and Pharmacological Activities of *Quercus* Species." Evidence-based complementary and alternative medicine: eCaliforniaM, vol. 2020 1920683. July 31, 2020. ncbi.nlm.nih.gov/pmc/articles /PMC7415107/#/.

Takeoka, Gary R. et al. "Headspace Volatiles of *Scutellaria californica* A. Gray Flowers." *Journal of Essential Oil Research,* February 2008. tandfonline.com/doi/abs/10.1080 /10412905.2008.9699982.

Takeoka, Gary R., et al. (2010). "Volatile Constituents of the Aerial Parts of *Salvia apiana* Jepson." *Journal of Essential Oil Research* 22. sd3b1043620c280fa.jimcontent.com/ download/version/1504299875/module/12319943325/name/naturwissenschaft liche_analyse_weisser_salbei.pdf.

Tan, Keng Hong, and Ritsuo Nishida (2012). "Methyl eugenol: its occurrence, distribution, and role in nature, especially in relation to insect behavior and pollination." *Journal of Insect Science* (online), vol. 12: 56. ncbi.nlm.nih.gov/pmc/articles/PMC3500151/.

Tavares, Wilson R., and Ana M. L. Seca. "The Current Status of the Pharmaceutical Potential of *Juniperus* L. Metabolites." *Medicines* (Basel, Switzerland), vol. 5(3), July 31, 2018: 81. ncbi.nlm.nih.gov/pmc/articles/PMC6165314/.

Thorne Research. *Sambucus nigra* (elderberry) monograph. *Altern Med Rev.* 10(1), March 2005: 51–54. archive.foundationalmedicinereview.com/publications/10/1/51.pdf.

Tierra, Michael. "Wild Cherry, One of the Great North American Herbs." Michael's blog, East West School of Herbology website. planetherbs.com/blogs/michaels-blogs /wild-cherry-one-of-the-great-north-american-herbs/.

————. *Planetary Herbology*. Santa Fe, NM: Lotus Press,1988.

Timbrook, Jan. *Chumash Ethnobotany*. Santa Barbara, CA: Santa Barbara Museum of Natural History, 2007.

————. "Virtuous Herbs: Plants in Chumash Medicine." *J. Ethnobiol* 7(2), Winter 1987: 171–80. ethnobiology.org/sites/default/files/pdfs/JoE/7-2/Timbrook1987.pdf.

Tiralongo, Evelin, et al. "Elderberry Supplementation Reduces Cold Duration and Symptoms in Air-Travellers: A Randomized, Double-Blind Placebo-Controlled Clinical Trial." *Nutrients*, vol. 8(4), March 24, 2016: 182. ncbi.nlm.nih.gov/pmc /articles/PMC4848651/.

Tomè, Franca, Maria Laura Colombo, and Luisa Caldirol (1999). "A Comparative Investigation on Alkaloid Composition in Different Populations of *Eschscholtzia californica* Cham." *Phytochem. Anal* 10: 264–67. academia.edu/12486673/A_com parative_investigation_on_alkaloid_composition_in_different_populations_of _Eschscholtzia_californica_cham.

Train, Percy, et al. *Medicinal Uses of Plants by Indian Tribes of Nevada*, revised edition. US Department of Agriculture, 1957. ia800504.us.archive.org/13/items/medicinal usesofp45trai/medicinalusesofp45trai.pdf.

Tumen, Ibrahim, et al. "Topical Wound-Healing Effects and Phytochemical Composition of Heartwood Essential Oils of *Juniperus virginiana* L., *Juniperus occidentalis* Hook., and *Juniperus ashei* J. Buchholz." *Journal of Medicinal Food*, January 2013: 48–55. juniper.oregonstate.edu/bibliography/documents/phpqTlBiK_Tumen2.pdf.

US Department of Agriculture, Agricultural Research Service. "Dr. Duke's Phytochemical and Ethnobotanical Databases." phytochem.nal.usda.gov/phytochem/search.

————, Forest Service. "Seasonal Changes in Carbohydrates and Ascorbic Acid of White Pine and Possible Relation to Tipburn Sensitivity." Forest Research Note SE-124, December 1969. srs.fs.usda.gov/pubs/rn/rn_se124.pdf.

————, Natural Resources Conservation Service. "Plant Guide for Jeffrey Pine." plants .usda.gov/plantguide/pdf/pg_pije.pdf.

————, Natural Resources Conservation Service. "Plant Guide for Toyon." plants.usda .gov/plantguide/pdf/cs_hear5.pdf.

United Plant Savers. "Species At-Risk" List. unitedplantsavers.org/species-at-risk-list/.

University of California, Berkeley. "The Jepson Herbarium." ucjeps.berkeley.edu/eflora/.

University of California, Riverside. Detailed Case Histories of Salient Worldwide Biological Pest Control Projects (Puncture Vine). faculty.ucr.edu/~legneref/biotact/ch -88.htm

Upton R. (2013). "Stinging nettles leaf (*Urtica dioica* L.): Extraordinary vegetable medicine." *J Herbal Med*. sciencedirect.com/science/article/abs/pii/S221080331 2000978?via%3Dihub

Upton, Roy (editor), et al. *American Herbal Pharmacopoeia: Botanical Pharmacognosy— Microscopic Characterization of Botanical Medicines*. Boca Raton, FL: CRC Press, 2011.

Veluthoor, Sheeba, et al. (2011). "Composition of the heartwood essential oil of incense cedar (*Calocedrus decurrens* Torr.)," *Holzforschung* 65. fs.fed.us/pnw/pubs/journals /pnw_2011_veluthoor.pdf.

Viola, H., et al. (1995). "Apigenin, a component of *Matricaria recutita* flowers, is a central benzodiazepine receptors-ligand with anxiolytic effects." *Planta Med.* 61(3): 213–16. pubmed.ncbi.nlm.nih.gov/7617761/.

Walker, Phillip L., and Travis Hudson. *Chumash Healing; Changing Health and Medical Practices in an American Indian Society.* Banning, CA: Malki Museum, 1993.

Wang, Jiayi, et al. "Antibacterial Activity of Juglone against *Staphylococcus aureus*: From Apparent to Proteomic." *International Journal of Molecular Sciences* 17, no. 6, June 18, 2016: 965. mdpi.com/1422-0067/17/6/965#cite.

Wang, Xiaogang, et al. (2016). "*Heteromeles arbutifolia*, a Traditional Treatment for Alzheimer's Disease, Phytochemistry and Safety." *Medicines* 3, 17. mdpi.com /2305-6320/3/3/17/htm.

Westrich, LoLo. *California Herbal Remedies.* Houston: Gulf Publishing Co., 1989.

Wheeler-Voegelin, Erminie. *Tübatulabal Ethnography.* Berkeley, CA: University of California Press, 1938. Accessed at Internet Archive. archive.org/details/tubatul abalethno0000whee.

Whitehead, Anne, et al. "Cholesterol-lowering effects of oat β-glucan: a meta-analysis of randomized controlled trials," *The American Journal of Clinical Nutrition*," vol. 100, no. 6, December 2014: 1413–21. academic.oup.com/ajcn/article/100/6/14 13/4576477?login=true.

Wilken-Robertson, Michael. *Kumeyaay Ethnobotany: Shared Heritage of the Californias.* San Diego, CA: Sunbelt Publications, 2018.

World Health Organization. WHO monographs on selected medicinal plants, vol. 1–4. apps.who.int/iris/handle/10665/42052.

Yarnell, Eric, ND, and Lauren Russel, ND. "Solidago: An Inflammation Modulator." *Naturopathic Doctor News & Review,* April 11, 2018. ndnr.com/autoimmune allergy-medicine/solidago-an-inflammation-modulator/.

# PLANT INDEX

**A**

*Abies* spp., 49
*Achillea millefolium*, 82
*Anemopsis californica*, 62
*Arctostaphylos manzanita*, 126
*Arctostaphylos uva-ursi*, 127
*Artemisia californica*, 86
*Artemisia douglasiana*, 92
*Artemisia ludoviciana*, 87
*Artemisia tridentata*, 88
*Avena fatua*, 67

**B**

bay, California, 58
bearberry, 127
black walnut, southern California, 147
blackberry, California, 210

**C**

cactus, prickly-pear, 121
*Calocedrus decurrens*, 29
cedar, 29
chamomile, wild, 100
cherry
    bitter, 199
    Catalina, 200
    hollyleaf, 199
chokecherry, western, 200
*Clinopodium douglasii*, 151
creosote bush, 223

**D**

datura, sacred, 214
*Datura wrightii*, 214
Douglas-fir, 49

**E**

elderberry
    black, 73
    blue, 72
    red, 73
ephedra, 44
    California, 44
    green, 45
    Nevada, 44
*Ephedra californica*, 44
*Ephedra nevadensis*, 44
*Ephedra viridis*, 45
*Eriodictyon californicum*, 113
*Eriodictyon crassifolium*, 114
*Eriodictyon tomentosum*, 114
*Eriodictyon trichocalyx*, 115
*Eschscholzia californica*, 190
estafiate, 87
eucalyptus, 186
*Eucalyptus globulus*, 186
everlasting, California, 104

**F**

fennel, 78
fir, 49
*Foeniculum vulgare*, 78

**G**

*Glycyrrhiza lepidota*, 132
goathead, 227
goldenrod, 109
gold-wire, 142
grindelia, 95
*Grindelia camporum*, 96
gumplant, 96

**H**

*Heteromeles arbutifolia*, 194
horehound, 154
*Hypericum anagalloides*, 142
*Hypericum concinnum*, 142
*Hypericum perforatum* subsp. *perforatum*, 143
*Hypericum scouleri*, 143

**I**

incense-cedar, 29

**J**

*Juglans californica*, 147
juniper
      California, 36
      common, 37
      Sierra, 38
      Utah, 40
      western, 39
*Juniperus californica*, 36
*Juniperus communis*, 37
*Juniperus grandis*, 38
*Juniperus occidentalis*, 39
*Juniperus osteosperma*, 40

**K**

klamathweed, 143

**L**

*Larrea tridentata*, 223
licorice, American, 132

**M**

manzanita, 126
*Marrubium vulgare*, 154
*Matricaria discoidea*, 100
*Mentha arvensis*, 158
*Mentha canadensis*, 159
mint, wild, 159
mugwort, 92

**N**

nopal, 121
*Notholithocarpus densiflorus*, 136

**O**

oak, 136
oats, wild, 67
*Opuntia* spp., 121

**P**

pine, 49
pineapple weed, 100
*Pinus* spp., 49
poppy, California, 190
*Prunella vulgaris*, 161
*Prunus emarginata*, 199
*Prunus ilicifolia* subsp. *ilicifolia*, 199
*Prunus ilicifolia* subsp. *lyonii*, 200
*Prunus virginiana* var. *demissa*, 200
*Pseudognaphalium californicum*, 104
*Pseudotsuga* spp., 49
puncture vine, 227

**Q**

*Quercus* spp., 136

**R**

raspberry, whitebark, 209
red-cedar, western, 30
*Rosa californica*, 205
*Rosa gymnocarpa*, 205
*Rosa woodsii*, 206
rose
      bald-hip, 205
      California wild, 205
      interior, 206
      Woods', 206
*Rubus leucodermis*, 209
*Rubus parviflorus*, 209
*Rubus spectabilis*, 210
*Rubus ursinus*, 210

**S**

sacred datura, 214
sage
    black, 171
    blue, 169
    hummingbird, 176
    purple, 170
    white, 165
sagebrush
    coastal, 86
    Great Basin, 88
salmonberry, 210
*Salvia apiana*, 165
*Salvia dorrii*, 165
*Salvia leucophylla*, 170
*Salvia mellifera*, 171
*Salvia spathacea*, 176
*Sambucus nigra* subsp. *caerulea*, 72
*Sambucus racemosa* var. *melanocarpa*, 73
*Sambucus racemosa* var. *racemosa*, 73
*Scutellaria californica*, 179
self-heal, 161
skullcap, 179
*Solidago velutina* subsp. *californica*, 109
St. John's wort, Scouler's, 142
stinging nettle
    dwarf, 218
    giant, 218

**T**

tanbark-oak, 136
thimbleberry, 209

*Thuja plicata*, 30
tinker's penny, 142
toyon, 194
*Tribulus terrestris*, 227
*Trichostema lanatum*, 182
*Trichostema lanceolatum*, 183

**U**

*Umbellularia californica*, 58
*Urtica dioica*, 218
*Urtica urens*, 218
usnea, 25
*Usnea californica*, 25
uva ursi, 127

**V**

vinegar weed, 182

**W**

woolly blue curls, 182

**Y**

yarrow, 82
yerba buena, California,
    151
yerba mansa, 62
yerba santa
    California, 113
    sticky, 115
    thick-leaved, 114
    woolly, 114

# RECIPE INDEX

Bearberry
    Manzanita/Bearberry Cider, 231
Black Walnut
    Poison Oak Liniment, 243
California Poppy
    California Poppy Tincture, 232
Cherry
    Cough Formula Tincture, 234
    Wild Cherry Cough Syrup, 249
Creosote Bush
    Herbal Steam Inhalation, 237
    Medicinal Ointments (Balms),
        239
Datura
    Sacred Datura Soak, 244
Elderberry
    Chaparral Cold, Flu, and Fever Tea,
        233
    Elderberry Glycerite Recipe, 236
    Elderberry Immune Syrup, 236
    Spring Sinus Herbal Infusion, 246
Ephedra
    Spring Sinus Herbal Infusion, 246
Eucalyptus
    Herbal Steam Inhalation, 237
Fennel
    Candied Wild Fennel Seeds, 233
Grindelia
    Cough Formula Tincture, 234
    Medicinal Ointments (Balms),
        239
    Poison Oak Liniment, 243
Horehound
    Horehound Cough Syrup, 238
Incense-cedar
    Medicinal Ointments (Balms), 239
    Herbal Steam Inhalation, 237
Juniper
    Herbal Steam Inhalation, 237
    Medicinal Ointments (Balms),
        239

Manzanita
    Manzanita/Bearberry Cider, 231
Mugwort
    California Dream Tea, 232
    Medicinal Ointments (Balms), 239
    Poison Oak Liniment, 243
    Rejuvenating Herbal Bath Soak, 244
Oats
    California Dream Tea, 232
    Milky Oats Tincture, 240
    Oatstraw and Nettle Leaf Mineral
        Supplement Tea, 241
Pine
    Herbal Steam Inhalation, 237
    Medicinal Ointments (Balms), 239
    Pinyon Pine Salve, 242
Pineapple Weed
    California Dream Tea, 232
Prickly-Pear
    Desert Love Tea Blend, 235
    Nopal (Prickly-Pear) Cactus
        Smoothie, 240
Sage, Black
    Black Sage Foot Soak, 231
    Chaparral Cold, Flu, and Fever Tea,
        233
Sage, Hummingbird
    Hummingbird Sage Chocolate Tea
        for Anxiety, 239
Sage, Purple
    Black Sage Foot Soak, 231
    Desert Love Tea Blend, 235
Sage, White
    Herbal Steam Inhalation, 237
    Rejuvenating Herbal Bath Soak, 244
    White Sage Water, 248
Sagebrush
    Herbal Steam Inhalation, 237
    Rejuvenating Herbal Bath Soak, 244
    Poison Oak Liniment, 243
    Sagebrush Liniment, 245

St. John's Wort
    St. John's Wort Infused Topical Oil,
       245
Skullcap
    California Dream Tea, 232
Stinging Nettle
    Oatstraw and Nettle Leaf Mineral
       Supplement Tea, 241
    Spring Sinus Herbal Infusion, 246
Toyon
    Dried Toyon Berries, 235
    Toyon Persimmon Bars, 247
Usnea
    Usnea Antibacterial Double
       Extraction, 248

Western red-cedar
    Medicinal Ointments (Balms), 239
    Herbal Steam Inhalation, 237
Yarrow
    Chaparral Cold, Flu, and Fever Tea,
       233
    Poison Oak Liniment, 243
Yerba Mansa
    Soothing Yerba Mansa Sore Throat
       Gargle, 246
Yerba Santa
    Cough Formula Tincture, 234
    Herbal Steam Inhalation, 234

# CONTRIBUTORS

## Recipes

James David Adams Jr., Abedus Press; abeduspress.com

James D. Adams Jr. and Cecilia Garcia, "Traditional Chumash Healing." *Wilderness Way*, vol. 12, no. 4; abeduspress.com/files/Wildernessway12_4_2006aGeneral.pdf

Amanda McQuade Crawford, PhytoHumana; amandamcquadecrawford.com

Cecilia Garcia and James D. Adams Jr., *Healing with Medicinal Plants of the West*; abeduspress.com

Laura Pasetta, Wild Rootz; wild-rootz.com

Jess Starwood, Herbalist, Forager, Chef; jstarwood.com

Helen Sweany

Enrique Villaseñor; abeduspress.com

Carol Wade, Earth Island Herbs; earthislandherbs.com

Carol Wermuth

## Photos

James David Adams Jr., Abedus Press; abeduspress.com

Bryant Baker; shrublander.com

Matt Below, Matt Below's iNaturalist Profile; inaturalist.org/people/matt_below

Linda Blue, Linda Blue Photography; LABluePhotography.com

Patrick Breen, Department of Horticulture, Oregon State University; landscapeplants.oregonstate.edu

Kim Chisholm, Wolf Camp & School of Natural Science; wolfcollege.com

Barbara Eisenstein, Weeding Wild Suburbia; weedingwildsuburbia.com

Kyra Epstein; kyraepstein.wordpress.com

Keith Farrar; farrarafar.com

Ben Grangereau; benjero.com

John Griffith

J. R. "Bob" Haller, Courtesy of Santa Barbara Botanic Garden; sbbgphotos.org

Steve Junak; email: sjunak@sbbg.org

Rondia Kaufer

Joshua Kaplan

Megan Keefe, Courtesy of Santa Barbara Botanic Garden; sbbgphotos.org

Sangeet Khalsa, Courtesy of Santa Barbara Botanic Garden; sbbgphotos.org

Angela Rockett Kirwin; AnthroMama.com

Richard Marcellin

Robert E. Merritt

Mark Moore; e-mail: mmoore1229@gmail.com

Keir Morse, Botanist and Photographer; keiriosity.com

Steven Mark Norris, California State University, Channel Islands; nativeplants.csuci.edu

Greg Pasetta, Wild Rootz; wild-rootz.com
Jean Pawek
Neil Reichline, Neil Reichline Photography & Fine Prints; neilreichline.zenfolio.com
Angelina Sanchez
Santa Barbara Botanic Garden; sbbgphotos.org
Stephen Sharnoff, Stephen Sharnoff Photography; sharnoffphotos.com
Holly Sherwin
Jess Starwood, Herbalist, Forager, Chef; jstarwood.com
Monika Szrek, Living Wisdom; livingwisdom.live
Anna Szymkowiak-Chung
Enrique Villaseñor; abeduspress.com
Carol Wade, Earth Island Herbs; earthislandherbs.com
James Wapotich, Songs of the Wilderness; songsofthewilderness.com
Tricia Wardlaw, Courtesy of Santa Barbara Botanic Garden; sbbgphotos.org
Smitty West; smittywest.com
David White, Center for Regenerative Agriculture; ojaicra.org
Dieter Wilken, Courtesy of Santa Barbara Botanic Garden; sbbgphotos.org

# ABOUT THE AUTHOR

**Lanny Kaufer** has been leading Herb Walks in Ventura and Santa Barbara Counties since 1976, educating scores of locals and visitors on the flora of the area, with a focus on herbs that can be used for food and medicine. As an herbal educator, Lanny also leads workshops and presentations throughout the Ojai-Ventura–Santa Barbara area on the edible and medicinal uses of California plants.

Lanny earned a biology degree at the University of California, where he completed independent studies in naturopathic medicine under physiology professor Dr. Henry Hilgard.

Lanny is a faculty member of the Osher Lifelong Learning Institute at California State University, Channel Islands. He served as chief consultant on medicinal plants for the redesign of the Swimmer Medicinal Garden in Playa Vista. Lanny actively shares his work online through his website (HerbWalks.com), newsletter, and social media.

Lanny lives in Ojai, California, with his wife, Rondia.